Bad Girls, Dirty Bodies

Library of Gender and Popular Culture

From Mad Men to gaming culture, performance art to steampunk fashion, the presentation and representation of gender continues to saturate popular media. This series seeks to explore the intersection of gender and popular culture, engaging with a variety of texts – drawn primarily from Art, Fashion, TV, Cinema, Cultural Studies and Media Studies – as a way of considering various models for understanding the complementary relationship between 'gender identities' and 'popular culture'. By considering race, ethnicity, class, and sexual identities across a range of cultural forms, each book in the series adopts a critical stance towards issues surrounding the development of gender identities and popular and mass cultural 'products'.

For further information or enquiries, please contact the library series editors:

Claire Nally: claire.nally@northumbria.ac.uk
Angela Smith: angela.smith@sunderland.ac.uk

Advisory Board:

Dr Kate Ames, Central Queensland University, Australia
Prof Leslie Heywood, Binghampton University, USA
Dr Michael Higgins, Strathclyde University, UK
Prof Åsa Kroon, Örebro University, Sweden
Dr Niall Richardson, Sussex University, UK
Dr Jacki Willson, Central St Martins, University of Arts London, UK

Library of Gender
& Popular Culture

Published and forthcoming titles:

Bad Girls, Dirty Bodies

Sex, Performance and Safe Femininity

Gemma Commane

BLOOMSBURY ACADEMIC

LONDON • NEW YORK • OXFORD • NEW DELHI • SYDNEY

BLOOMSBURY ACADEMIC
Bloomsbury Publishing Plc
50 Bedford Square, London, WC1B 3DP, UK
1385 Broadway, New York, NY 10018, USA

BLOOMSBURY, BLOOMSBURY ACADEMIC and the Diana logo
are trademarks of Bloomsbury Publishing Plc

First published in Great Britain 2021

Paperback edition published 2022

Cover design: Charlotte Daniels
Cover image © Biwa Studio / Getty Images

A catalogue record for this book is available from the British Library.

Library of Congress Cataloging-in-Publication Data
Names: Commane, Gemma, author.
Title: Bad girls, dirty bodies : sex, performance and safe femininity /
Gemma Commane.
Description: London ; New York : Bloomsbury Academic, 2020. |
Series: Library of gender and popular culture | Includes bibliographical
references and index. |
Identifiers: LCCN 2020010860 (print) | LCCN 2020010861 (ebook) |
ISBN 9781788311267 (hardback) | ISBN 9781350117358 (pdf) |
ISBN 9781350117341 (epub) | ISBN 9781350117365
Subjects: LCSH: Women in motion pictures. | Sex in motion pictures.
Classification: LCC PN1995.9.W6 C625 2020 (print) | LCC PN1995.9.W6
(ebook) | DDC 791.43/6522–dc23
LC record available at https://lccn.loc.gov/2020010860
LC ebook record available at https://lccn.loc.gov/2020010861

ISBN: HB: 978-1-7883-1126-7
       PB: 978-1-3501-8535-7
       ePDF: 978-1-3501-1735-8
       eBook: 978-1-3501-1734-1

Series: Library of Gender and Popular Culture

Typeset by Integra Software Services Pvt. Ltd.

To find out more about our authors and books visit www.bloomsbury.com and sign up for
our newsletters

For Elizabeth, Sandra, Paul, Lisa, Clare, Louisa and Mariella.

Contents

Series Editors' Foreword

Just what constitutes 'popular culture' is something that many of the books in this Library explore, testing the boundaries of culture and subculture. As society continues to become more liberal and tolerant, with laws introduced in all parts of the world that extend the boundaries of gender equality, so too does the cultural context in which gender is performed. Gemma Commane's study here is relevant, as she explores the world of constructions of the femininity that have been in turn taboo and celebrated. As the title of the book shows, there is a moral value judgement of what is acceptable of femininity that can be reflected in the adjectives 'bad' and 'dirty'. In exploring the subversive nature of female performances from subculture to popular culture, Commane is able to show how the policing of heteronormative sexual norms has led to these labels being attached.

This book shares several themes with others in the Library, most closely with Claire Nally's *Steampunk: Gender, Subculture and the Neo-Victorian* (2019) and with Anna Watz's *Paradoxical Pleasures* (forthcoming), but also in tangential ways with Esperanza Miyake's *The Gendered Motorcycle* (2018) and Cristelle Maury and David Roche's edited collection, *Women Who Kill* (2020).

Commane's use of ethnographic interviews and own personal experiences of identifying as an intersectional queer feminist allows readers to see a world that is on the edges of popular culture. Like the participants in Victoria Cann's *Girls Like This, Boys Like That* (2018), Commane's evidence shows how complicated it can be to negotiate identity in a contemporary setting. Both studies have found that there is a boundary between what is 'cool' and what is 'uncool' or even 'gross'. In Commane's study, this relates more to expressions of sexuality and she is able to show that these boundaries are both challenged and created. What she is also able to show is that the policing of women's bodies in the ever-present patriarchal gaze of popular culture is also mirrored in the subcultural level.

She explores how this contradiction operates in terms of what is it to be 'bad' and what it is to be 'dirty'. In both cases, dangerous femininity is in operation. Just as other authors in the Library have explored pornography in terms of gay sexuality, Commane's study shows how similar issues are apparent in queer feminism. She offers case studies drawn from interviews with a range of well-known and lesser-known performers who engage with expressions of sexuality, gender non-conformity and 'taboo'. The performers' witty and playful expressions of identity test the boundaries of 'safe' femininity. The book leads to an exploration of the more mainstream articulation of the Bad Girl and Dirty Body, in the form of heteronormative burlesque, before offering a critique of binary opposite of the Bad/Dirty Body – the good/clean body – and suggests that the fierce femininity of the Bad Girls is something that helps us challenge the patriarchal expectations of the good/clean girl.

Acknowledgements

I would like to thank my colleagues in Media at Birmingham City University and BCMCR for their continued support and encouragement. In particular, I am so grateful for the support of Hazel Collie, Oliver Carter, Stephanie Fremaux, Neil Hollins, Sam Coley, Xavier Mendik, Annette Naudin, Dima Saber, Karen Patel, Paul Long, Nick Webber, Kirsten Forkert, Dave Harte, Olivia Swinscone, John Mercer, Sarah Raine and Nick Gebhart. Thank you to my fellow Bean Flicks co-organizers, colleagues and friends: Annalise Weckesser, Keeley Abbott, Gemma Williams, Pip Langstrompe, Andrew Bradbury and Michell Chresfield. Another source of energy and insight has been my students on my Gender, Sexuality and the Body module. Thank you for daring to write about topics that politically matter. This has greatly encouraged me. One person who encouraged and inspired me during my teenage years is Val Bissell, my English teacher. Thank you for recognizing things in me that other teachers did not. My journey started at eighteen, with the wonderful support and mentoring from Will Barton (my dissertation supervisor) and Andrew Beck. I want to acknowledge and thank you both for helping me build my confidence which enabled me to give myself permission to experiment with ideas and stand my ground.

I also want to recognize and thank some of my academic heroes for their generosity but also how they have inspired me to do research in the areas that I love. Thank you Feona Attwood, Debra Ferreday, Paul Hodkinson, Clarissa Smith and Susanna Paasonen. I am eternally grateful to the series editors Claire Nally and Angela Smith, as well as the anonymous reviewer for seeing the significance of the book. To the anonymous reviewer: thank you very much for recommendations and guidance, all of which made the book stronger. A special thank you to my dear friend Crow Dillon-Parkin for the suggestions, your patience and for proofreading the manuscript.

One key person who has been with me since the beginning of the research is my PhD supervisor Shane Blackman. Thank you for your insights, mentoring, unwavering support, kindness and energy. Thank you for your friendship too. You believed in the research, in me and the voices of women in my research. Solidarity!

A massive thank you to the generosity of Liselle Terret (Doris La Trine), Ms T, Empress Stah and other participants and gatekeepers involved in the ethnography.

To my family and friends, thank you for always being there and providing much-needed love, laughter and adventures.

To my late Grandma and Great Aunties: thank you for showing me the strength to do the right thing. You always remind me of how important it is to be generous, empathetic and loving, but most of all to practise what I preach. I will love you, always.

Introduction

This book is based on original ethnographic research exploring Bad Women, Dirty bodies and dangerous femininities in a range of settings in subculture and popular culture. 'Bad', 'Dirty' and the policing of heteronormative sexual norms are core themes and tensions which are explored through confrontational, fun, perverse, deliberately dirty and kinky performances. Alongside the celebration of Dirt, Bad Girls in this book demonstrate how giving yourself permission to do what you want opens more inclusive space to reflect the diversity of femininity and the importance of embodied knowledge. The central stories in this book are from the voices and experiences of women who have been maligned as Bad/Dirty (i.e. non-conforming). Burlesque is used as a vehicle into debates about femininity, but also to elicit a deeper critique of how women's stories are mediated. Drawing from the accounts of research participants and emergent themes in the ethnography, this book argues that the construction of femininities within the contemporary revival of burlesque does not challenge or offer an alternative to mainstream heteronormativity.

When we think of alternatives to the mainstream, this may conjure up images of individuals or groups who question or challenge 'the norm'. Questioning or challenging the norm can be articulated through alternative practices and belief systems, expressing intimacy beyond socially approved ways (i.e. polyamory, BDSM that is not Fifty Shades of Grey, non-monogamy, etc.) and through visual means (i.e. body modifications, striptease, etc.). Furthermore, this can include a political statement that is performed on stage in ways that undermine established ways of performing beauty, sexiness, self-identity and so on. Alternative constructions of femininity can also be applied here when exploring 'subcultures' where progressive space is apparently opened for women who do not follow expected social scripts aligned with 'good femininity'. A safe progressive space can be positive, especially when it supports women articulating their self-identity on their own terms. Whilst the opening of space is important for possibilities to happen, we still need to investigate the extents to which these alternative constructions are really *that* alternative, or if some women are still punished or dismissed for going beyond socially approved ways of 'doing' the alternative. This dismissal can even be articulated by some women about Bad/Dirty/Other women in the same scenes, which evidences the pervasiveness of heteronormativity and how this value system is used to validate or vilify.

Stories, performances and case studies used in the book are a way to explore alternative constructions of femininity, embodied knowledge and the Bad Girl. Central to the book is the articulation of femininity, specifically femininities demarcated as 'Bad', problematic, indecent, pornographic and unsafe. How gender and sexuality are negotiated in various spaces, and the issues that emerge are key features of the case studies (Ms T, Empress Stah and RubberDoll, Mouse and Doris La Trine) and how they offer a challenge to binaries (i.e. cleanliness/dirtiness and the good/Bad Girl). These situate the Bad Girl as a site of power and transformation.

My voice and self-identity

As the book explores voice and experience, it is important for me to position myself within the research, sexual politics and feminism. Firstly, I am a cultural theorist and an ethnographer who is invested in exploring the lived experience of marginalized women who identify as Bad, dirty, alternative and queer (although these identifying features are sometimes imposed on marginalized women). I am an intersectional queer feminist, although some may see me as a 'third wave' feminist (i.e. positioning myself alongside and within post 90s feminist discourse). The approach of the book, and indeed my own political ethos, is sex-positive, holistic and queer. I am white and from a working-class family. I am a goth and a queer woman. Being Bad myself has given me access to the Bad Women in this book, but it is important to note that critique and reflexivity are central in unpacking what these femininities mean.

Since my teens, I have been interested in identities, lifestyles and sexualities that deviated from the norm. Some of this interest was stoked by my own feelings and experience of marginalization and exclusion. Every person experiences marginalization in different ways, dependent on a myriad of intersections. How marginalization operates and is negotiated by individuals is something which has always intrigued me, both on a personal and professional level. Growing up in the 1990s and 2000s in a very conservative setting meant that I was unaware of why I felt different. In Sixth Form and through my Saturday job at Coventry Market, my friendship group reflected more of what I identified with: goths and metalheads. Mixing with different people on the goth and alternative scenes opened up possibilities for me. Although I wasn't comfortable with my sexuality until my early thirties, I felt that the clubs I frequented in my youth allowed myself and my friends to be ourselves. In these spaces, I started to mix with people who were queer, lesbian, gay, bisexual and kinky. These people were kind, cool and understanding. Mainstream culture did not really see them this way.

One thing I noticed (and continue to notice) was the hypocrisy of popular culture. Some aspects of subculture and alternative expressions of femininity were accepted (i.e. mainstream fashion, film and TV, celebrity culture, etc.), whilst other types of alternative women and sexual expressions were demonized or maligned as bad and dirty (i.e. too kinky, too naughty, too sexual, too weird, too different for male approval, etc.). These contradictions have never disappeared as they were also found in my research too. Contradictions/contestations can feel quite negative and constricting; however, what has always fascinated me is how women navigate, queer and challenge heteronormative expectations.

We will see how Bad Women (as evidenced in the research) demonstrate how space can be both challenged and created to allow more possibilities to be present (i.e. not at the expense of other women, nor by telling 'women' that they all need to be the same). The policing of women's bodies and self-expression, as we will see in this book, also operates within subculture and between women too. This was something I observed both in my personal life and in the research. Possibilities and contradictions are central in the investigation into Bad Women and how both Bad/Dirty as the underpinnings of the book bring both together.

Bad Girls, Dirty Bodies

Bad Women and Dirty Bodies have direct links to dangerous forms of femininity, such as the slut, the woman who is far too kinky, the bisexual and the woman who expresses her self-identity in disapproving ways (i.e. too honest, too confrontational, too gay, etc.). Dangerous femininities challenge patriarchy in various ways, such as outspoken women who speak their own truth, women who revel in their own sexiness/filth and sexual women who do not need male approval (or other women's approval for that matter). Challenging gendered scripts can be through troubling social norms around how your femininity is expected to be performed (i.e. in any group setting, and not just within popular culture). Dangerous femininities are important to explore, and in relation to this book, the case studies offer ways in which self-identity can be given space through voice, biography, context and experience.

'Bad' and 'Dirty' (we can add here: 'problematic', 'pornographic' and 'unsafe') can also conjure up a variety of images in the readers' mind through their own cultural awareness of what a Bad Girl is and how she may be framed in popular culture at any given time. These images are usually related to iconic figures in popular culture, such as the femme fatale, a woman who is sexually ravenous, the girl you would never want to take home to your parents, or marry, the black widow, the good girl gone bad, lustful lesbians, boyfriend-stealing harlots, bisexual vamps and the man-eating nymphomaniac. The issue of using words or associations with the Bad Girl – even to valorize the potential of the Bad Girl in challenging heterocentric discourses – means that the Bad Girl is always fighting against and speaking to binaries (i.e. good/bad, normal/pathological, burlesque/stripping, straight/gay, etc.). This can be problematic if the same language systems we use to communicate, interpret and express can trap how the Bad Girl can be read, perceived and valued. How then can we see the potential of the Bad Girl and clearly understand the messages she is projecting (i.e. in the manner she wants us to see her message too), if we cannot see beyond or between binaries?

The concept of the Bad Girl is not something new, with feminist and gender scholarship and media and cultural theorists engaging with debates connecting to popular culture, new/alternative femininities, post-feminist discourses and the 'sexually independent' woman (e.g. Attwood, 2005, 2007a, 2009, 2007a and b; Attwood and Holland, 2009; Holland, 2004, 2010; Walters, 2010; Ferreday, 2008; Budgeon, 1998, 2011; Evans and Riley, 2014, but also see fourth wave feminist critiques of digital/social media). Porn studies also offers new and exciting avenues in exploring women's desire, affect and resonance, and porn consumption/production (see the extensive work of Feona

Attwood, Clarissa Smith, Susanna Paasonen and Paul J. Maginn). All of these contexts enable femininity to be seen, understood and researched in ways beyond the heteronormative.

There are, however, still absences in popular culture. Women whose lifestyles, sexual identities and bodily practices are maligned as 'dirty', strange and pathological are still not acceptable or represented in good light. This is despite positive developments in socio-sexual, political and gendered contexts where conditions are such that more femininities are supposedly included and celebrated in popular culture. For example, being too slutty, too queer, too butch, too alternative, too kinky and too 'bad' still relegate women being labelled Bad/Dirty (i.e. Other), as being both unworthy and insignificant. It is OK to be alternative, be independent and sex-positive or 'bad' in ways that are still deemed to be feminine or socially permissible. Being too authentically bad can still class that individual as socially corrosive, dirty and contagious. These labels are not politically neutral nor do they emerge out of thin air: they have a history. Dirtiness and stigma do not happen overnight, nor are they aimed sporadically. Dirt, abjection and filth are still terms that ensure the Bad Girl is seen in a negative light (see Cohen, 2005; Douglas, 1966; Mort, 2000; Weeks, 1991). On the other hand, versions of the Bad Girl – in contemporary media and popular culture – create opportunity for controversy. This opportunity is not in favour of women who step beyond the mediated image, and adopt or express characteristics which contravene the mediated/permissible Bad Girl image (i.e. this is not just in subcultural spaces, but in popular culture too).

Applying these terms and expressions to a person or body is a systematic way of abstracting and disqualifying a person's agency, rights and value. We may think that this is a symptom of the mainstream holding onto a sense of stability to retain heteronormative sensibilities, but it is very difficult for a particular identity to shake a history away so easily. Certain histories pass from person to person and generation to generation; thus, negativity transposes time, it sees no borders and it sticks. When a word and its associated contexts are situated in language and within social scripts, it is hard to distance oneself when we are labelled/read as bad or dirty. Being in proximity with these words or associated identities can bestow you with stigma. Even when you are trying to unravel or illuminate the limitations of heteronormativity, the negative implications of words continue to stick to certain identities, bodies and groups. For an individual, therefore, to embrace the Bad Girl is actually a radically political act of defiance, but also it is simply embodying who they are.

The concept of the Bad Girl is, however, interchangeable, and her (superficial) value in popular culture, the wider media landscape and within subcultural entertainment contexts continues to devalue women who seek to reclaim or even just embrace the Bad Girl on their own terms. The integration of the Bad Girl within cult media and popular consciousness reinforces certain qualities and characteristics that try to disarm political resistance against repressive sexual attitudes towards sexual women. This book acknowledges this integration alongside the issues of assimilation of Bad Girl practices, objects and self-expression (i.e. performance art, music, burlesque, etc.) from subculture to the mainstream.

The Bad Girl always comes with assumed and associated problems (i.e. stigma, not fitting in, not being taken seriously, being read the wrong way and devalued), which women have to continually negotiate to fit in, to stand out and to create dialogue that rejects the Bad Girl as something negative, something putrid or contagiously wicked. Beyond the binary of the good/bad, can the range and varieties of 'Bad Girls' found in subcultural settings actually be problematic for good reasons? What about the women who fall between the good/bad binary – what do they have to say about being bad?

Dangerous femininities

The book presents a range of case studies (Bad Girls with Dirty Bodies) that challenge sexual puritanism (see also Attwood, 2007a; Jackson and Gilbertson, 2009; Kristeva, 1982; Reger, 2015; Lim and Fanghanel, 2013; Wilkins, 2008; Tyler, 2009; Sprinkle, 1998; Williams, 1993), which open up space for more possibilities to happen, which include multiple ways of doing/embodying femininity. The case studies[1] are: Ms T, Empress Stah, RubberDoll, Doris La Trine and Mouse. With the exception of Doris La Trine, the other case studies used tease and performativity through the lens of explicitness, kink, BDSM and the erotic. Doris La Trine, RubberDoll and Mouse not only provide commentary on the aesthetics of femininity, but also challenge patriarchal expectations around women's worth, desire and place. The case studies offer an insight into the ways in which some women navigate and comment on sexual self-expression, sexuality, gender non-conformity and 'taboo' (i.e. pornography, sex work, BDSM, kink and fetish). The case studies were selected by their difference from the repetition of alternative looks, performance style and 'political' message in the rise and success of neo-burlesque both in popular culture and within some subcultural settings.

The case studies situate the Bad Girl as something transformative and able to destabilize heterocentric worldviews around gender, sexuality, femininity and sexual self-identity. Themes that emerged through these case studies[2] also mapped onto other examples in popular culture and subculture, where Bad Women were articulating their femininity in powerfully confrontational and explicit ways.

Through the combination of case studies, this book offers a challenge to those who think that sexual, slutty, Bad and Dirty Women are not worth listening to. The case studies evidence women who fall between expectations, whose commentaries open up new embodied knowledge. These offer an important insight into a history, where alternative women and femininities continue a legacy of challenging societal expectations surrounding what makes a good/Bad Woman. The specific case studies demonstrate inconsistencies with wider socio-cultural attitudes around sexualized women and how Bad Women use their bodies.

Embodied knowledge is at the heart of the book, which enables a more inclusive examination of femininity, self-identity and what women can do with their bodies. As a consequence, the case studies draw our attention to liminal and 'in-between' spaces, where 'Bad Girls' continually open sexual and political possibilities for women. The book argues that these possibilities offer scope and validity into how women's bodies, sexual expressions and femininity are lived, critiqued and can be re-presented in a variety of media texts and social contexts. Consequently, critical discussions around sex, sexuality and femininity are needed to enable a reconceptualization of the Bad Girl and her importance. Despite these women being historically stereotyped and maligned as 'dirty', thus possibly undermining the manner in which their political 'message' is understood by the mainstream, the book critically explores the detrimental role the Bad Girl potentially plays in fighting for a range of socio-political changes, specifically around what women can do with and to their bodies.

Significantly, the book develops a much-needed unpicking of the issues generated by women who are complicit in the subjugation, policing and marginalization of Bad/Dirty (i.e. Other) women, both in popular culture and in sites of subcultural resistance.

From Bad Girls to the shadows of safe femininity

Bad Girls need to come first, especially as they have been maligned and sidelined for centuries. So, what is a Bad Girl and what makes a body Dirty? Chapter 1 contextualizes the core concepts of the book (i.e. Bad, Dirty, and the policing of heteronormative sexual norms), leading to initial examples of Bad Girls in the research: Mouse and Doris La Trine. The rejection of and challenge to feminine norms are discussed in relation to Mouse and Doris La Trine whose performances rework the abject, stigma and objectification through the value of the vagina (Mouse) and the importance of biography (Doris La Trine) in challenging heteronormative presuppositions.

Chapter 2 explores the vampy, queer burlesquer and self-proclaimed Bad Girl, Ms T. The focus of critique synthesizes the negotiations Ms T has had with a range of fetish, gay and queer communities, alongside the outcomes of her performance themes and attitudes towards her body. The groups she identified with and the people she has been rejected by provide an approach which informs how gender, sexuality and sexual expression are conceived, specifically regarding social relations. Ms T's performances and self-identity are used to explore how being a Bad Girl is not necessarily a negative thing and that women, who are seen by wider social attitudes to be overtly sexual, should not be seen as strange.

Chapter 3 focuses on Empress Stah, a global neo-burlesque, twisted cabaret and trapeze artist. Through *The Queen of the Night*, and the themes of magnification and the unknown, we will explore how the use of the absurd and the ridiculous can undermine social norms around dangerous sexualities, Bad Girls and Dirty femininity. It will be argued that Empress Stah contradicts the revival's focus on preserving respectability. What is explained is the extent to which being one of the 'futures' of burlesque allows Empress Stah to direct herself through her own experiences, rather than relying on the formulas presented in revivalist burlesque. We will see how being a 'Bad Girl' does not necessarily mean that femininity or self-expression is compromised.

Chapter 4 presents RubberDoll (http://rubberdoll.net/) a hard-core fetish latex model, performance-artist and full-time kinkster.

RubberDoll's latex-encased lifestyle and artistic expressivity are cleverly mixed across and within a range of hybridized forms of technologies and leisure-time environments, where she continuously presents a journey to the outer limits of fetish and kink. Through managing herself and expanding how (her) sexual expressivity and kink can be communicated, the chapter argues that RubberDoll queers the cis-gendered male gaze and develops the political significance of sexual otherness. The chapter seeks to explore disruptions to the many layers and locations of repressive ideological values which deem Bad/Dirty (i.e. Other) women such as RubberDoll as insignificant due to their failure to comply with heterosexual standards (i.e. relating to coupling, intimacy, desire and pleasure). The chapter develops and addresses the implications of 'reading' RubberDoll within the contexts of commodification, as this limits scope and the significance of sensorial-affective and sensuous journeys into an individual's own kinks and perversions. Through exploring RubberDoll (her performance repertoire, self-management and her sexual desires), the chapter will argue that Bad/Dirty women are actively producing alternative routes to desires that are politically, financially and personally significant.

From the Bad Girl to the clean, Chapter 5 presents examples of revivalist burlesque that demonstrate the contradictions within the rise and popularity of burlesque in popular culture. This examination includes the issues of commercial appeal and the standardization of Bad Girl aesthetics. Chapter 5 examines heteronormative scripts and expectations in mainstream burlesque style, femininity and performance. The chapter explores and critiques the popularity of burlesque within mainstream culture and in the clubs/venues the research was conducted in. Focusing on the femininities present in the language, construction and representation of burlesque, it will be argued that the main body of revivalist burlesque promotes heteronormativity, despite how empowering burlesque can be for some women. To explore the reasons why, the second half of Chapter 5 focuses on the rise, demise and re-emergence of neo-burlesque, because the history reinforces what is legitimate within the contemporary movement.

Cleanliness and the good girl have a lot to do with maligning and marginalizing the Bad Girl (thus silencing her and subduing her power), and this is something which Chapter 6 explores. The central theme the case study chapters highlight is the importance of context as a means to challenge and create space (i.e. space to include the diversity of femininity and more possibilities for women).

In this book, we will see how Bad/Dirty women disrupt heteronormativity by showing femininity as fierce, diverse and a challenge to sexual norms. Bad Girls and women with Dirty Bodies are not victims. They shout back to patriarchal policing of their bodies and sexual freedoms. They offer a challenge to cleanliness and heteronormative policing of women's bodies and sexualities. Bad Girls highlight that gendered and sexual norms are fabricated (i.e. socially constructed and for the benefit of upholding patriarchal power systems). Bad Girls continually challenge/destabilize heteronormativity and, indeed, the predominance of the good/clean default.

Notes

1   Ethnographic interviews were conducted with Empress Stah, Ms T and Doris La Trine. Although all case studies are of equal importance, it was Empress Stah and Ms T who initially shaped the direction of the research outcomes, with Doris La Trine, Mouse and RubberDoll further opening scope. Conducting ethnographic interviews with Empress Stah, Ms T and Doris La Trine was important as it gives empirical richness and opens up the scope of interpretation. Using

interview data is another way to continue the presence of participant voice in the text. Exploring personal history and biography of the main case studies is another important tool to undermine assumptions, but to also humanize accounts.

2   The research that informs this book combines ethnography from a range of subcultural night-time events and entertainment venues, as well as websites and visual performances accessed via online platforms such as Vimeo, YouTube, Facebook and – at the time when the research was conducted – Myspace and Informed Consent. Information on club nights and performers was sourced via their websites and information, such as galleries, description of performances and dress codes, was also included in the data collection. The locations in the ethnography included the following cities: Birmingham, Manchester, Brighton, London and Blackpool. Over forty-two events were visited (club nights, private parties, erotic art exhibitions and adult lifestyle shows, cabaret nights with dining, theatre shows in city centres, community events and fetish fashion markets). Over 170 performances were observed (involving 109 different performers), which revealed themes such as tensions between different types of alternative femininity (the good/ bad but not too Bad Girl, versus femininity that was seen as too risky, dirty and sexual), cleanliness demarcating safe alternative 'empowered' femininity, and women policing and subjugating other women who did not fit the standard of commercial burlesque and alternative femininity. For further details about the ethnographic study, see Commane (2010, 2011, 2016) and Blackman and Commane (2011).

1

Bad Girls, Dirty Bodies

I was interested in the rise and popularity of burlesque striptease, but also the ways in which women 'expressed' themselves within BDSM and fetish clubbing spaces. The research became an exploration of gender and sexuality within a range of subcultural, digital and clubbing spaces, with a specific focus on Bad Girls. Although the book mainly focuses on a UK context, where most of the case studies are drawn from (except RubberDoll, who mainly performs in America and lives there), it is important to highlight that digital platforms and technologies circulate and distribute performance content across borders. Bad Girls and their Dirty Bodies travel, which means that anyone having the ability to access these communities can have an opportunity to identify with them (although 'access' always depends on a variety of affordances). The circulation and popularity of burlesque also have gathered speed in the last decade or so, with mainstream success stemming from revivalist roots in alternative clubbing and performance spaces. Discussions of girl power, sexual confidence and independence were (and still are) common themes in popular culture, helping women recognize themselves and be recognized as sexually agentic. Sex-positive space and greater social/economic opportunities for women have enabled some women and young girls to refuse the feeling that they need to fall into demarcated roles because of their gender. However, having the opportunity or space to express yourself in 'alternative' or non-conforming ways is not always straightforward or as simple and easy for all.

So, what happens, then, when your identity goes beyond the sanctioned and safe form of that alternative, even within groups that are supposed to support and validate you? The acceptance of certain forms of alternative lifestyles and femininity in popular culture is not always a negative thing as the presence of 'alternatives to' in the mainstream allows people to identify and recognize themselves, and then seek out like-minded others in other spaces beyond mainstream depictions, spaces and approval. Although these forms might take aspects of behaviours, lifestyles and expressions that are more palatable, visibility can act as a vehicle into other areas that are not as socially approved by the mainstream.

Bad Girls: What is a Bad Girl?

What we understand to be Bad (i.e. Dirty and Other) manifests through a range of social and cultural conditions. This enables people to use language and meaning systems to identify with a group, as well as judge other people by. If we step back and observe our surroundings, we can see this manifestation in the media and in other cultural, social and political institutions that touch our everyday lives. The norms we identify with (i.e. if you are a Bad or good girl) circulate in what we consume (i.e. what we watch on streaming services, what we listen to on the radio and our engagement on social media platforms), or in our everyday interactions with friends, peers, family and colleagues. In everyday life, our social relationships help certain norms circulate and become accepted (see Foucault, Nietzsche and other philosophers from Plato to Butler too). Discourse plays a massive role in maintaining social equilibrium, where you can stray slightly, but only within the permissible edges of what is 'normal' (i.e. this applies to any social group). These permissible edges can change when consumer culture recognizes trends and profitability within areas of subculture or deviance. Styles, attitudes and musical sounds can become integrated within the mainstream (see Klein, 1999), making new alternatives to the 'norm' repackaged, made safe and available to consume within popular culture. This is not necessarily a bad thing, as individuals may relate to these alternatives and then seek a like-minded community, which may exist on the periphery of popular culture. We can also see popular culture to be a space where possibilities can happen (see Hall, 1997; Halberstam, 2011; etc.).

There are alternative discourses and people can reject conditions imposed on them, because discourse is not static, and meaning is always negotiated in everyday contexts (i.e. the micro-layer). It is, however, important to highlight that value judgements and the use of stereotypes still fall back on age-old assumptions that have produced a heterocentric worldview. Shaking ourselves completely free from this can feel like an impossible task, as all roads through language come back to what is intelligible. Intelligibility and recognition can develop over time, as more identities become visible in positive ways and are seen to be valid. What is valid generally means what is accepted (to a greater extent) in mainstream culture and in legal terms (i.e. think of same-sex marriage, etc.), but there are spaces, personal relationships and social contexts, where identity can still be questioned, rejected and be seen as dirty. This is irrespective of legal rights and the visibility of, for example, women having sexual agency.

Bad Women, bad sexualities?

Bad Women are associated with certain forms of sexual behaviour and sexual practices. Whilst women consume and produce pornography (e.g. see the work of Susanna Paasonen, Danielle Lindemann and Katrien Jacobs), as well as being seen as sexual consumers who embrace pole exercise, hen dos at strip clubs and areas of sex work (e.g. see the work of Feona Attwood, Clarissa Smith, Samantha Holland and Debra Ferreday), Bad Girls continue to receive bad press despite there being many positive experiences in being Bad, which we will see in the case study chapters. Bisexuality, kink and other fluid forms of sexuality are themes which run through the case studies in this book so it is important to explore non-normative sexualities in relation to Bad Women.

Bisexuality and other non-normative identities, such as women who identify as kinky or into BDSM and fetish, are still associated with Bad Women. This builds onto wider beliefs that Bad Women are people to be suspicious of. In popular culture being bad is still taboo and dirty. It is a subject position that is looked at in particular ways (i.e. not to be taken seriously, a freak show) and is often seen as 'strange' (i.e. being too kinky). The line that separates perversity and profit/cleanliness may seem blurred in popular contemporary culture; however, value hierarchies within groups can still demonize and sully certain identities or expressions of femininity. For example, femmes can be rejected from lesbian spaces and bisexual women can be viewed by women and men as predatory or fence sitters.

Bad Girls generate a lot of money and have huge commercial appeal, especially Bad Girls who love other girls. One of the problems, however, facing bisexuality is its commercial visibility in popular culture as a temporary identity connoting risk and subversion even when there may be none, as opposed to stability in gay culture and identity (see Michael Warner (1993) on gay culture and patterns of consumption within music, adverting and clubs, and Attwood (2011a:86) on 'gay lifestyle' being 'mainstreamed as a form of cosmopolitan leisure and conspicuous consumption'). It must be noted that we cannot read gay culture as one thing, as there are various invisibilities within gay culture and a rising resistance against assimilation and corporate brands capitalizing on aspects of gay culture (i.e. during Pride month, etc.). Assimilation and consumer culture are important areas to look at, especially when exploring how certain sexual orientations are used to reinforce stereotypes. If we look at girl-on-girl representation in popular culture, we can see a temporary visibility of same-sex desire and performativity (i.e. Madonna and Britney kiss at the VMAs in

2003; Rihanna Te Amo, 2010; Christina Aguilera Not Myself Tonight, 2010; Die Antwoord, Banana Brain, 2016; etc.). Gay or straight identity is presented by consumer culture as an active identity, whilst bisexuality is still visible as temporary and titillating, as social attitudes towards 'two distinct orientations' actively reduce the value of bisexuality as 'merely a behaviour which is fairly common but does not have an identity to back it up' (du Plessis, 1996:19). Even if bisexuality is seen to be visible, but only in threatening ways (Weeks, 1995; du Plessis, 1996), its perceived lack of exclusiveness allows heterosexual normativity to continually be elevated as the default.

Suspicion and lack of exclusiveness are something alluring and incredibly erotic. Bad Girls are sexy, no matter if they are bisexual, heteroflexible (see Lisa Diamond, 2008) or lesbian. Pop culture and the flirtation with girl-on-girl culture validate 'heteroflexibility', but this is a temporary thing (i.e. falling back into heterosexuality). Heteroflexibility is about experimentation and, in media texts in popular culture, there have been 'numerous women hinting at or experimenting with same-sex sexuality, a phenomenon that has been called "heteroflexibility" (Essig, 2000)' (Diamond, 2008:104). The aesthetic of girl-on-girl culture is still white, cis, good looking and desirable in terms of attraction and profits. In terms of profits, we can briefly turn to Naomi Klein (1999) who identifies that brands in the 1990s recognized the youth market (i.e. the MTV generation) and (this can also be applied to celebrities too) the need to resonate with youth culture. Subversion or counter-cultural elements are therefore assimilated within mainstream popular consumerism, which means that the visibility of 'alternative to' the normal is more about status and competition rather than progressive politics (Heath and Potter, 2006:69). Even lesbian representation cannot escape from commercialization (see Jackson and Gilbertson, 2009). Lesbian chic in popular culture is still pretty, slim, hot and standardized, thus heterosexualized and palatable. This is even the case within homonormativity because distancing and Othering of those outside the binary will always make certain positions exclusive and powerful. The process of recognition may be open to more identities, as culture allows it to be, but what this still relies on and is informed by is how culture (at large) deals with, understands and re-presents difference.

Another issue, then, is the reactions towards sexual identities seen as Bad/Dirty. For example, Jeffrey Weeks (1995) explores how bisexuality signals a crisis in sexual certainty. Having a sexuality that has an aura of being 'in-between' actually destabilizes essentialist presumptions around sexuality (i.e. 'homo' and 'hetero' only). Despite Alfred Kinsey's (1948, 1953) sex-positive attitude and his scale-disrupting binary assumptions, wider social, cultural and academic discourses can still fall back into heteronormative intelligibility. This is despite discussions in feminist discourse (i.e. the third and fourth 'waves') around how consumer culture, sexual/gendered freedoms and the internet/social media are opening new avenues and possibilities for women to network, collaborate and shout back at misogyny. Gender and sexuality are seen to be intertwined in such a way that assumptions around identity still gravitate towards something that 'should be' stable or fixed. Stable and fixed identity reinforces the idea that your gender expression and sexual identity will not change during your life-course, which has been disputed by a range of studies and life experiences (e.g. see the seminal work of Lisa Diamond, Meg-John Barker, Lisa Downing, Michael Foucault, Kath Browne, Yvette Taylor and Alfred Kinsey). Bad Women cannot win, especially when their self-identity is so obsessed over and subject to study. For example, psychiatry and other forms of popular psychology often see anything that is outside of 'normal' sexual behaviour as abnormal, in need of being cured or studied, and something that can become a measure to prop up the 'normal'. If we cannot measure up to strict binaries, then surely, we are all dysfunctional. Prevailing (hetero) normative ideological systems will never adequately explain how the world comes to, or is interpreted/challenged by, the individual experiencing it.

We will see, through the case studies, that Bad Girls challenge heteronormativity as the default through highlighting that more femininities exist beyond the binary. Whilst the Bad is exciting to heteronormative visitors, embodying this subject position is something that is still dangerous (i.e. temporary badness is fun, but being constantly Bad is weird and dodgy). For Weeks (1995), the reason why sexualities, such as bisexuality, are rejected or seen as a threat is that its characteristics are viewed as changeable and not able to be predicted or measured.

For Surya Munro (2005) the issues facing bisexuality and its interpretations by feminism are varied. Although liberal feminists embrace bisexual and straight women, in the main, Munro (2005:104) argues that bisexual women are still marginalized specifically as they are viewed by some lesbian feminists as cop-outs and fence-sitters, undecided about their politics and sexuality. Munro (2005:104) states that 'anti-bisexual feminist sentiment amongst the feminist and lesbian communities has contributed a great deal to the marginalisation of bisexual women within these communities' and what this suggests is that credentials are still used to mediate the Dirt/cleanliness binary. Thus, bisexual identity and its associations (i.e. spreader of disease, fence sitting, predatory, greedy, etc.) make it appear to be untrustworthy and destabilizing. The threat of instability highlights the presumed value of 'stability' in heterosexual and homosexual exclusivity. 'Lack' in this instance is not exclusively tied to sexual desire or sexual preference, but to the closing of available (physical, social, embodied, etc.) space where place making, identification and belonging happen.

Potentiality and being in-between is vital in challenging restrictive norms (i.e. hetero/homonormativity, heterosexual and homosexual exclusivity, etc.) and to highlight that more sexualities and expressions of femininity exist, despite being excluded from wider struggles for recognition (i.e. homosexuality). As bisexuality falls outside of the binary into a grey area, there are presumed 'lacks' of connection to a 'stable identity', a visible community, a physical space where bisexuality can be recognized in its own terms (even when a person is dating someone of the opposite sex) and a linear identity narrative (i.e. dating, then marriage, falling back into exclusive homo/hetero, hiding the bi; and other forms of success measured by the binary). What the above outlines is that marginalized identities still have to continually justify their existence, their choices and their subject position. Heteronormativity, therefore, disregards the importance of contexts, biography and lived experience. Space and positive visibility within the social world and representation (Harris, 1997; du Plessis, 1996), therefore, are still needed. This is something that the main case studies in this book will demonstrate.

Bad Girls, space and popular culture

Although popular cultural images of the Bad Girl might be playful, they do still hide a socially constructed history that enforces a gendered reality in which girls have to grow up good, even in contemporary Anglo-American contexts. This is perpetuated by the use of the Bad Girl in popular culture, with artists such as Christina Aguilera in Not Myself Tonight (2010), toying with the bad and the sexually adventurous woman (i.e. same-sex desire, group-sex, BDSM, latex fashion) who then, in the same narrative, falls back into linear heterosexual tropes, vanilla-sex and monogamy (thus the 'good'). Being Bad can be OK if it does not last: you grow out of it, you 'do it' for one night only, you wear it for a hen do and a themed night-out. In the context of Not Myself Tonight, the product placement of Aguilera's self-branded perfumes near the end of the music video demonstrates that feeling bad or embodying the 'bad-ass' can be packaged up and bottled: spray it on and then wash it off as you go to bed at night. Commodity culture, from the 1990s onwards, has used the 'Bad Girl' as a means to represent 'girl power' and female (sexual) empowerment. Although the Bad Girl in this form (i.e. connecting to the slut, active female sexuality and alternative femininities) is recognizable in popular culture, what needs to be explored are the ways in which this figure plays out in everyday contexts and through women's experiences.

A range of alternative constructions of femininity are therefore explored throughout this book, alongside an examination of the extent to which these forms of femininity are progressive or contradictory. Included in this examination is understanding what forms and types are demarcated as dangerous and dirty dependent on who is performing, how they are performing, the spaces they are performing in and who is casting judgement on them. What 'identity' is and how we 'read' identity is dependent on how we interpret someone based on our own assessment of their social identity, sexual identity, cultural identity and so on. How we read identity is dependent on our own standing point and relationship with that person, as well as the group we feel we belong to. This means alternative constructions or even norms are based on social ideals that enable us to articulate our place within a social group, whilst using perceptions as leverage to confirm our status within the group we have affinity to. Leverage and cultural awareness can mean that one's place in a group can be confirmed by rejecting what one is not. This can be through Othering women whose activities are similar to yours but you do not want to be associated with them (or their behaviour, style and politics) as your agency could be questioned (i.e. 'what I do is burlesque: it is empowering as I am not stripping for men because that is "bad" and not feminist').

It is interesting how tensions play out in spaces where alternative forms of self-expression, self-identity and femininity are supposed to be celebrated and supported. This is further complicated by the presence of these 'alternatives' in popular and consumer culture: enabling socially approved ways of articulating 'alternative constructions' of femininity. Socially approved ways of performing the alternative exist alongside the backdrop of third wave feminist politics, women being addressed as sexual consumers, and certain forms of sexual self-expression being perceived and celebrated as valid and empowering. History has a massive part to play here in relation to cultural and social memory around certain forms of self-expression that are considered harmful, dirty and questionable. History is obviously shaped by present perceptions and is, to various extents, conditioned by some ideological mores that remain unchanged. This is despite new openings and visibilities, developments in society, and tolerances around identities that were once subject to criminalization. New visibilities and tolerances emerge through popular culture as a space where debates can happen (i.e. the public sphere explored by Habermas (1962), but also see Stuart Hall's work on popular culture) and where commodities – relating to various identities, lifestyles and beliefs – are accessible. These can become enabling tools for people to identify and put a name to who they are, and this is important when someone might feel they do not belong to the 'mainstream'.

Conversely, non-mainstream and alternative lifestyles or beliefs can be an alluring ingredient when launching a new celebrity or artist, or even selling a new range of clothes, a book series or films. The commodification of non-mainstream identities and behaviours is not something new, but the presence of BDSM, fetish, burlesque and other forms of alternative lifestyles in popular culture is significant when we examine the extents to which sanctioned forms present temporary or long-term possibilities for women (i.e. do these forms give access to commodities that – when used in particular ways – become tools enabling new forms of knowledge that potentially transform socio-political, sexual and cultural landscapes?). The presence of these in music videos, self-help books and magazines, in the movies, and other areas of consumer culture and leisure-time pursuits may create a space of tolerance. However, we must assess what this tolerance extends to and to what extent it encompasses more radical ways of articulating femininity and sexual subjectivity. If someone toys with taboo or socially approved ways of doing the alternative, then this might only be a temporary location for that individual as the standardization and mass appeal of challenging the norm can still damage careers, social standing and your gender (i.e. you become a gender violator, someone that needs saving, the girl a guy would 'fuck' but not take home to their parents, etc.).

Our identities (at any given time), then, are shaped and surrounded by a range of contexts. We make sense of who we are in a variety of spaces and in our relationships with others. Simply put: identity and sense-making happen in space and through social relations. Identity does not happen in isolation. Within any social space, dominant meaning is sustained and, subsequently, re-produced through behaviours and identities that are sanctioned as normal (i.e. the normal/abnormal, good/bad binaries operate here). What is normal is contingent and can change dependent on a range of factors, enabling more identities to be present as legitimate in popular culture. Scope can open in specific public/private/online/physical spaces, but how spaces of recognition manifest in positive ways is up for debate. If scope is there, and possibilities can and do happen, then why does the agency and visibility of 'Bad Girls' diminish? What are the spaces (or spontaneous temporary generated spaces) that give individuals more opportunity to express agency beyond wider social restrictions? The negative associations cast onto Bad/Dirty (i.e. Other) women, such as seeing them as destructive and lacking value/significance, are problematic. It is problematic as narrow heteronormative attitudes do not see Bad/Dirty women in context. Individual agency and scope are taken away, reducing their significance.

Tattooed, screwed and lewd

Samantha Holland's (2004) study of alternative femininity adds an interesting and important contribution to debates around alternative constructions of femininity – particularly opening up scope around how femininity is embodied by Bad Girls. For context, Holland's study focused on women with tattoos and other body modifications. She explored the self-representation of female participants who might not commonly be associated with traditional 'safe'/clean femininity. Although tattoo culture is massive now and more mainstreamed in the UK, with more women getting heavily inked, what is significant about Holland's study is that modifications can be viewed as a means to explore how femininity is articulated and embodied. In the section 'This Is Me' Holland identifies the value of choices her participants have made, with modifications being seen as an 'intrinsic part of their identity as "alternative" women' (Holland, 2004:104). Importantly, Holland and her participants express that alternative femininity is more than just about resistance. Modification is also about a state of mind.

Holland argues that the personal value of tattoos and their intrinsic inclusion into participants' sense of self-identity allow the tattooed female body to overstep gender boundaries. Although her participants related to men more so than women, specifically male tattoo artists, their own sense of femininity was not seen to be compromised by choosing to have tattoos or by being an 'alternative' femininity (i.e. not the traditional articulation of femininity). In fact, 'traditional'/ clean femininity was seen to be 'fluffy', which can be interpreted as less defined, less individuated, soft, present in unthreatening ways, pretty standard (i.e. think pink, cutesy and not fierce) and not individuated (i.e. the 'standard' does not, perhaps, recognize more possibilities in being a 'woman').

The body being seen as an essential platform to modify, explore and develop is something that is discussed by modern primitives and academics exploring body modifications (see Pitts, 2000, 2003; Mercury, 2000; Nan, 2004; Vason, Watson and Wilson, 2001; Woods, 1996, 1999; Zpira, 2005). Significantly, Maureen Mercury (2000) and Lukas Zpira (2005) both state that the body is something that is not an endpoint but a vessel which needs to be evolved from its primitive status. In the ethnography (for this book), this attitude towards the body concerned the importance of the sensuous and experiential. This allowed an opening of scope in gender identification and sexual expression through the exploration of the body, style and identity. Knowledge is therefore drawn from the body and experience (i.e. embodied). Victoria Pitts (2000, 2003) argues that assuming the modified body is a signifier for self-harm, abuse and psychological injury is a way for psychologists to devalue non-normative behaviours and practices (we can tie this to discussions of lacks too). This negative attitude implicates any alternative constructions of femininity, be it the body modified beyond what is considered socially acceptable or even a woman challenging norms by shouting back or being Bad/Dirty.

Taking up and creating space is a central theme in this book, specifically evidenced through the case studies, where the personal focus of performances outlines new embodied knowledge emanating from Bad Girls. These themes challenge the dismissal of Bad Girls as strong, important and empowered. Bodies that are different in ways that seem to 'contravene' safe/clean femininity can easily be assigned labels that have history as we have seen in previous sections (see also Chapter 2). This history connects to how certain behaviours were seen as deviant, dirty and pathological (i.e. the sexual woman, the wayward/fallen woman, femininities that did not correlate to the family or function as a productive cog in maintaining capitalist progress). For Pitts (2000, 2003) the modified body is a space where individuals carve out their own identity, and where identity and sense of self can push further the value and meaning of that individual's body, bodily experience and self-identity. This is supported by Maureen

Mercury (2000), Mistress Nan (2004) and Lukas Zpira (2005), as well as participants involved in my ethnographic fieldwork (i.e. clubbers, friends and other people fieldwork connected with; see Commane, 2011), who expressed that their choices evidenced strength, resilience and power. These elements enabled participants in my study to challenge and undermine the restrictions, which wider dominant discourses and culture place on identity.

Self-management of self-identity, alternative possibilities and bodily aesthetics is recognized by Holland (2004:107) in a range of body-conscious women who are into cosmetics, fashion and fitness. Self-awareness, self-worth and understanding the body by feeling closer to it demonstrate how women can occupy space in their own way (i.e. created by and for the individual, without having to seek approval from another person). The notion of making space on your own terms is essential when articulating identity (see case study chapters). This is important to recognize when trying to understand women who do not fit neatly into mainstream definitions of femininity. Significantly, alternative women do not see themselves as unfeminine, but reactions from other people to their appearance enabled them to 'create a new discourse of femininity' (Holland, 2004:151), enabling empowerment and self-identity to continue despite tensions between traditional and alternative femininity. Although her participants still used aspects of traditional feminine beauty, such as make-up, dresses, active self-pampering and perfume, these were not only about claiming general 'allegiance' to this type of femininity. This was also to recuperate their own self-identity without reducing themselves to an either/or distinction (Meg-John Barker – in *Queer: A Graphic History*, 2016 – highlights how it is more productive to queerly go beyond the binary either/or by considering both/and).

Despite a range of femininities being felt and experienced on an individual level, where individuals will feel they exist in their own terms, wider discourses and consumer culture still perpetuate ideal types and stigmatize others (i.e. be it through continued use of stereotyping, or making certain aspects of gender, sexuality and self-identity invisible). This is not about 'lack', as lack is an artificial product of discourse. Instead, what is highlighted is the limitation of language. The limitation of language is not a negative thing, as we will find out in the coming chapters, because existing in-between binaries and outside of language is deeply unsettling (in a positive way) and exposes normative moralities and values as socially, historically and culturally constructed. The limitations of language might cause issues on an individual level (e.g. stigma, rejection, devaluation, being subject to ridicule, arrest and violence), but moments of tension, unease and being unsettled call attention to a space where subjectivity escapes from heteronormative discourses and survives.

Dirty Bodies: What makes a body dirty?

As we have explored in the book's Introduction, Dirtiness is at the heart of this study. Dirt sticks to certain bodies and femininities making them appear to be either something alluring (i.e. temporary in popular culture – think of the Bad Girl or seductive femme fatale) or someone we must be afraid of as they are strange, abject and able to pollute/corrupt you. Dirty Bodies are associated with certain expressions of gender, sexuality and self. For example, the female bisexual is often seen with suspicion as the 'spreader of disease' (i.e. STIs), having a massive sexual appetite (i.e. thus includes wanting to seal your boyfriend) and being sexually adventurous (see Weeks, 1991, 1995; Harris, 1997; Weeks, 1991, 1995; du Plessis, 1996; Munro, 2005). Dirt also has a history, and what dirt means (in relation to women's bodies and sexual practices) has a lot to do with the crystallization of gender/sexuality during the nineteenth century. The focus on eradicating dirt during this period was through the regulation of the female body and sexuality. The obsession with Dirt during the nineteenth century (resulting in the elevation of the importance of 'purity' and 'cleanliness' – see William Cohen, 2005) is significant. Social pollutants, usually working-class women, prostitutes and other 'loose' women (see Mary Douglas (1966), but also Frank Mort (2000) and Jeffrey Weeks (1995) on Contagious Disease Acts and social regulation) were targeted and subject to 'correction'.

In contemporary culture, the public shaming and policing of women's bodies (i.e. slut shaming, degradation of the working-class woman, etc.) can be found in the media and popular culture, with some academics, such as Angela McRobbie, interrogating Reality Television. For feminists like Angela McRobbie, Reality Television makeover shows function to publicly humiliate women (working-class women, single mums, and loud or sexually active women) *by* other women policing taste (i.e. clean femininity – set by white middle-class women). Dirty Bodies are, therefore, entertaining as they can be laughed at. Insulting women who have failed femininity is one way for women's bodies and femininity to be demeaned. The rise of industrial capitalism and commodity culture has also had a hand to play in identifying/classifying Dirty Bodies through normalizing certain gendered roles and sexual practices (i.e. through heteronormative representations in the media, as well as assimilating more palatable aspects of subculture into the mainstream).

In an interview with Rebecca Drury (who teaches burlesque), she discussed what she believes is the central problem surrounding women's bodies. Feeling Dirty or ashamed is a feeling that is derived from religious institutions and misogynist attitudes. On burlesque as a means to challenge norms, Rebecca Drury outlined:

> I think with striptease and burlesque it can teach you that you have that beautiful sexuality and to not be ashamed of your body. It can be an absolute liberation from the chains of Christianity that

demonised the female form, you know whereas we celebrate every single shape and size, and age and disability whatever in burlesque and striptease these days, you know so it's a liberation from all that crap. I don't just teach [students] how to do it. I go into the psychology of it all, try and relax them; try to find out where their issues are and try and reason with them that they shouldn't feel that way, there is no need to feel that way. It is only since Christianity that the female form has been demonised. We have been suppressed and been made to feel that anything we do may be seen provocative, is wrong. So, I tell [my students] all about that, you know and they are like oh right, good and off [their bra] comes!

Being sexual and Dirty is something not to be ashamed of. The demonization of the female form restricts the potential of Bad Girls and their Dirty Bodies, so sharing stories (i.e. embodied knowledge) and seeing Dirt as something fun, sexy and a valid form of self-expression troubles the view that female sexuality is a sin, a sign of lack and something forbidden in contexts beyond heteronormativity. We will see that the case studies in this book magnify the importance of women who are seen to be Bad/Dirty (i.e. Other), thus challenging heterocentric worldviews about Bad/Dirty women.

Dirt, filth, stigma

Despite sexual liberation and women being seen as sexual consumers, women's bodies and their sexualities are still policed. What makes a body dirty is the application of filth/stigma, disgust as a means to reinforce social conformity, the abject and how Dirty Bodies occupy space. Stigma and the abject are placed on certain bodies by outside agencies. These attachments are used by individuals or groups to dismiss independent, outspoken, fierce and sexual women (see also Ms T and Chapter 5). Although dirt and stigma are applied to reinforce dominant ideological perceptions to punish those who contravene societal cleanliness, application is purposeful too, as it enables the entitled person projecting negativity to feel that their identity is safe/default. They place the Bad/Dirty (i.e. the Other) outside of their immediate world to give themselves a healthy distance from an identity that is 'spoiled' (i.e. socially undesirable). In other words: if you want to fit in, then you do not want a Bad/Dirty identity spoiling or tainting you by any association. The clean can dip in and out of Dirt but the Dirty cannot do the same with cleanness. This process is continuous and the contexts in which certain bodies are stigmatized do not happen overnight. Processes take time. Processes (or discourses) are historic, pervasive and have designed a specific way for gender to be seen, valued and expressed in wider culture.

Although there are multiple possibilities and ways of doing gender and sexuality during a person's life course, the legacy of doing these a specific way to confirm allegiance to social norms is still present today (i.e. if society was OK with LGBTQ+ then there would be no need for a closet to exist, etc.). The 'norm' is there for people to easily measure themselves and others by. Measurability and hierarches happen in a range of social spaces, within institutions and through social interaction. This means that meaning is constantly negotiated and performed. Alongside social expectation, rules need to be navigated by the individual in order to fit in to the group they identify with or, in some cases, to blend in because stepping outside the norm could be dangerous. One of the key features of intelligibility is (as stated above) measurability and prediction (Nietzsche and Foucault talk about this at length). We can also see that binary understandings of gender and sexuality also draw upon what is intelligible (i.e. social expectations). The incorporation of socially acceptable 'norms' into governing value systems draws upon social expectations around behaviour, performativity (i.e. strict rules around what it means to be feminine or masculine) and the benefits of conforming to the social good. This framework holds a certain type of reality in place, creating spaces where politics, communication and a sense of 'place' help people come together to support one another. These are 'available' identities. Available identities have a history and a sense of place and purpose (i.e. to communicate, to procreate, to live life in a way that commands intelligibility). As Weeks (1995:97) states: 'Available identities are taken up for a variety of reasons: because they make sense of individual experiences, because they give access to communities of meaning and support, because they are politically chosen.' Sexualities, such as bisexuality, have the potential to highlight what restrictive norms (i.e. hetero/homonormative) are.

To be in reference to or measured by normativity is something that subcultures and marginalized groups have to constantly navigate. Members of subcultures and other marginalized groups are often the object of analysis by wider social and popular cultural commentaries. Being an object of analysis and judgement, rather than a subject – in defining their own terms of reference and definition – can be restrictive, as self-representation and biography are removed. In this social process, self-representation is removed through certain self-expressions (in this book's case: alternative constructions of femininity) being associated with non-productivity (i.e. not beneficial to wider culture, unless in a profitable commodify form), and dirt and illegality (e.g. sexual practices seen to be deviant, and possibly subject to social and judicial prosecution – see the face-sitting protests of 2014 as an example of how women's sexual pleasure is being continually dismissed, regulated and seen as evil). This is why biography is central to the case study chapters. The ways in which people negotiate relationships, self-identity, possibilities and their (social) environment rely on how they are constituted in language and the systems of representation (e.g. the media and popular culture have a part to play in this).

Prevailing heteronormative discourses can, therefore, use Dirt as a means to hold alternative constructions of femininity in states of disempowerment (i.e. rather than opening space for new embodied knowledge to exist in its own terms). What the issue comes down to is perception. Perceptions impose meanings, rather than meanings emerging through the self-presentation and self-representation of the women in question. Context can be an issue when re-presenting identities that are situated precariously in popular culture and academic critique – not to mention in relation to moral beliefs, cleanliness and what is deemed tasteful. If women's agency is questioned and if they are seen as having multiple layers of lack, then the consequences tend to mean that the everyday experiences and biographies of women are bypassed. In the same vein as the Centre for Contemporary Cultural Studies (CCCS) variabilities are and should always be considered when critiquing and understanding non-mainstream practices.

Not all practices or self-expressions can be simply or irreducibly read as 'perverted', 'abnormal' or 'lacking decency'; instead, there are multiple ways we can understand femininity. If we all feel different about how we self-identify, then why should we flatten how we interpret other people, who might express who they are in different ways? Surely diversity (beyond the types of diversity sanctioned by popular consumer culture) is exciting and shows the irreducibility of self-identity and experience. Although we can see what constitutes a Bad Girl as socially, culturally and historically inherited, we must not see this as an essentialist fact, as subordination is external and artificially created. It is, however, interesting to see how 'dirt' becomes attached to certain bodies, and how these bodies – through social processes, reforms and puritanical attitudes – become second rate and linked to deviancy/disgust.

Disgust reinforcing social conformity

Ann Campbell's (1981) observation on second rate assumptions about the second sex is still relevant today. Those who fail good girl discourse and become 'delinquent'/Dirty are still not automatically viewed as important. She extensively explores the reasons why, particularly the implications of the absence of women in academic work on deviancy (i.e. the main studies being focused on men, resulting in analytical frameworks and interpretations – from a male perspective – being imposed on women in subcultural/deviant settings). Although there is an established and growing area exploring Bad Girls (i.e. Bad Women) such as in porn studies, media and cultural studies and feminism critiques (as explored in this book), more work still needs to be done especially within popular culture.

The prevalence of the good/Bad and clean/Dirty girl dichotomy, even in popular culture (e.g. Britney Spears *Work B**ch* 2013, and *Gimme More* 2007, Taylor Swift *End Game* 2017 and Nicole Scherzinger *Poison* 2011), may seem positive but actually the framing of being Bad/Dirty as a temporary identity further demeans and subordinates Bad/Dirty women outside of the pop culture context. Building on this theme, Edwin Schur (1984:8) critiques the impact of labelling women deviant and suggests that the general subordination of women adds to the ease to which subordination is fitted. Labelling someone 'deviant' can be used for political means, such as producing a legal strategy to quash and control it, or as a political label to devalue individuals (Becker, 1963:7; Blackman, 2011; Cohen, 1972:9). Dirt is always attached to the Other, such as dirty women, dirty immigrants, even dirty animals, and used as a reason for their subjugation and/or exploitation. Although Peter Aggleton (1987:13) states that labelling someone as deviant can change depending on age, class and ethnicity; the presence of the word is still problematic despite variability and the importance of embodied knowledge in 'deviant' settings and groups (see the Chicago School, the CCCS and beyond).

Despite popular culture recognizing areas of deviancy, dirt and Bad Women as profitable (i.e. women are seen as sexual consumers, social influencers and pop culture icons – think of Lady Gaga,

Rhianna, Nicky Minaj, Amber Rose, Pamela Anderson, Kim Kardashian, etc.), women who are stigmatized through being labelled as 'deviant' (thus dirty, strange, not normal) still have a 'spoiled' or tarnished identity (see Schur (1984) as one example, but also the work of Sara Ahmed, Julia Kirsteva and Imogen Tyler). The examples of celebrities above are women who are still acceptable for the male gaze and patriarchy, as they are mostly heteronormative and their flirtation with dirt is only temporary. Dirt, as a label, means that certain behaviours are socially seen as a violation of clean femininity, thus reiterating discourses that propose that women already have a devalued status (i.e. they are also told they are sluts, bitches, hoes, too outspoken, feminazis, 'cunts' and so on). Thus, the actions of the person labelled Dirty or 'deviant' do not only show what is socially inappropriate for females, but reveal a sustained idealization of a pure/clean femininity that is unrealistic and unachievable (yet people are punished or punish themselves for not fitting the 'standard'). Socially sanctioned and clean – thus safe – femininity is an identity shaped from what is ideologically approved, highlighting the value of heterosexuality in maintaining binary norms. The concept of spoilt identities leads on to more recent critiques of stickiness (see Ahmed, 2004) and the abject (see Kristeva, 1982; Tyler, 2009). Similar to labelling, the abject has dehumanizing effects and something which is a social experience (Tyler, 2009:87). This envelopes Bad Girls and their Dirty Bodies.

Bad Women, Dirty Bodies as abject

The abject connects with disgust, layers of 'lack' and it is a process by which dominant social groups stigmatize and devalue other people (i.e. be it socially, politically, judicially, psychoanalytically and so on). As Krauss (1999:236) expresses: 'Abjection is not just a psychic process but a social experience. Disgust reactions, hate speech, physical acts of violence and the dehumanizing effects of law are integral to processes of abjection. Indeed, abjection should be understood as a concept that describes the violent exclusionary forces operating within modern states: forces that strip people of their human dignity and reproduce them as dehumanized waste, the dregs and refuse of social life.' The label cuts deep; it excludes and is an enabling mechanism that promotes physical responses (i.e. revulsion, dismissal, violence, etc.). To take away someone's existence and rights, to count them as nothing and to strip away their dignity is about trying to elevate the agency of the person judging (usually a person who reflects the heteronormative). Demarcating the pure from the dirty is not just a physical or social thing: it's a psychological, personal and emotional attack that is all about nulling and taking away that Bad/Dirty (i.e. Other) person's existence. This act of violence can have devastating consequences, but as we will see with the case study chapters, there are ways of challenging, upending and questioning negativities to produce new embodied knowledge. It has always been there: it has just been ignored or framed in problematic ways.

Once an individual is perceived to be deviant/dirty/abnormal, this terminology takes over their whole character. Highlighted here is a social system which focuses on 'a renewal and development of the moral principles of human growth and health' (Sumner, 1994:107). The 'need' for stability ('cleanliness', normativity', 'belonging', 'health', etc.) is seen as an enabling factor for society to function, again heralding the shape of industrial capitalism. Those who contravene the norm by being Dirty are, therefore, perceived as being unhealthy, unruly and throwaway. Consequently, this discourse casts out 'trouble makers', gender outlaws and sexual deviants as violators of the social order. Responses to violations include social shunning, media stigmatization, rejection from peers or loved ones and work colleagues and – in the past – incarceration and punitive violence (e.g. think back to pregnant unmarried young women being admitted into asylums, 'witches' being hung/burnt/drowned due to suspicions about their femininity, etc.; see Sollee, 2017).

Deviants are always intrinsically linked to 'social problems' or are at risk of causing upset. Tying deviant or 'different' behaviours to the violation of 'norms' within a dominant group means that the people being labelled as 'deviant' are not defined by their own terms (n.b. this is not new: see Polsky (1967) on the hustler, etc.) and are objects, not subjects. It is important to challenge imposed definitions, especially when meaning is flexible, felt and negotiated by the individual. Meaning can be, and is, defined by the individual and groups in their own terms, which can redirect, challenge and upend dominant discourse. Thus, the direction of meaning flows through and is informed by individuals and their experiences, voices and stories. This is why ethnographic fieldwork *with people* matters, as situated knowledge opens the possibility to learn from lived experiences and what is actually happening in micro-contexts. Although it might feel like Bad Girls have an upward and slow battle to force change, the badges and definitions they are presented with can be played about with in creative and transformative ways.

Turning 'deviant'/Dirty women and their choices into expressions of negative sexuality, pathological illness, abuse and lack is harmful to the study of women, alternative constructions of femininity and (sub) cultural contexts where they can manifest. Supporting this Campbell (1981:62) argues that 'the real danger of psychoanalysis for the present discussion is that it inevitably turns a social and psychological issue into a psychiatric one, once again underlining the view that only a woman who is "sick" engages in antisocial behaviour'. Consequently, women need to conform to an agreeable clean femininity to escape being seen as anti-social, damaged, a Dirty bitch, and someone to be suspicious of. Casting any threat away from your position as a 'normal' clean woman is a process where you self-differentiate and elevate your own subject position at the expense of that other person. Seeing deviants as 'mentally ill', 'filthy', 'diseased' and lacking agency or control means that those classified will always need to prove themselves. Choice has been taken away. The context of illness and disease focuses on a specific history defining differences through dirt, but additionally what these associations suggest is that the application of filth and dirt not only makes identities conceivable; these readings can be actively felt in the everyday lives of individuals (see the previous sections on the abject, filth and stickiness, etc.). What emerges is a space that allows distancing to continually happen to protect communities (or self-identity) from 'disease' and risk. What is interesting about the case studies in this book is how they re-interpret, play with and challenge themes around sexuality, dirt, deviancy, filth, health and the Bad Girl. These examples show an embodied history that continually plays with norms and shows that women – who fall between the good/ Bad – are creatively narrating possibilities. What the case studies do in this book is to open scope when interpreting and recognizing Bad Women within their own contexts.

Dirty Bodies, place, space

Within any social space dominant meaning is sustained and, subsequently, re-produced through certain behaviours and identities being sanctioned as appropriate and normal (i.e. through language, performativity, etc.). This can create a sense of superiority over a group you want to devalue. We must remember that this is not just something found within wider popular culture, but also within subculture too. This is something we will revisit in later chapters. Individuals occupy a multitude of spaces, and their identity may be visible, presumed, hidden or evident dependent on where they are, who they are with and their access to modes of communication (i.e. being able to use language to identify, differentiate and express). Recognizing that these multiple spaces exist is important when we try and understand identity and how people interpret their own identity *and* the identity of others. This can reveal multiple readings and multiple changeable layers, which shift depending on who is looking, reading, judging, expressing and so on. The freedoms we might afford our own identity should not stop when we are interpreting others; thus, we need to seek multiple ways of understanding situations, contexts and people (see C. W. Mills' *The Subcultural Imagination* as an example of how to open interpretation through layers, situated knowledge, the mundane/banal and reflexivity).

On social spaces, Nirmal Puwar (2004:8) argues that they are not 'blank and open for any body to occupy. There is a connection between bodies and space … it is certain types of bodies that are tacitly designed as being the "natural" occupants of specific positions'. Building on this, we can see that perceptions shape individuals and groups in particular ways (see Burkitt, 1999; Burr, 2003; Hall, 2012; McNay, 2000; Thrift, 2004:69). This shaping can – as we have already seen (and will see in case study chapters) – exclude individuals and demarcate who has the right and privilege to belong. In the same vein as matter out of place (see Douglas (1966) on social pollutants), Puwar (2004:8) argues that some bodies are considered to have the (automatic) right to belong, 'while others are marked out as trespassers, who are, in accordance with how both spaces and bodies are imaged (politically, historically and conceptually) circumscribed as being "out of place"'. Thus, binaries operate in ways that are *intrinsic* in producing 'difference' (even indifference), and this is a process that happens within all spaces and through social interaction with like-minded others. It is important to highlight that subcultural spaces are not exempt from these concerns, and despite being open for individuals to express in 'safe space', superiority and hierarchies still govern who fits in, who is accepted and who you should connect with to be in the 'in crowd'. There are more contexts beyond the visible norms, which shape social meaning. Social meanings are shaped through how people negotiate macro-politics in the spaces they are in, alongside the micro-politics of the friendship groups they are part of (see Commane, 2011).

The structuring of gendered and sexual norms is, therefore, socially agreed upon, along the lines of mutual recognition. 'Meaning' and identity are also defined in negotiation with emotional–sexual relationships (Stein, 1997). These relationships are informed by wider belief/value systems, which are then tailored (i.e. negotiated) geographically to the groups individuals identify with. This may or may not provide a larger scope of inclusion, as identification is conditioned by a sense of togetherness. Togetherness manifests via feelings that are felt when a person's identity is recognized and seen to be of value by friendships within the community they identify with. Friendships and spaces are also 'inextricably linked with one another' (Hodkinson, 2002:65), so if we are to see challenges to mainstream norms we have to look at opportunities that enable individuals to reinsert themselves in their own terms (see case study chapters). For like-minded individuals to find other like-minded people/groups (see Foucault on reverse discourse), this means opening scope for relatability. This gives potential access to feelings of belonging and strength to exist in spaces that might be hostile beyond the safe spaces of the (sub)culture the individual might be part of. Marginalized individuals and the groups/friendships/spaces they connect with open opportunities to redefine and challenge social scripts that keep these at the margins. This actively challenges the binary of belonging/not belonging, having a place/being matter out of place (i.e. Dirt), good/ bad, abundance/lack, whilst at the same time further illuminates the constructions that try to make individuals/groups abide by binary norms.

The case study chapters will articulate and evidence new embodied knowledge through opening scope in how femininity is performed, expressed and experienced. The case studies cannot be relegated to an either/or binary, because that bypasses biography, experience and self-expression. Although some of the ethnography is absent from this book (relating to details of venues of fetish clubs and their punters – see Commane, 2011), some of the case studies performed in BDSM, fetish, kinky and queer clubs/spaces (e.g. Mouse, Empress Stah, Ms T and RubberDoll). Participants in the wider ethnographic study felt that BDSM fetish clubs and the queer scenes allowed authenticity and ownership over how sexuality was personally conceived and celebrated. How this was established was through exploring clubs and scenes with friends who 'did things differently'. This also correlated to participants in research who felt the BDSM, kinky and queer clubs allowed them to dress how they wanted, to make friends with like-minded individuals, to explore sexuality in relatively safe-space, to 'heal' (see Lindemann (2011), etc.) and to not feel that they were sick, pathologically strange or dirty. They did not have to over-emphasize or prove their sexuality.

Although subcultural spaces, and indeed popular culture too (see Stuart Hall's seminal work), enable space for individuals to express their voice and freedom to self-define, these spaces are complex and there are tensions. We will see with some of the case studies that there are evident points of tensions in subcultural spaces, where some women did not fulfil expectations in the ways they performed, how they looked (i.e. style, beauty, etc.) and how they expressed self-identity. Fitting expectations and 'norms' are still present, which beg the question: to what extent do subcultural spaces give individuals greater opportunity to express self-identity and agency beyond those wider social restrictions? The extent to which we can see these spaces as *both* temporary reliefs *and* spaces where possibilities emerge is something we will be exploring in this book. Linear time is something associated with heteronormativity, so when we look at 'temporary' locations, such as alternative subcultural clubs, music events, BDSM performance clubs, burlesque performances and protests, we can see disruption to linearity. Instead, the sensuous and experiential enable more identities to be visible through a carnivalesque atmosphere (for more detail on the carnivalesque, see Mikhail Bakhtin (1984), Daniel Mannix (1976), Adrian Werner (1976) and others). The carnivalesque opens space to ridicule, poke fun and to shine a light on social problems and repressive social categories (we will see this identified by Empress Stah on the clown/fool). This space shows other ways to behave through entertainment and temporality, enabling the visibility of many ways of doing gender, sexuality, identity and self-expression.

Linear time and history are commonly associated with heterosexuality and heteronormativity, as its logic operates in a manner that situates 'norms' within 'nature', 'fact' and the 'common good'. This even applies to romance, with children being brought up playing mummies and daddies as a means of educating them into roles they may be expected to occupy in later life (i.e. marriage, children, etc.). Despite changes in relationship dynamics and the visibility of same-sex couples with families, the closet is still there, and different types of relationships, such as polyamory, are still taboo. We will always have to unpack the complexity of belonging, even in spaces where gender and sexuality are seemingly given more space, such as fetish and BDSM club spaces and communities, LGBTQ+ community groups and clubs, punk and goth nights, burlesque events and so on. This does beg the question: is space what you make of it? We will be interrogating these themes through the case studies. In any case, in areas of post-colonial studies, sociology, cultural studies and media theory, the concept of the 'third space' calls attention to possibilities, as well as opening routes to overcome exclusion, abjection and prejudice. This is where transgressions transpire, and new routes to live, express and identify are recognized by individuals and groups. These routes are also sustained through the repetition of style, language and performativity within this group or community. This is not always a negative thing (as we will see through the case studies), as other ways to express and be valued can open new worlds of possibilities to individuals who might feel suffocated or trapped by wider social (heteronormative) norms. The ambivalence of this space means that wider cultural and political knowledge and ways of seeing the world are questioned, disrupted and no longer concealed.

The above calls into question the 'nature' of being, of gender, of sexuality, because all are up for interpretation. We will see through Empress Stah, Ms T and RubberDoll that it is a productive thing to be Bad/Dirty, to fall between binaries and to disrupt expectations, space, socio-cultural and sexual norms. These transgressions might have a personal cost, but the opening of space and the discussions it creates in the public sphere continue these possibilities. Possibilities continue a backdrop of hope that is female-centred, radical and led by Dirty/Bad Women. Dirty possibilities are not so impossible: they open space. We will now explore these themes through two important case studies: Mouse and Doris La Trine.

What's this? It's messy, dirty

As the fieldwork developed and a variety of shows were observed, there were several performances which stood out in terms of approaches to sexual expression and femininity. We will be exploring three main case studies in the following three chapters; however, it is important to include two examples where femininity is deliberately dirty and the commercial form of burlesque is radically challenged. The performances and performers directly question heteronormativity and clean femininity valued in mainstream burlesque. The performers also demonstrated the importance of recognizing the *contexts* of Dirty/Bad (i.e. Other) women's bodies, rather than presuming certain women are compromised, abnormal or needing to be fixed. Both performers occupy space where they give themselves permission to resist and to articulate their self-identity in their own terms. Negative social attitudes towards certain bodies are arguably produced through the lack of understanding that femininity can be many things. Both Mouse and Doris La Trine interrogate the body, femininity, sex and dirt.

Mouse, Dirty Dog

At Scarlet (a fetish, BDSM and performance art club in Birmingham), the performer Mouse reworked the idea of the 'reveal' to confront audiences with orifices, dirt and female sexual desire. Even if mainstream revivalist burlesque fails to address anything other than clean femininity (we will explore this in Chapter 5), Mouse used some attributes of this comedic style to present dirt, the grotesque and explicitness as amusing, awe-inspiring (i.e. pushing orifices beyond perceived limits and moving orifices away from penetration by a penis) and fun. Comedy in her show connected to the characters Barbara Winsor played in the *Carry-On* films, mixed with the explicit use of her vagina and her ability to squirt soapy liquid out of her vagina (i.e. like an enema rather than sexual fluids).

As I stood talking to participants, I noticed that the dance floor was being cleared of clubbers and a large blue plastic sheet was being laid out. The show was going to cover a vast amount of space, and the interaction level of performer and audience would be on the same level, breaking the fourth wall. Props placed about the plastic sheet included a washing-up bowl filled with suds, other small props such as sticks, and a large tin of dog food. The audience crowded around the front of the plastic sheet and slightly around the other two sides. Some of the audience crouched or sat on their knees, trying to get on the same physical level as the performer. A few sat at the front, including one clubber who was holding an umbrella which he used later on in the performance. The use of the umbrella did not make sense until near the end of the performance, making what happened ever funnier because of the participation.

From a corner, Mouse came on to the dance floor from one of the rooms leading upstairs to the VIP bar, which was always used by artists as a changing room. She was on all fours dressed as a pink poodle complete with pink tail and hair, and heels, mirroring the animal iconography inscribed onto the deportment, dirt and 'breeding' of particular working-class women (see Mort (2000) on the wayward woman and prostitute during the Victorian period). Extreme aspects in the performance included anal self-fisting, pushing a bib out of her vagina and placing the bib (which had the words 'Dirty Dog' on it) around her neck. The bib provoked laughter in the audience. The bib was tongue-in-cheek putting into words a description of her identity: dirty. As the performance developed, the bib's use of keeping dirt away was replaced by the dirty things she was doing with her body and the use of her orifices for fun and not heterosexual penetrative sex or masturbation.

Mouse also lit three sparklers after their handles were inserted into her anus and vagina. After taking these out, she sat down in a bowl of soapy water and intensified naughtiness and 'dirt' by using the water to give herself two enemas squirted out towards the audience on three sides. The guy in the audience with the umbrella put it up as she aimed, to which the audience responded with more laughter. Usually the audience in burlesque striptease are involved at a distance, with the performer not exposing their body in extreme, dirty or confrontational ways. Breaking the limits of taste and decency illuminates that preferred clean femininity is not the only way to do femininity or to showcase the power of the body, orifices and individual creativity. Showcasing the explicit use and value of orifices sees the body as a site of power, with the vagina becoming a multipurpose space of strength and expression. The vagina is not weak; it is strong just like Mouse's femininity. Questioning the use of the vagina also destabilizes the meaning of the word 'dirt' as something that is negative and socially abhorrent. This playfulness highlights the inability of categories to fully capture the range of expressions of femininity, as well as exposing how meaning is not something that is fixed or certain.

Mouse's use of her body and the control she exuded over the props she used shows that the body, the imagination and identity have more potential and are spaces to create. The vagina was not connected with shame or devaluation, nor did she devalue/parody other women. The vagina was present as something with power and ability. The use of the orifices, eating dog food and presenting femininity in a way that can repulse, asserts an agency which is individually specific, allowing her to revel in context. Significantly, Mouse destabilizes the use of her orifices through detaching heterosexual sex as the definitive genesis and purpose of 'sexual' holes. Not only does she highlight social norms confirming dirt, she goes beyond this to assert an agency which is not abhorrent. Confidence and lack of shame in this performance demonstrate the ways in which femininity can be presented, highlighting agency through rediscovering how femininity can be conceived through the body. Conceiving femininity need not to be in the absence of sexual holes but their re-definition through strength, use and context.

Doris La Trine: Burlesquing Bulimia

The stage as a space for stories, protest and women's voices is also evidenced by Doris La Trine. Similarly to Mouse, Doris La Trine (Liselle Terret) reworks the reveal, but in her context she burlesques bulimia with her toilet prop called Len. She also challenges the visual ideal of beauty and feminine success by delivering a spectacular, honest and gritty narrative that directly confronts audiences' ideas around the body, the abject and women's constant navigation of their agency. Liselle Terret (in Nally and Smith, 2012:128) explains that 'referring to it throughout as "him", the toilet (for Doris La Trine) debunks the glamorous object (champagne glass) of von Teese, to explore the current social climate where women desperately grasp for a visual ideal and attempt to navigate feelings of powerlessness and abjection: ... (so as) to reposition people's ideas about bulimia'. The personal is political, and for Liselle Terret the platform she uses enables her to challenge perceptions, to celebrate her own identity and to show women that their stories need to always occupy space.

The performance re-appropriates burlesque and uses the reveal as a political weapon to give visibility to stories of femininity, but also as a feminist praxis to confront the commodification of women's experience into a neat, clean and safe narrative. Dirtiness, the abject and feelings of unease are areas which Doris La Trine plays with, specifically turning the body into a site of protest. This site of protest confronts audiences with an inescapable truth about women's experiences. Performing this for the penultimate act on a Valentine's day burlesque night at a theatre in Birmingham drew out significant reactions from the audience who had viewed a range of cheesecake and classic renditions of burlesque before she entered the stage. The other burlesque artists could be easily recognized as 'burlesque' as the style of performance, makeup and pin-up themes correlated to more mainstreamed ideals.

After pushing the golden toilet bowl on stage, Doris La Trine's monologue explores her relationship with the toilet, her body and her sexuality. As the story unfolds, she starts to take off her clothes and confronts the audience by revealing her story and her life experience. The penultimate reveal is her mimicking being sick in her toilet, which is accompanied by the sound of retching and sick splattering into a toilet bowl. On speaking about her bulimia, Liselle Terret (Doris La Trine) explained: 'I cannot escape the bulimia ... I carry this with me ... this toilet is part of who I am: it is my identity. It's like having a bulimic mentality that is constantly pushing me to a place that is very uncomfortable, where there is constant danger, so that everything in my world could collapse. The bulimic act might have ended but it is in everything I do. I am in constant recovery.' The reveal explores women's realities, which include their relationship with their body and how they navigate people's opinions of what they do with their body, femininity and voice. Some women in the audience did speak to Liselle Terret afterwards and expressed that the performance resonated with them. However, the more extreme reactions to Doris La Trine included disgust (verbal: in the theatre space through whispers), audience members leaving the theatre space during the performance and online abuse. For Liselle Terret she felt that she had 'shattered the male gaze, the facade, the titillation of the other performers before me, those objectified burlesquing–women. The men were angry. Perhaps my bulimic act parodied the entire night as a powerful metaphor'. Abuse included comments on online forums stating she was too old and that the performance was not appropriate, one fellow performer dismissing the performance as odd, and general hostility from the audience who wanted to be entertained. The latter undermines the idea that burlesque is a space for resistance, women's stories and feminist praxis. What the performance has provoked is patriarchy's refusal to see women as more than objects and, when confronted with an unapologetic account of agency, this is violently abjected.

> **Liselle Terret:** What's this? It's messy, dirty! It doesn't turn us on. Why would we want to hear that your dishes at home are dirty, we aren't interested in your dishes! Keep your dishes, we want your tits. We want the object. We want your body. We are not interested in what's going on for you at all, and we are violently going to get rid of you because it doesn't fit into our agenda.

Preforming in non-queer spaces can be confrontational, with the performer experiencing a clash of social, personal and gendered scripts. Although it might appear to be safer to perform in queerer spaces, the autobiographical and raw tease presented by Doris La Trine enables a needed queering of normative space through upending performative expectations, desire and discourse.

If women's stories cannot be told in a performative space where they are apparently revered, this shows how the commercial availability of burlesque ideals irradiates personal politics and renders Bad/Dirty (i.e. Other) women's voices unworthy.

2

Bad Girls happen to things

Ms T is a young queer British burlesquer who identifies as femme. She addressed her sexuality as queer, with a preference for women. She maintained that her queerness does not box or categorize her within any particular type of romantic or gendered relationship. For reasons of confidentiality the name 'Ms T' is a pseudonym. To protect her identity, themes that emerge through her burlesque performances are presented, rather than a detailed description which could explicitly identify her. Central to this case study is the concept of the Bad Girl. Through Ms T's life story, we will see how 'Bad Girls happen to things' is a radical act of self-love that articulates the importance of women's sexual self-identity. Themes in this case study have emerged through a holistic view of meanings derived from different data sets (i.e. conversations in the field, participant observation, ethnographic interview and interview transcript, fieldwork diary). It will be argued that being a Bad Girl is not necessarily a negative thing and that sexual women are not strange, dirty or lacking something. Evidence will be drawn from Ms T's lived experiences, how she has negotiated her identity in various cultural sites and how she articulates experiences via performances on stage.

The kinky and queer Bad Girl

Growing up in the 1990s, Ms T never felt that she was an average conventional girl. After finishing her GCSEs, she was looking forward to A-Levels with dreams of meeting new and exciting people. She felt that the other students she met were not like her or how she identified. During this period, she started to go to BDSM fetish clubs and she found the contrast between going to one particular club and coming back home the next day to the rituals of Sixth Form thrilling. The most important thing for her was being in a space and inside a community that she identified with. Socializing with a variety of people can open up space which allows the individual to express self-identity in ways that might be hidden elsewhere. Hiding aspects of identity can be due to fear of being judged or being seen as someone that needs to be saved (see Chapters 1 and 3). Importantly, for Ms T she felt she had found a variety of people in the BDSM fetish club that accepted her without judgement. Identification with this group allowed her a visibility she had previously not felt. She was able to take up space and explore her self-identity in new ways. Identifying with the atmosphere and a shared mentality of doing things 'differently', she stated:

> **Ms T:** Even though everyone was so diverse I really felt like I really fitted in with this community of – not outsiders – but people who did things differently ... I felt that I had more in common with them.

Ms T disclosed that she had struggled with her sense of identity until she experienced BDSM clubs, finding that she could be anything she wanted to be at any given moment in time. Significantly, she does not use language to 'Other' or marginalize those in BDSM fetish clubs, as the label of 'outsider' can stigmatize bodies and lifestyles that are socially perceived as abject, dirty and strange. Ms T was careful in her choice of language when articulating her self-identity and biography, especially as she previously had counselling to explore why she had same-sex feelings. These feelings had been a point of shame for her. Part of this struggle was through feeling that she did not live up to the expectations of rigid definitions of sexual orientations, even within gay and lesbian groups. On gay clubs and hearing women having similar experiences, she expressed:

> **Ms T:** I had to over lesbian myself, like really over emphasize every same sex experience, denounce everything that could possibly make me look like I was in doubt. And I don't wanna have to hide my past or hide a part of myself to prove myself to people who aren't going to believe me whatever I say ... I had this conversation [...] [and] it was incredible to hear other women saying exactly the same as me and hate the way they have to re-emphasize everything, constantly defend themselves and sort of down play personal aspects in their lives that could make them look questionable and sort of really constantly re-stressing ... There is like this constant self-denial and defence all the time. It was rewarding to hear other women who have also had it.

Having to defend her sexual identity and choices was a point of frustration; however, Ms T expressed that the BDSM and fetish community she connected with allowed space for her to be comfortable with her sexuality and body. Interestingly, this sense of belonging connected with her not having to worry that she would offend, be seen as a straight tourist or somehow have to re-emphasize the preconditions of a fixed 'sexual identity' associated with binaries (gay/straight, etc.). Instead of suppressing her self-identity, the BDSM fetish club she frequented enabled her the freedom to style herself in her own terms and gave her the opportunity to be creative, especially when designing performances for stage shows. Making friends with the management of the club enabled her to create new nights combining BDSM and kink with music and dancing. Her success and popularity with the management and others in this club made her a valued member who had input in the community. She was an insider, which demonstrates the central role friendships play for individuals accessing that sense of value and acceptance. Not everyone may have this experience in BDSM clubs, and it is important to note that Ms T was outgoing, good looking and a very charming person. However, for Ms T and other research participants alike, the fetish BDSM club experiences became a space where she could amplify aspects of her identity without the fear of being judged based on her appearance, sexual expression and gender identity.

Friendships are integral to self-esteem, self-acceptance and self-expression, so the BDSM club was an important factor for Ms T and the development of her performance themes. Also, having more in common with a particular group is an enabling factor in recognizing that you are not alone, which can give the individual a sense of belonging and credibility. One theme that kept repeating itself in the interview was identification. In the ethnography Ms T discussed how her style and physical appearance were factors that had initially denied her access and credibility in more commercial parts of gay culture and community. This is something we need to explore, as her performances are contextualized through her life experiences and informed by her sense of identity. She expressed:

> **Ms T:** … At the time I hadn't quite grasped that it was really because of my appearance that no one was interested, but I think that I obviously looked like a straight tourist so then I didn't get the same welcoming feeling. I didn't meet anyone there because no one would really wanna talk to me. I didn't end up going to anything like that, so it was quite nice to be part of the group where it didn't really matter what your sexuality was 'cause there's so many different ones within it and if you were feminine looking, it didn't seem to matter.

The inability of certain groups to recognize queerness due to physical appearances highlights that binaries cannot capture lived experiences, or a variety of shifting contexts. Ms T's identity can easily be captured in the category of 'straight' and 'feminine', but this categorization is informed by perceptions rather than taking into account the embodied knowledge of that particular individual. What Ms T identified above is two elements of identification: physical recognition and how styling identity in specific ways supposedly connects to your sexuality. Although one could argue Ms T's personal style is political in itself, the gothic femme image does not really connect with wider cultural connotations to mainstream gay and lesbian culture. Schacht (2000) and Wilson (1993:108) both explore the typical styles associated with lesbian and gay identity. Communal allegiance and style as political (i.e. butch haircuts, bears, camp queens, etc.) are read as forms of resistance against heterosexual gender positions. Although certain styles and politics can become homonormative and restrictive, Wilson (1993:108) outlines the ways in which the political statements invested in dress are tied to a history of struggle (see Stein (1997) too on politics, physical aesthetics and lifestyle). Much like the streamlining of burlesque femininities (see Chapter 5), those considered insiders use the 'correct' style to demonstrate they are part of the community (see Chapter 1 on bisexuality).

Aligning yourself with the wider norms and communicating this through certain styles and behaviours mean you are not questioning gendered, bodily and sexual politics of the group. If someone questions group politics or goes against the grain, then their motives might be questioned, they might be ostracized and they might not be trusted. For Ms T being read as a tourist, a bisexual and kinky rendered her an outsider. Her femme looks and alternative style of dress set her at a disadvantage. Being associated with the bisexual, the Bad Girl, the whore, the slut and the femme fatale are factors which groups may use to reject the idea that this identity is political, stable and something of worth. The pollutant, the spreader of disease, the woman who likes to do dirty things to her body, destabilizes group norms and exposes the limitation of language. Thus, the attitude is: if you do not get this identity, just disavow it and use wider cultural perceptions to denounce it. Associations stick to identity and it is easy for a dominant group to use the language afforded to them to cast off anything they deem as Other or unreadable. Consequently, bisexuality, BDSM and kink, and queerness can be questioned and rejected by lesbian and gay politics as sexualities in their own right (Weeks, 1991, 1995). This is damaging. Ms T maintained that for her, being in a group where it did not matter what your sexuality was opened up the possibility of other sexualities which were genuine and legitimate for her (i.e. BDSM, kink, bisexuality, queerness, etc.).

> **Ms T:** As far as I am concerned, sexuality is an incredibly fluid thing, and to put it into three tick-boxes of 'gay/bi/straight' is absolutely insane. Of course, some people really do fit into those categories, and that's great for them, but I much prefer to be a big mish-mash of desire and express myself however I choose, sleep with whoever I choose and not worry about which box that puts me in, or if I am somehow tainting someone else's definition of that label with my behaviours. Like: 'Well, if you call yourself a lesbian then go prancing around taking your clothes off in front of men, you can't be a proper one, and you make the rest of us look bad.'

What the above highlights are issues to do with hierarchies and ideals. Ms T explained further in the ethnographic interview that she felt her feelings towards women were dismissed by some lesbians who asked if she was going through a 'stage', which directly links to the tourist label: a person who is only present for a short period of time and will bring nothing of value to the wider community. However, we cannot paint the gay and lesbian 'community' as one monolithic entity as there are differences in attitudes, acceptance and perceptions depending on the location, geography and individuals who reside in particular social settings. Although Ms T felt that BDSM fetish clubs did not constrict her gender and sexuality to a specific style, when she moved to another city she began to socialize in the butch-femme community. In this community, she began to understand that her femininity was celebrated and that differences did not matter.

She felt the people she met acknowledged her sense of identity and appearance in positive ways.

> **Ms T:** Since I moved I found it a lot more welcoming overall, of all different types of sexualities, and all appearances, and being femme is a good thing, not something to be criticised. I have felt much more at home meeting people in the butch/femme lesbian community and genderqueer community in general.

Scope of self-expression

Through her experiences, we can see that there is scope open for including more ways to desire, to express yourself sexually and to be feminine. What Ms T also suggests is that sexuality can change at any point, meaning that gender should not always be a determinate factor for attraction or identification with a specific 'type'. Instead, attraction, desire and identification are specific to an individual person at any given time. One point of contestation is that this openness only really translates to in-between spaces (i.e. queering space) and people who already share the same belief systems as you. The spaces which Ms T performs at and identifies with provide her the opportunity to express herself in a particular way, giving her a feeling of belonging, solidarity and agency which are not always present in a variety of social settings. Although the scope of Ms T's gender expression and style are based in the spaces she has chosen to situate her identity within, it is important that we explore the themes in her stage performances. Ms T outlined that there are no differences between who she is on stage and who she is off stage, as the attributes represent an amplified version of her self-identity, rather than a parody of specific women. The extent to which she can express these ideals beyond the relationships she has built in certain spaces she socializes and performs will be critiqued. It is vital, therefore, to see what we can learn from her attitudes towards gender, sexuality and sexual expression. How, then, can Dirt, filth and being a Bad Girl enable sexual women to be seen as progressive and important in re-articulating femininity in powerful ways?

Ms T expresses herself in a visual form and this recurs throughout her biography. For Ms T, the themes presented in her performances and her sexuality are inseparable, as both reflect her self-identity. She maintains that she bares her soul on stage and that the amplified version of herself actually reflects what she represents and identifies with. Instead of poking fun at women or demonizing them, Ms T uses the stage to extend *her* self-identity and to exist in various spaces on her own terms. On narrating her self-identity, Ms T expressed: 'I like the sort of collective idea of this [Ms T] expressing all those sides of me and the other me being the rest of me, but even then, both sides complement each other and feed into each other. Things I pick up in my everyday life I will use in [Ms T].' Agency comes through positioning herself within sexual politics and this is maintained through the spaces she performs in and where she negotiates her self-identity through (i.e. on and off stage). As she amplifies parts of herself, she is not applying stereotypes. Despite her vampy image easily connoting to wider cultural notions of vampy women as provocateurs, her flirting with female audience members disqualifies binary notions of desire between heterosexuals. This amplified space demonstrates other routes to embody self-identity, and these routes do not have to be tied to heteronormative or homonormative linear narratives and endpoints.

We will see further on in this chapter that Ms T incorporates and oozes overt sexuality within her performances, but interestingly does not degrade or make strange the sexual desires or the sensuality of the performer. The personal can connect with women in the audience who might be attracted to her or somehow identify with her sexual expression and identity. This is significant as the performer can be more than someone who entertains, but also a vehicle where counter-discourses and new ways of doing femininity can be articulated, lived and felt. The Bad Girl happens to things: *she is subject*, not object. Visual means of transmitting the personal on stage, and audience members receiving and interpreting this in positive ways, are still reliant upon the space where the performance is located and the beliefs/values of the individuals in the space. Although her shows still rely on the acknowledgement and the capacity of seeing sexual women in positive light, the ways she re-presents and articulates the 'Bad Girl' demonstrate a powerful way for women to embrace their sexual assertiveness and sexual self-identity. The application of this positive image opens space and allows Ms T to co-opt cultural assumptions and to challenge them, through repositioning agency as central in articulating sexual assertiveness and sexual confidence.

Adapting from the BDSM fetish performances she used to do, Ms T continues to perform specifically through burlesque striptease. Ms T performs on a local circuit and does burlesque as a local cultural practice rather than internationally or as a career like Empress Stah, who we will see in the next chapter. As Ms T's shows are informed by her lived experiences and her negotiation with gender and sexuality, it is therefore important to contextualize her shows and how they are conceived.

Intimacy, Dirt and the Monster Stomp

The themes which were repeated in her performances included: female sexuality, gender, self-pleasure, same-sex attraction, horniness, Bad Girls, BDSM, foreplay, sensuality, sexy dirtiness and being filthy with the body. The 1950s pin-up style was something that Ms T appropriated, much like the themes found in wider BDSM and burlesque circuits. Her style also included goth, rockabilly, pseudo-military uniform, 1950s domesticity and kitsch American culture. In the ethnography Ms T explained that inspiration for shows can come from listening to a piece of music or from an outfit. Ms T's performance repertoires are also formed through set themes for whichever nights she is performing at, with some ideas being constructed a week or a few days in advance of gigs. Ms T customized the outfits she performed in and used the props and clothing in her everyday life too. This tailoring signifies the importance of DIY cultures (McKay, 1998) but also the importance of self-expression and individual creativity. Using items in everyday life saves money too. Ms T explained that she mixes cheaper pieces of clothing from high street shops, with expensive corsets and lingerie so she gets more use of the outfits as they can get ripped easily. Themes in her performances range from cutesy naughty girl and the charming domestic goddess to the vampiric sexual sadomasochist pouring candle wax all over her body. The diversity of her shows is important to address, as they demonstrate several ways of presenting extensions of femininity. Although traditional styles of teasing were applied in some performances, such as fan dances and parasols used to conceal and reveal parts of her body, the inclusion of stripper heels and the way she grinded the wall and slapped her bottom cheeks articulated sexual intent. The application of burlesque was intimate, horny and personal. The normative ideals around the Bad Girl and femme fatale are queered by Ms T in her performance of monstrous femininity in the following performance: Monster Stomp.

As the bright lights lit up the stage, Ms T strutted on dressed in vintage lingerie, six-inch heels and a horror mask. She stomped across the stage like a sexy feminine monster causing havoc in a 1950s American city (think attack of the 50-foot woman). She glared at the audience from behind her mask. Her monstrous femininity was alluring and dangerous as she danced seductively. The horny and sexy dance made the creature exciting and other worldly. The Bad Girl and the femme fatale were present, but the queering of these through alluring intimacy and comedy demonstrated that sexual women are not really that monstrous. The performance space included regular audience members, and as Ms T performed several times in a night new audience members would become familiar with her style of tease. The tongue-in-cheek tease makes femininity fun, and pop-culture references to 1950s queer pulp help her convey self-identity in her own way. The performance is choreographed and constructed with a queer audience in mind, allowing her to re-write rules and question norms. In this tease (indeed all of her shows), she outlines that sexual women can actively desire and be desired and this does not compromise how she defines her femininity. Although hiding her face may conversely connote that the bad sexual woman has to protect her identity, the unknown is alluring. The cultural standards that are projected onto sexual women may make them appear monstrous, but this is shaken off by the shimmy and the allure of a confident woman who does not care about what others think of her. The cheers and support from the audience highlight that sexual women cannot always be seen as strange or negatively dangerous.

Slippages away from burlesque ideals (i.e. through same-sex attraction, the performer being desired and mutually reciprocating desire, etc.) enables the presence of same-sex desire and shines a light on the Bad Girl being visible, having agency and being recognized as powerful and a desirable subject position. What was consistent in her burlesque was the permanency and consistency of sexual confidence and the invitation of intimacy between audience and performer. Gazing at women intensely whilst slapping her buttocks or dripping wax down her body acknowledges the importance of same-sex desire and self-pleasure. Tassel-twirling, the bump-n-grind (i.e. 'doing sex' – see Liepe-Levinson, 2002:113) and feeling her own body with her hands are standard attributes of the classic striptease; however, how she looked at audience members and how she flirted with them broke the fourth wall in interestingly sexual ways. The aesthetics of burlesque emphasize the anatomy of the performer and make her hyper-feminine (Liepe-Levinson, 2002:113), which is integral for Ms

T's political stance on queering expectations and norms surrounding the body, desire and femininity. Although Liepe-Levinson (2002:113) maintains that critics' emphasis on the anatomy of the performer 'epitomises ... the very mechanics by which women are objectified in Western culture', Ms T's assertiveness and the repetition of themes (i.e. body, desire, intimacy, filth, sex, etc.) actually demonstrate confidence and clarity. The outfits she wears during performances are horny, sexy and kinky making her look confident and sexually powerful. Sex and horniness are not 'bad' things, but routes to explore self-identity. Sexual confidence is projected beyond the stripper heels and lacy underwear through how she actively invites the audience to desire *her*. What she performs is not a parody or a reconstruction of gender stereotypes.

Women's desire is usually repackaged in popular culture as safe, with aspects of burlesque and kink becoming normalized practices in women's consumption and practices of 'new' femininities post-90s (see Evans and Riley, 2014; Ferreday, 2008; Attwood, 2005) and, indeed, through the 'fourth wave' focus on social/digital media. The representation of women's sexual pleasure in popular culture is usually commodified as 'fashionable, safe and aesthetically pleasing and feminine' (Attwood, 2005:2), as seen in Anne Summers for instance and the feminization of the space as safe and not seedy (see Evans and Riley, 2014). The visibility of sexual pleasure and women being seen as sexual consumers (i.e. through the popularity of burlesque on the high-street, sex toys and other consumer goods, such as vintage lingerie) domesticates the goods (i.e. commodities) and, indeed, 'alternative' ways to perform sexiness and appeal (i.e. the temporary Bad Girl in the bedroom). Domestication means that these items become 'everyday' and part of an accepted range of expressing the 'sexual' woman. The politics are nullified to an appropriate level of respectability, which then produces safe femininity, safe space and a safe position for women to occupy. This is at the expense of women who choose not to conform to these standards. Although Ms T uses items of clothing and dance moves associated with burlesque and other forms of striptease, sexual intensity and sexual invitation take this temporary performance into something embodied and radically feminine. Despite only existing in moments and perhaps individuals seeing her only once, her burlesque is still a significant display of resistance. Ms T creates a space where possibilities are exchanged. In this instance, possibilities focus on actively desiring the individual audience member and the possibility of the audience member desiring her in return. Her power and confidence on stage re-presented sexual femininity and same-sex desire as achievable and real.

The use of her body and the intimacy suggested between audience and performer allow her to exude desire and challenge the idea that female sexual display is about exchange into submission and powerlessness. Sexual horniness, sexiness, orgasm and enjoying her own body make intimacy real and of great importance to the woman feeling it in her own body. Although the construction of her shows still relies on cultural understandings of Bad/Dirty femininity, the inclusion of intimacy and the themes of dirt, sensuality and an embodied account of bodily desire demonstrates the expansive qualities of femininity. Although the meanings she plays with do not fully sit outside of language (i.e. she needs to connect with the audience and entertain them, etc.), it is the embodiment of intimate knowledge that allows the 'Bad Woman' to be visible beyond the remit of dominant discourses that reinforce the value of safe and clean forms of femininity. Ms T does not vilify Other or distance herself from women who are culturally seen to lack agency (i.e. strippers and adult performers), and her choice in designing shows for particular venues and for specific events is an active and conscious choice to assert control over her sexuality and the way in which her femininity is expressed.

Bad Girls happen to things

During the ethnographic interview Ms T discussed one performance that really intrigued her. After the music stopped due to technical problems, both the audience and compere started to sing a parody of the song she was teasing to. The song the audience and compere were singing linked her performance to disease and STIs. Although being linked to disease might appear to be unsexy, Ms T maintained that the contrast this had to the sexy traditional striptease actually improved the performance. Dirt did not taint her femininity, in fact performing 'both/and' the sexy/dirty, the good/bad was positive. Being both at the same time opens queer possibilities and other avenues to exist in-between, in grey areas and beyond the binary. The perverse and the clean are unstable categories, and although overt sexuality was present in her performances, Ms T did not degrade or make strange the sexual desire or the sensuality of the performer. The audience (mainly comprised of women) has access to this mutual desire. The performer is more than someone who entertains. Burlesque and desire are the vehicles to get 'the personal' across to the audience. Despite shows still relying on the audience's capacity of seeing a sexual woman in a positive frame, sexual assertiveness and confidence were prominent and recurring themes. The repetition and application of positive sexual self-identity open up space and allow Ms T to use and actively challenge cultural assumptions by reclaiming 'Bad Girl' identity through the use of subcultural attributes. This correlates to Emily White's (2002) stance that the embrace of the freak and subcultural identity offers a variety of ways to 'represent and articulate the "slut" experience', and for many women this is 'a powerful way of rescuing themselves from their sexual victimisation'. Agency and choice come from the position she places herself in, and this is maintained through the spaces she performs at and the spaces she creates in intimate moments between performer/audience. The amplification of parts of herself enables her to question the notion of stereotyping as she does not objectify, poke fun at or judge any other expression of femininity. As Ms T's performance themes and intent do not 'Other' or make sexual women strange, it signals that the application of heteronormative paradigms is constrictive and corrosive because it imposes artificial barriers intent on holding the power of Bad Women back.

'Dirtying it out'

The themes of dirt and overt sexual expression are central issues in Ms T's performances and her attitudes towards the body, gender and sexual expression. Although it was found in ethnographic fieldwork that there was a distinction between clean and dirty female sexual expression in burlesque (see Chapter 5), the raunchy nature of Ms T's performances and their permanent place in themes and all aspects of who she is highlights an approach which does not judge or categorize what female sexual desire should live up to. This expression is individual and personal. Significantly, her performances did not nullify sexual desire linked to objectification and, most importantly, same-sex attraction was not abandoned for heterosexuality as seen in many burlesque performances in the ethnography (i.e. pop culture's flirtation with the Bad Girl can be placed here too, such as Christine Aguilera's *Not Myself Tonight* video, 2010).

Intrinsic to her creativity is the belief that female sexual expression is not a bad thing. This is applied to all women, not just clean forms of femininities seen in burlesque. Radically she does not distinguish herself from or judge herself as more valid than any other women. Burlesque and BDSM are queerly used to enable Ms T to re-articulate her lived experience and sexual self-identity as something that is acceptable and permissible. In several performances seen, Ms T made it clear that she liked women, although her femme pin-up style does not correspond to 'typical' gayness. The femme pin-up style (Luther, 2000) and the Bad Girl image Ms T likes to play with open up space (i.e. social, political, bodily, etc.) where women can exist on their own terms, instead of being rejected due to their style of dress being culturally associated with the dismissal of sexual certainty (Stein, 1997). If there is no space for you, then make it or find places that welcome you. Two key themes that emerged out of interview data and performances were sexual desire and the lack of positive recognition for women like Ms T (i.e. pin-up, Bad Girl, slut, etc.). This was a point of contestation and challenge for Ms T, particularly as the image of the Bad Girl was so important for her. The Bad Girl was a theme which was central to her self-identity, performance style and belief system. I wanted to know what Ms T understood about the image of the Bad Girl and how she negotiated this image through the meanings constructed within her performances. As the Bad Girl was a standing point which she valued both on and off stage, it was important for the research to give space for her to explore what this subject position meant for her. Connecting the 'Bad Girl' to her physical appearance, I asked if she thought that the Bad Girl image (in general) pointed towards bisexuals and femme fatales which she embodies on stage. Replying to this question, Ms T expressed:

> **Ms T:** Yeah … the tainter of the pure … like this bad force dragging everyone down and the idea of a bisexual female tainting the lesbian community with disease which [they've] got from a man, 'cause of course a lesbian can't have a disease just all on her own(!). Yeah that whole idea of taking something good and dirtying it out.

'Dirtying it out' can be a metaphor for binaries, but also there is queer potential here as dirtying out makes the 'good' an unstable category amongst an undefinable number of subject positions. Ms T maintained that she identified with the 'Bad Girl' but argued that this figure was something more than being reduced to sexual parts, or something negative implying that the Bad Girl usually 'infects' and makes women's choices dirty. Consequently, the tainter of the pure represents something which can destabilize established moral codes and political subject positions. It is an identity that is seemingly lacking any sort of value for the 'common good' and socially abhorrent if the 'bad' is not commercially viable or palatable (i.e. attitudes can link to taste, values and hierarchies). Social approval indicates solidarity and integrity, both of which signify agency. This usually applies automatically and without question to normative identities that are visible, valuable and socially acceptable. Heterosexuality erroneously implies 'completeness' which is maintained through gender distinctions (Krieger, 1996:28). The Bad Girl seems to lack these qualities within heteronormative contexts.

The challenge Ms T presents is the questioning of these values through the re-articulation of the Bad Girl via positive ways (i.e. complete, not impure in the traditional sense, and not shameful). Although living by your own rules might seem to be something negative, it is something of great value for Ms T and her understanding of embodying the Bad Girl: the woman who lives in that in-between space, not fitting either side of the binary (she is both/and). I was interested in the value Ms T places on the 'Bad Girl', so I asked her to explore what she meant by this term.

GC: When you say Bad Girl, what do you mean by that?

Ms T: It's someone who lives by their own rules, instead of someone else's. It's someone who says 'this is me, and I love me, whether you do or not', who does not hide her sexuality even if others don't understand it. I don't worry about whether that makes me impure. I think a lot of women who express their sexuality differently, in whatever manner, are stereotyped as Bad Girls but whereas if you go and have one monogamous relationship to another, that's OK 'cause you are always in a monogamous relationship, so you're playing by the rules, you can be controlled.

Bad Girls, sex and stereotypes

Ms T connected the connotations of the Bad Girl to sex (i.e. the physical/intimate act) and the bodies of particular women who are stereotyped. Her performances and description of the Bad Girl outline her opposition to the restrictions placed on women who question and reject social control. Heterosexuality and the value placed on monogamy are vehicles of control and degradation. What Ms T highlights is that there are a variety of ways in which women can express their sexuality in their own terms. Although Ms T states that playing by the rules (i.e. the binary) allows women to be controlled, what is different is her perception of the Bad Girl having the ability to be who she wants to be (i.e. on her own terms – which is a similar theme found in Holland's work on tattooed women, which we explored in Chapter 1 in relation to fluffy femininity). This does not mean those who play by the rules are unconscious, or not of significant value. Ms T's opposition enables her to position herself in a space where she can comment on self-identity, sexuality and spectrums (we will see similarities with Empress Stah in the next chapter). Defining the Bad Girl in her own terms is positive; however, there are some issues. One issue is having to open space for identity to be visible (i.e. the clubs she chooses to perform at), which makes this particular expression of identity legitimate. This positive visibility and recognition may not generally be the case in popular culture or the wider social environments Ms T negotiates. Although Ms T maintains that Bad Girls do not depend on the approval of others, this is difficult as everyone still needs to feel recognized as having value and agency. However, her actions enable her to 'happen to things' instead of social pressures holding her back and denying her agency. It is a radical and political act of self-love and gives justice to her self-identity.

> **Ms T:** A Bad Girl is too often seen as being a bad thing, when in fact it is society's definition that makes it that way. For me, a Bad Girl

makes her own rules, makes her own adventures. She does not wait for things to happen to her – she happens to things. Society wants women to remain in serial monogamous relationships (otherwise she is a slut and 'Bad Girl'), whereas it is fine for men to be 'studs' and sleep around as they please. Bad boys are praised, Bad Girls are not. Or if they are praised, it is only on the merit of that one facet of their sexuality, something temporary. They are OK to fuck, but not to love. It's fine to sleep with one of them, but you don't want your girlfriend to be one. Bad Girls depend on themselves, not on the approval of others, and do not play by the definitions set upon them by a society trying to box them in and control them.

Maintaining that Bad Girls depend on themselves implies that if your identity invites societal disapproval, just continue what you are doing anyway and stay strong. Conversely, acceptable forms of sexual expression are still mediated by mainstream culture and other institutions of power. Keeping strong can be difficult, but *not impossible*. As solidarity and integrity are vital in any human relationship and social group, it can be difficult for anyone to always challenge norms for fear of losing friends, loved ones and respect from others you may identify with. This was something Ms T reflected on; however, having a sex-positive approach to life was something very meaningful to her. Having a sex-positive attitude is significant because for Ms T, Bad Girls can have sex with who they want, the way they want and where they want. This is a defiant attitude to how, where and to what degree women choose to have sex or 'fuck'. Here, there is a repackaging of female sexuality as a lifestyle choice, which is not commodified. Women 'do sex' rather than sex being 'done' to them. Although Ms T's approach to sexuality and gender is defined by her as fluid, this is against the backdrop of the variety of femininities presented in consumer culture that are still re-packaged in binary good/bad positions. Pornography, bisexuality and attitudes towards 'dirty Bad Women' are still used as a means of disempowering sexual women who fall beyond socially sanctioned ways of embodying their gender. The words Ms T uses when she refers to 'Bad Girls depending on themselves' acknowledge this because Bad Girls that fall outside the commercial repackaging do not yet have the luxury of the visibility she carefully upholds in her own life. Bad Girls depending on themselves highlight that independency is perhaps not just a choice, but actually a survival strategy too. The presence of Ms T demonstrates that not every woman is uniform and not all women feel obligated to fall into mainstream normative trappings as they do not identify with those specific contexts. In striptease Liepe-Levinson (2002:187) outlines that not all strip contexts can advocate social change, but they do show disruptions in uniformity. What this highlights is that sexuality need not to be seen as something dirty or filthy (i.e. in a negative way) as there are sites that women create and congregate to challenge hetero/homonormativity. Sexuality does not need to be seen as dirty or filthy if the person does not follow binary norms. For Ms T, her performances articulate sexual expression as central to self-identity, and her way of seeing and being in the world in queerly disruptive ways. Scope is opened up, even if scope is only negotiated by the individual and the contexts they prescribe to.

> **Ms T:** I definitely want more people to realise that sexuality is not a dirty thing. I'd find it worrying that people are hidden about their sexuality and find it such a wrong thing, that they somehow should not be expressing. If people were more open and comfortable with themselves as sexual beings there would be a lot less problems in the world ... [I] really want people to get that message.

Furthering this, Ms T felt it important to recognize that there are many ways to be female and that there are multiple ways in which femininity can be read, presented and approached. Through appropriating various approaches to sexiness, this allows a variety of possibilities to be evident. This is especially pertinent as the personal is expressed on stage, demonstrating that biography, experience and self-expression are not bypassed. Exploring this and touching upon the 'both/and', Ms T expressed:

> **Ms T:** [I] really want people to get that message and as well the idea that women who will strip or be sexual 'don't know any better', or that you are either Madonna or a whore. You can be everything. And also, I think I would like women to see that you don't have to be some tanned, bottle blonde stereotypical porn star with huge plastic tits, to be sexy. There is so many ways [of] being sexy, and I really want women to be able to see different kinds of bodies and think: hey, she's up there doing that, maybe I'm OK the way I am.

Being OK with who you are (as maintained by Ms T) is significant as it highlights a means to actively shout back and exist in a variety of spaces that may deny your representation. Self-confidence and being connected to like-minded communities enable individuals to navigate identity in their own terms. We will see in the next section that individual journeys are important when exploring and understanding sexual self-identity and the value of the filthy body.

Filthy bodies and sexual security

> **Ms T:** I like my filthy body and I like being filthy with it. I want all women to be able to feel like that and to think it's OK, but not just in a way that's there to pander for men. There's a lot of feminist arguments about "oh so you're trying to reclaim this idea of sexiness, but all it's coming down to is pleasing a man again", which completely disregards any sense of a woman being able to choose what she does with her own body, and having the self-awareness to do so. If a woman just wants to do it by herself; if she just wants to prance around the bedroom with a corset and high heels, or if she wants to perform on stage or just for her lover or whatever else, then who is anyone else to say what she should and should not be doing? Who are we really making happy by denying ourselves and telling other people how to feel about their bodies?

Themes about the body, filth and individuality emerged through the ethnography, and Ms T highlights that there are multiple spaces where Bad Girls can exist in multiple ways and in various terms (e.g. the bedroom, the street, the club, for themselves, for their lover, etc.). Individuals can destabilize and disrupt the status of heterosexual normalcy if they wish to do so. For Ms T, to queer expectations is to continually disrupt and not accept assimilation into norms found in the mainstream. What queering showcases is the importance of individual journeys and changes people make over their life course when exploring their self-identity, desire and gender. The importance of individual journeys is demonstrated by Ms T articulating the personal and allowing her sense of identity to be formed by and through embodied knowledge. Understanding her self-identity is about re-understanding what filthy means through her own experiences. Ms T explores the value of filth and being filthy with her body, opening up new embodied knowledge for her and – potentially – for others engaging with her too.

GC: So, do you think [through] filthy practices and [through] perversity you can actually reclaim your body?

Ms T: I think so. For example, in many 'normal' jobs, you know daily grind stuff, women are subconsciously told they have to be pretty to get anywhere, have to work themselves to the bone to get nowhere. Then at the same time are put down for the very things they have been told in the first place they have to be. I [would] feel more exploited doing that [as] someone's taking advantage of me. So, I think, well if people are going to try and exploit … not exploit but use my physical appearance as a way to get ahead: I may as well do that myself and get where I wanna go with it.

GC: Like self-direction?

Ms T: Yeah definitely. If I want to get somewhere in life, I will make sure I get there myself.

GC: Do what you want, when you want to [and] go where you want …

> **Ms T:** Instead of being a good girl who also has to look a certain way to get somewhere but it's still under someone else's control, I'll think: well I'm just going to be a Bad Girl and use what I have to get where I want to be.

What is significant for Ms T are the feelings attributed to specific bodies, such as women who like to express themselves as sexual beings, and that if women choose to be filthy or sexy with their bodies, then they should not feel shame. This is a radical position to take when we look at the commercial success of burlesque and the Othering of certain performers (e.g. like Mouse and Doris La Trine in Chapter 1) who are doing things to challenge norms that the mainstream burlesque aesthetics uphold as clean, empowering and 'feminist'. However, what Ms T conceives as good/Bad (i.e. despite applying 'a queer perspective') is still culturally recognizable and understood, highlighting that even straddling in-between can still allow Ms T to fall into the same category as 'bad' depending on the attitudes of the audience and if they get what she is trying to bring across. Ms T is an entertainer, so she needs to make sure that her performances connect to audience expectations and cultural knowledge. Although Ms T still uses a culturally understood identity onstage, she provides scope in seeing and embodying a sexually confident woman. One key thing here is that the approach Ms T uses to frame the overtly sexual woman into taboo sexual behaviours is not a bad thing. What developed from this part of the ethnographic discussion directly repeated themes around sidelined identities and social stigma (i.e. sexual women and strippers, etc.). The types of women connected to this are seen to be vulnerable, bad or someone who can taint a community, such as the bisexual or queer woman. This connects back to Stein's (1997) exploration of lesbian identification and the rejection of identities seen to disrupt the equilibrium of emotional–sexual relationships at the heart of lesbian dynamics, politics and discourse. This is something we have already explored earlier in the chapter, but is a repeated theme. What Ms T re-presents is choice irrespective of her identity being visible or included within specific communities. Her queerness disrupts any complacency, which can also be apparent through homonormativity and in parts of LGBT+ communities.

Key themes that emerged through this discussion are approval and sexual security. For Ms T, the idea of approval and issues of stripping at lesbian clubs are something she finds absurd. In response to the suggestion that some lesbian feminists might accuse women who are in stripping spaces/clubs (i.e. as dancers or consumers) as misogynists, she exclaimed:

> **Ms T:** Assuming that a queer woman would never want to strip for another queer woman is problematic to me in the first place. Having a space to do that is actually a wonderful thing for the lesbian community as a whole. If they don't like the idea of paying to look at semi-naked women, there are dozens of other bars they can go to and leave the ones who do want to do that to just enjoy it without being accused of being misogynist, which is absolutely ridiculous. And what on earth is wrong with lesbian women looking at other women being sexual and enjoying it? The point is that they fancy women, so it's OK to want to look at them! Besides, it's not about whether it's better or worse being a man or a woman and looking at strippers, the point is that who is anyone else to say it's wrong in the first place?

What the quote demonstrates is that women do not have to justify themselves, and having the choice to be sexual or think sexually with the gender they desire should be respected (i.e. it is not shameful). The idea that women cannot strip for other women and enjoy it is something which can be easily tied to misogyny (i.e. see the work of Andrea Dworkin and Shiela Jefferys). This relation is not something all women experience, so context and situations need to be recognized, rather than universals overtaking or sidelining lived experiences (see Attwood (2005, 2007a, 2011b) and Budgeon (1998, 2011) on the importance of context in relation to consumer culture and new femininities/sexualities). The approach individuals have to their sexuality and sexual expression cannot always be understood by, neatly fit into, or relate to, binary notions of identity. These themes were repeated by Ms T, and we will see these also emerge through Empress Stah. Although the choice of friendship groups and spaces to socialize/express within can open up scope, it is important to explore how individuals construct their own space to control access and ownership over their self-identity. Ms T's negotiation of social sites and her beliefs about her personal desire shows that sexuality cannot always free women from wider debates and expectations. The idea that a woman may want to perform a striptease for a group of women she identifies sexually with is something that wider culture would see as blasphemous, as it questions the status and approval of mainstream female sexuality and, indeed, the application of a mediated 'alternative' femininity in the burlesque ideal (as explored in Chapter 5).

Queering burlesque can be used as a vehicle for some women to be sexual and express their sexuality in a way which does not distance women from each other or see sexually deviant women as strange. However, the success of this depends on context, *where* a type of sexuality is staged and by what means, specifically as Ms T expresses herself through a local cultural practice. Ms T maintained that she performs for self-expression, despite not acknowledging that the terms of this expression are still mediated by the venue space (i.e. its politics and clientele) and the belief systems of the audience. However, she expressed that what is performed on stage should be real for the performer (i.e. not a parody), which means biography is explored and burlesque becomes a feminist praxis (e.g. such as Doris La Trine's queering of burlesque through bulimia and her relationship with Len the toilet).

Ms T: [I'd] much rather look at someone up on stage and see them as a real person, who has fun and is doing something because she loves it, not just going through the motions, getting her money and getting out of the venue as fast as she can. I mean obviously if it's a job it's a job, but I don't really want it as a job. I want it as self-expression and art and fun. I want to meet people who've just seen me take my clothes off and pour [substances] on myself, and see how they react to it, and show them that overt sexuality does not make a woman strange or messed up in the head. I can be normal just like them.

Mingling with the audience after the performance has ended, Ms T feels that she is giving back to her community: the social group she feels she is part of. For Ms T those in the audience are the sorts of people she would choose to be intimate with. In consequence, the rationale for performance in those spaces is safety but also solidarity. Ms T's choice to perform in her leisure time outlines a personal draw to the activity. There is, however, a huge personal commitment (e.g. much like Doris La Trine) in teasing both in her leisure time and within spaces that she identifies with. One issue concerns restrictions and the extent she can be fully open because the spaces she performs at contain the people she identifies with (i.e. can she really open up fully as kinky in some queer spaces, etc.?). The other issue concerns the extent to which she can apply this honesty and the personal to wider social spaces which may reject her (e.g. like Doris La Trine at the Valentine's Day performance). Both social spheres still mean that she has to negotiate access, approval and credibility. As Ms T performs locally, there is much more for her to lose if she exposes parts of her identity which does not correspond to the community she is part of. Any criticism from those who are close would be devastating.

This magnifies the importance of identity management and knowing the extents to which you can disclose aspects of your self-identity and personal sexual politics. This does not necessarily undermine her self-identity; instead, it gives her knowledge that not all spaces or people will accept her, but other spaces will. The extent to which people censor what they express, even in spaces they identify with, is important to highlight. Being recognized and celebrated is something of great significance when connecting with like-minded others. Ms T has been careful when negotiating and engaging with groups she has felt solidarity with. She has actively had to create context and credibility for herself, and this is how she negotiates the social spaces she performs at and is invested personally in. Access to agency and credibility depends on not only the contexts Ms T is dismissing or resisting, but the contexts which shape herself-expression. This concerns approval.

Ms T: Some people will see any woman being blatantly sexual as being in need of approval, usually male approval, and so weak in herself she cannot possibly value herself as a woman, or that she is so damaged in herself she needs to do this to cover that up. To me, it is the exact opposite. To reveal so much of myself to so many strangers means I need to feel completely secure in my own expression and my own identity because if people are going to have something to say about it, it could very well be something intensely personal. If I felt insecure in my body or in my actions and heard someone turn around and say: 'yeah, well she's fat anyway, and look what a slut she is grinding up there on stage', it could be horribly damaging. As it is, obviously I wouldn't be best pleased, but at the end of the day I like myself and I like the way I look, and if I was looking for approval I certainly wouldn't be doing it this publicly. So, if they don't like what they see, they don't have to look at it. Further to that, I really want to challenge the idea that sexual women cannot be secure in themselves, and that being a 'slut' is a bad thing. Insecure people are often the first to project their issues onto other people, and I for one do not appreciate being the target of their baggage. I want everyone looking at me to challenge themselves and their own ideas of Madonna/whore, good/Bad Girl and what makes a woman feel secure or insecure.

The use of the Madonna/whore binary in the extract above is not completely dependent on normative descriptions of the binary or powerlessness. Instead, Ms T opens up scope by including a personal approach to terms. Actively engaging in subcultural settings allows Ms T to express in a way that is sanctioned and allowed (i.e. the slut is a good thing). This highlights the importance of embodied knowledge. What this acknowledgement enables is seeing the slut in diverse and individual terms, which recognizes the multiple ways an individual styles their body, attitude and approach. This celebrates the slut, rather than falling into tropes that are there to socially control the sexual woman (see Attwood's (2007a) exploration of the term slut as a historical term, which connects to class, women's sexual relation to men and pollution). Gender is given space to be expressed and felt in meaningful ways for the individual woman. Although popular culture, 'girlfriend industries' (Kipnis, 2006) and the rise of burlesque have opened more avenues for women to explore sexual desire and their femininity, these areas are still normative and there is pressure for women to still feel approval from other women. Ms T may be able to perform in 'straight' venues, but her identity as a queer woman may not be recognized in the ways she projects. Her use of burlesque requires the audience to be open to kink, BDSM and the availability of same-sex intimacy.

The slut and Bad Girl are therefore contextualized by the venue and the group who are already open to celebrating sexual expression, rather than condemning or banishing the performers' self-identity by seeing her body as abject, dirty and polluting. As scope is dependent on the venue and the themes it allows, then challenging concepts in wider culture is still a problem. Another issue confronting self-identity and agency is how both of these relate to the etiquettes, attitudes and ethos of the venues and the punters the venues want to attract. How Ms T presents herself and expresses still relies upon the codes and conduct valued by the venues she performs at, and the types of performances they promote and are invested in. The ways in which she negotiates the Bad Girl identity she identifies with opens scope for her to self-express, but she still has to negotiate taste, discourse and values which may challenge her identity in other spaces. However, this contradiction is fruitful as these tensions provoke a queer disabling of binary tropes. Even if 'Bad Girls' may feel just as empowered as women performing in more mainstream burlesque, the meanings that connect to the common interpretation of empowerment still apply dirt as a medium to measure agency. This is why context needs to be applied, rather than reinforcing a universal critique of what agency is and what this means for the women who comment on this through language, performance and 'unsafe'/dirty femininity.

What Ms T demonstrates is that through the use of her burlesque, she seeks to deal with her sexual identity in a space where she has control, irrelevant of the social codes which try and bind her performances to wider discourses that would devalue her. Although this control is given specific space and cannot always be transferable to other women, the presence of this highlights a disruption of heteronormative certainty. Although Ms T's identity and stage performances do show another approach to sexualized women, this approach is still constricted by value systems which classify and categorize who she is through wider cultural factors. The negotiation with and definition of the Bad Girl, and being filthy with her body, show that context needs to constantly be applied when critiquing sexual women. While a variety of femininities and female sexual expressions are visible through consumer culture selling woman clean and safe identities, the scope of expression is still tied to the binary concept of clean and Dirty Bodies.

What Ms T seeks to demonstrate is that sexual woman need not be seen as strange or negatively dirty, rather that they can and do provide avenues for women to obtain control and access over their rights to express in the way they want. Although wider cultural assumptions regarding misogyny and the contexts of clean pure agency provide idealized versions of female sexuality, these definitions cannot always be applied to non-normative sexual women. As Ms T does not parody, devalue or 'Other' sexual women, this suggests that scope is inclusive of all women. The issue presented here still hangs onto justification and contexts, even if some women do have the opportunity to express themselves in sexualized ways or demonstrate an approach to femininity which opens scope through non-normativity. However, the ways in which Ms T creates justification and solidarity for herself, through choosing the places she identifies with in order to express her sexual identity, demonstrate that wider culture still does not recognize these contexts. Therefore, the extent to which the scope of gender and sexuality displayed by Ms T can expand within wider culture is still dependent on several factors. These factors include the access women have to their body through the positive recognition of culturally approved identities. What Ms T demonstrates is that women, who are sexual and are considered to not be pure, *do not* have to justify themselves in order to be seen a stable, albeit this issue being contradictory and dependent on situations.

3

Magnification and the unknown

This chapter draws on the outcomes and emergent themes produced by an ethnographic study of Empress Stah, an Australian-born neo-burlesque, twisted cabaret and trapeze performer. What Empress Stah said, how she performs and the implications of this will be demonstrated through how she negotiates and engages with the concepts of gender and sexuality, through the use of her body. What will be investigated are the meanings and issues which she brings forward in her stage performances, her thought process when conceptualizing a show and the concerns involved when examining these two elements. The impact these have on wider knowledge, concerning gender and our attitudes towards sex, will be assessed through scope, agency and context. Most importantly, what will be focused upon is the diversity to which sex, femininity and desire can be embodied and understood, particularly referencing bisexuality and other acts of non-standard female sexual expression. Analysis will critique the approaches used by Empress Stah to see if these structures can offer ways in which gender, sexuality and desire can be re-assessed.

The approaches she uses will be critiqued in relation to wider social structures. The key performance explored in this chapter is *The Queen of the Night* and the themes of magnification and the unknown. Over a period of a year I travelled to see Empress Stah perform in various locations in London. Fieldwork diaries and thick descriptions of performances were combined with details of performances from Empress Stah's website and online interviews sourced from various

websites and YouTube. A discussion-styled interview was included in
the data collection, at Empress Stah's home.

Background context and performance style

Empress Stah was born in Australia in 1974 and emigrated to the UK
in early 2000. Through her involvement with Torture Gardens (TG),
her performance styles developed and her notoriety has taken her all
over the world. Empress Stah is a global artist and her performances
can be explored and viewed via her website and YouTube. Having the
best education and opportunities afforded to her, Empress Stah always
felt that she was a born performer. She had started to perform when
she pierced her ears in the school toilets. Performing also included
when she started to make her own pornography after reading her
father's *Penthouse* magazine. These themes arise in her performances,
and she maintained that looking back at these elements and who she
is now, it makes her think that she was 'born this way'. A common
narrative that appeared in the ethnography and discussion-styled
interview was 'scope'. In relation to scope, Empress Stah maintained
that she does not want to box her sexual identity, nor did she want
to box her performance style. Although she entertains for a living,
it is still evident that self-identity and self-expression are explored
through the vehicle of performance and that themes in performances
tackle scope (i.e. what women can do), non-normative self-expression
and explicitness (i.e. the Bad Girl, the freak, the woman challenging
norms). Describing sexuality as a spectrum, Empress Stah explained
that in her late teens she had identified as a lesbian but then felt that
attraction was based on the person, regardless of gender. During the
time of the research, she identified as predominantly heterosexual,
but preferred queer looking men in 'frocks' or non-drag 'make-up'.

Empress Stah: I define myself as liking very queer boys mostly. I am heterosexual, but I am not straight and straight men don't do it for me. I was [thinking] they're not my cup of tea, and it occurred to me one day, a few years ago ... I thought, you know what Stah: you're probably not theirs either! [laughs]

Entertaining is her life and although she did go to university in Australia for a while, university was not for her. Similarly, to Ms T, her identity was based on what she identified with and this did not include her university colleagues. The combination of social groups she identified with were those who interested her and who she predominantly socialized with, such as drag queens and other subcultures. Building on this diversity of social groups, after leaving Australia, Empress Stah moved to Amsterdam where she became involved in the large squatting scene. During this time, she did improvisational street performances, a style which she is not keen on. Since 1998, Empress Stah has dedicated her life to her career as an entertainer. Taking a leap of faith, Empress Stah moved to the UK and started to perform freelance at fetish clubs. Her early gigs were at clubs such as FIST and TG, which initially booked her on the merit of her looks. The production team and management at TG became like family to her and she felt she had been embraced. Being involved with cutting-edge creatives in London and having bigger gigs enabled Empress Stah to further develop her performance style and the shows she is famous for (i.e. the Queen of the Night, Gold Stah, etc.). With touring shows in different locations and clubs, she was able to broaden her style. However, it was within fetish club environments like TG where she felt the style and content of her performances could be more challenging (i.e. more extreme) because of the types of people watching in the audience. Although she found the fetish crowd at TG intimidating, she wanted to entertain the crowd and liked the challenge. Empress Stah discussed how her shows evolved:

Empress Stah: Before burlesque there wasn't any cabaret audience. Here was I, this little girl from Australia, like Oh God! All these people are so hard-core and what am I going to do to entertain them! They've been it, seen it, done it all: they are really jaded. I'm not going to shock them. I've never had the desire to shock. I want to entertain and I consider myself an entertainer, so I started devising work more and more for these audiences. I keep challenging myself to come up with new concepts and new ideas 'cause I don't want to repeat anything that I have done in previous shows and that's how the work has really evolved. Torture Garden kept booking me and I kept going on tours and I kept needing the work from them. So, I kept devising more and more work.

The diversity offered by TG and her touring with TG meant she could do a variety of styles depending on the location and crowd. This diversity included being able to do a trapeze show, a body piercing show and a cabaret show. Empress Stah's diverse creativity and range of skills have paved the way for her becoming an established trapeze artist, and neo-burlesque and twisted cabaret performer on the London performance and fetish scene.

Her expertise has grown since working at TG and the Royal Opera House, but also through attending clown school and working on her own production company. The diversity of her skills means that she is internationally renowned for both her trapeze and circus skills, as well as being infamous for shocking audiences with her humorous, perverse and horny neo-burlesque cabaret shows. As well as performing at nightclubs, theatres and restaurants, Empress Stah's cabaret and trapeze shows have also toured festivals all over the world. Festivals have included Glastonbury, Splore and the Adelaide Fringe Festival. Producing theatre-style shows with a variety of other performers was something she wanted to continue doing. The shows she has produced for theatre-style venues and theme events included *The Ice Palace of Malice*, which I attended in 2008 at The Brickhouse in London. Segments of this have been performed at TG too. At the time of the research, Empress Stah noted that she wanted to expand her creative control of the types of entertainment she wanted to do, such as having permanent theatre bills. This would mean she could continue to be challenged by the spaces she is performing at, and develop content that gives the audience a particular experience.

The popularity of having 'experiences' in leisure time is big business, especially with the new economies of cities focused on themed events. This also prompts entertainers to continue to develop material for expanding audiences. Empress Stah wanted to have more of a permanent bill at a theatre so she could have creative control over every aspect of the show, environment and over-all experience (i.e. lighting, set design, working with her own crew, sound, etc.). She maintained that although this new direction may take her away from pulling diamonds out of her vagina (i.e. Diamond Pussy performance), she would not hide her past as her self-expression is valuable and important to her. Despite this, she reflected on how she would need to market herself differently and in a specific way to appeal to new audiences. Alongside this is making sure her original following of fans were aware of her direction and new material, so they are not disappointed.

Empress Stah is an entertainer who likes to keep her material fresh, which means that her material will reflect her current creativity, life course and the opportunities afforded to her with performance space, the narrative she wants to convey, her skills and expertise. Her new website launched in 2011 reflects this direction, with material presented in ways that open her up beyond fetish BDSM clubs (i.e. art spaces, theatres and so on). During the ethnographic fieldwork, her look was futuristic arty punk with a distinctive style, including a shaven head, pencilled-in eyebrows, double Marilyn Monroe piercings, double tongue piercings, star tattoos on the back of her neck and her exquisitely outrageous dress sense.

Performance style and notable themes

Empress Stah has developed her range of performances since the research was conducted. We will explore the context and narrative style of performances between 2008 and 2011. This chapter emerged through analysis of themes in the ethnography, which included: Empress Stah's website at the time of the research, the interview and observations at events she performed at. Themes include love, sex, magic, futurism and fantasy, fairy tales, kink, death, sexuality and the Bad Girl. These themes are framed through comedy, which leaves interpretation open for the audience to be entertained (or to take pleasure from) through laughter, feeling shocked and amusement. Her notoriety and style of twisted cabaret and neo-burlesque allow Empress Stah the scope to play with themes that revivalist burlesque steers clear of. The pornographic, blasphemous, the politically incorrect, horniness, sexual self-confidence and extremes (i.e. pulling a string of diamonds out of her vagina, revealing a cheeky butt plug with a pink tail and bloodletting) are recurring themes. Between 2007 and 2010 performances on Empress Stah's website were arranged in particular categories, such as: *Twisted Cabaret, Trapeze* and *Neo-Burlesque*.

The transition she spoke about in the interview reflects the changes on her website in 2011 to these sections, which are now: *Aerial Artist, Cabaret Performer* and *Show Producer*. Within these categories shows are described, alongside music, props and themes to give contextual information for audiences and anyone wanting to hire her. Her aerial performances include *Roses Are Red, Love to Love You, Ice Palace* and her signature piece *The Chandelier*. The ornate chandelier that she performs aerial acts on was a prop designed after winning the Jerwood Circus Award in 2003 for her aerial skills. These skills include hoop, rope and cloth. Empress Stah's shows are entertaining, orgasmic and high energy. She blurs distinctions between performance styles and genres making her stand out and diversify from mainstream neo-burlesque and cabaret. As entertaining and producing are her full-time jobs, how she markets her work will be different from local artists like Ms T. The trapeze performances are beautiful to watch.

Mirroring Annie Sprinkle's performance themes (see Sprinkle, 1998), in *Roses Are Red* Empress Stah pulls a string of diamonds out of her vagina whilst she is upside down during her aerial routine. The big reveal does not end on a shimmy or tassels; instead, there is an explicit confrontation with the body and a reframing of the vagina as something more than a site for sexual intercourse. The vagina is a site of pleasure, femininity, power and magic (i.e. like a magician's hat, but diamonds are pulled out instead of a rabbit). The craft of performances display the care, strength and training needed when executing routines.

Her cabaret performances include *Gold Stah, The Queen of the Night, Glamour Pussy, Hey Santa Claus* and *The Grinch*. Themes running through all these cabaret performances include overt sexual expression, sodomy, BDSM, kink, fetish, dildos, gender queering and multiple use of the orifices. Her nipples and genitals are often shown, demonstrating ease and confidence with her naked body, drawn from her experiences as a life-drawing model at art classes. Although there is a presence and a form of penetrative sex in *The Queen of the Night* and *Glamour Pussy*, the blow-up sex doll (*Queen of the Night*) or dildo/butt plug with fluffy tails (*Glamour Pussy*) is used to convey humour, naughtiness and sexual self-expression *within* femininity. Sex and sexual self-expression are not taken seriously. This offers a challenge to ideas around women not having access to their own bodies and patriarchal society defining women's sexual orifices as a space for a penis to fill.

It is vital for context and attitudes to be considered rather than assuming male supremacy over how sexual expression is conveyed (i.e. see de Beauvoir, 1949; Brownmiller, 1975; Millett, 1977; Storey, 2001). The cutesy fluffy pink tail attachment on the dildo in *Glamour Pussy* and the fluffy pink cutesy tail (attached to a butt plug) we see hanging from her anus, as she bends over at the end of the performance, make the performance appear sensual and feminine (see Attwood (2005) on sex toys, etc.). At the same time the performance is explicit and does not correlate to mainstream reveals. The destabilization and queering of normative associations around the use/function of sexual orifices continue with acts of sadomasochism and sodomy in *The Queen of the Night*, the use of a diamond butt plug and pulling a string of diamonds out of her vagina in *Roses Are Red* and pulling a golden balloon out of her anus (then inflating and popping the balloon over her head) in *Gold Stah*.

The vagina becomes something which is celebrated by Empress Stah and allows visibility through her self-identity and sexual expression, much like Annie Sprinkle (see Sprinkle, 1998). What was continually seen in the ethnography included high camp, high heels, diamonds and tongue-in-cheek politically incorrect humour. The outfits worn by Empress Stah are tailored to each show but there is a synthesis of luxury, punk and camp. Outfits are luxurious and expensive, complete with fake diamonds, furs, classy props like her chandelier, and obscure hats. Make-up has been inspired by drag queens and the high heels inject readable characteristics of femininity.

The themes and types of performances all link together giving visibility to her self-identity and femininity, even if she feels that people take her more seriously in her trapeze shows. Initially she had short deadlines when producing shows earlier on in her career, with one performance at TG being finalized in the corridor backstage just before she went on. This no longer happens as she strictly plans and choreographs shows in advance, because audiences now expect a certain standard when paying a lot of money to see her shows at clubs like TG. Pushing the boundaries is something which was inherent in the early stages of performance where she would want to entertain the communities she would be performing in. This is not necessarily out of the need to shock, but to do something different to what they may be expecting to see, even in subcultural groups. Through the use of comedy, neo-burlesque and her notoriety, these allow Empress Stah to highlight, undermine and twist (i.e. queer) gender norms that are taken for granted and accepted as 'natural'. What this indicates is that heterosexuality is not the only way in which gender can be presented, performed or done (see Butler, 1990a, 1990b, 1993).

Conceptualization and the value of the body

Performing freelance, for Empress Stah there is no differentiation between who Empress Stah is on stage and who she is off because she lives for her work (she changed her birth name to Empress Stah via deed poll). Empress Stah explained how her body is so central to her art, her livelihood and self-expression, by saying: 'My body is a major factor in how I style my performances. I've just did a clowning course last week, and the teacher who's this brilliant master clown, made a comment [stating] work with your assets and I thought: work to your strengths.' Empress Stah's performances are informed by the contexts of her biography and the environments she has been in. Performances included elements of modern primitivism, with piercing included in shows, as well as other styles of body performance such as ballet, comedy, neo-burlesque, twisted cabaret, spoken word and circus trapeze. Empress Stah maintains that she performs to entertain rather than shock, which can be easily associated with her trapeze because physical skill, strength and talent are demonstrated. Her more 'extreme' shows are still entertaining but there are elements which do shock as some audience reactions include complaints and non-interaction. When a multitude of people converge in social spaces for a variety of reasons, there are instances where differing interpretations are expressed.

For example, after watching Empress Stah at The Brickhouse in 2009 I got talking to some of the venue staff. The two young men behind the cloakroom asked me if I had enjoyed the performance. I said that I did, which they said was different to another female diner. They explained that this particular woman had complained and subsequently walked out. What was surmised was that the woman was offended by what she saw in Empress Stah's show, which involved a balloon being pulled out of her anus.

The space where the performance was programmed was known for putting on diverse performances for audiences who may not usually have access to certain types of burlesque or performance art (i.e. the audience may not attend fetish clubs or burlesque nights in an alternative bar or club). Spaces, therefore, become complex and performances may not be interpreted in typical ways, especially as this more 'vanilla' audience may not have been used to more extreme styles of burlesque. In this case, the audience was there just to watch (i.e. passive, like they were in a traditional theatre), instead of interacting or being part of the atmosphere. This was experienced in other venues in the ethnography, where the audience and artist divide was less defined.

Another example (at the same venue) involved another woman in the audience who was offered a phone by Empress Stah and over the sound system came the sound of someone on a sex-chat line. What amplified the hilarity was the woman's shock and her inability to interact with Empress Stah. Instead of interacting with Empress Stah, she was frozen to her seat. The differences between the types of people in the venue allow a distance to grow between the performer and the majority of the audience. Who were insiders or outsiders at this event was hard to measure, as those who were disgusted may think that the artist or anyone associated with them was strange. On the other hand, those laughing at the performance were entertained especially as reactions from the audience make the performance even funnier. Other ways in which audiences can participate include going with the flow. For example, when Empress Stah approached me with her Grinch mask on during another performance, I pretended to French kiss the mask. The audience therefore becomes part of the performance, despite their different reactions. The enjoyment of watching the performance is amplified through the response of the audience too.

How these performances are developed is important to explore when looking at self-expression. I asked where performances develop from, and Empress Stah stated that performances 'completely evolve from a song or a costume, a theme, a prop … something that I want to buy, just to have for myself.' This mentality is consistent as some outfits she wears onstage she also wears or uses in everyday life. What this demonstrates is that she not only wears the style but lives it too, indicating individuality and permanency, also expressed by Hodkinson's (2002) participants. Empress Stah also stated that she has complete creative control over the material and that once an idea is set she cannot deviate. What is seen on stage, no matter how extreme it may seem; is calculated, safe and controlled. Therefore, what distinguishes 'talent' from perversion is based on the attitudes, tastes and reactions of audience members. Specifically, this centres on social and cultural attitudes towards how women use their bodies and how women should entertain.

Empress Stah: I do every aspect of the production, I make it all, it's really just an organic process as you said. I'll start off with one thing then I'll start Googling music, have a theme or an idea, then I'll think well what would I put in it … I don't want to do that 'cause I've got that in that show, how can I do it differently, you know challenge myself. I write down lists, I think of what the character is and what things I could associate with that character, find some more tunes and think that will go with that and try edit the music and go oh that music just doesn't fit, it doesn't flow into that next track, I need to put something in the middle. At some point in the process of getting it all together I'll have a bath and it'll all just go [makes a noise]: that's it! That's it! Ah!! Get outta the bath! [Drums on table] Finish editing the sound track ... It's like that and [I] give myself a deadline and it has to happen. I have complete faith in the divine, the inspired nature of it all and the fact that if you put it along the line and you really put it out there, it'll all be alright on the night. I've worked like that for twelve years and I continue [to] work like that ... [It's] choreographed, it's set.

Much like Ms T, Empress Stah does not parody femininity in the ways other forms of revivalist burlesque do. The messages are not specifically political as Empress Stah maintained that she just enjoys being on stage and finds entertaining audiences fun. However, she does admit that themes do connect to love, gender and sexuality, but that there is no message as such. She explained:

Empress Stah: I don't really think about them, I just make them. Never had to write an essay about them, don't have theories about them, they just are. Having said that love, gender, sexuality ... it's more about entertainment you know there are different themes: blow-up dolls, dildos, blood, piercing, needles, flowers, champagne. It's all tongue-in-cheek, I'm having a laugh and I'm entertaining but I'm using these elements because it is appropriate to the audience that I am trying to entertain. I think it's hilarious, I think it's really funny. I know when I'm on a good streak when I'm devising a show and I'm like wahaha! Oh that's so wrong that's brilliant [amused] oh that's going to be really funny!

Stating that her performances 'just are' implies that ideas are routine and part of her creativity. Despite the idea that her performances develop organically, the performances still have to make sense and the routines have to be entertaining. She still has cultural awareness of what is appropriate for the audience and what elements might provoke certain responses. She is also aware of the political and social attitudes that surround women's bodies and taboo sexual behaviours, so her performances still offer an informed commentary and response to debates. What she uses to structure the shows is inevitably informed by various credentials that are conceivable to a range of people. As she acknowledges problems of heteronormativity, the styles of the shows she creates still have to be designed to what is appropriate to the audience, as audiences would expect her shows to be entertaining in a specific way. As Empress Stah has artistic control over the content and promotional material, performances are situated within the parameters of her expertise and notoriety. Her application of neo-burlesque and twisted cabaret is injected with personal contexts and biography. The mixture of styles and skill demonstrates that different embodied constructions of femininity *are* conceivable and that assumptions and binaries can be undermined by the presence of doing gender and self-identity your own way.

The extent to which her shows can destabilize and challenge heteronormativity, through including another approach to femininity, needs to be critiqued. This is especially the case when heteronormativity articulates the parameters of femininity in the mainstreaming of burlesque, which we will see in Chapter 5. The factors which condition the definitions of these 'alternative ways' of doing gender, sexuality and expression are queered by Empress Stah. Interestingly, what is included in Empress Stah's various performance base is neo-burlesque, which is not structured as 'revivalist', but is conditioned by what she feels is the 'future' of burlesque. This is articulated through a description advertising Empress Stah at The Brickhouse, stating that: Stah's work as a 'Neo-Burlesque' starlet picks up where tassel twirling and fan dancing leave off. Not for the faint hearted, 'neo' or 'new' burlesque is about taking the art form and making it relevant for the twenty-first century. There is no retro-styling here; neo-burlesque confronts contemporary life in a way that is at times humorous, blasphemous, pornographic, light hearted, challenging, camp, politically incorrect and above all entertaining (www.thebrickhouse.co.uk, 2009). The combinations present in Empress Stah's performances, the context of her biography and the construction of shows are not specifically binary opposed to burlesque or mainstream femininities. Instead, scope and possibilities are enacted and made visible through embodied knowledge.

Doing it sideways: The future of neo-burlesque

> **Empress Stah:** Right from the get-go when a club would try to book me six years ago, I was like well I don't really do burlesque but I never really knew what to describe what I did, so I just started to pick up on the term neo-burlesque and started exploring that. I thought well neo is like new burlesque, it actually pushes boundaries and parodies and makes a comic art about what is taboo in today's society. The other burlesque doesn't do that, it's just revivalist.

Empress Stah stated that on the whole the burlesque revival is 'a renaissance' and that the popularity of this revival creates certain expectations about what should be performed (i.e. stylistics, etc.) from the perspectives of promoters, production companies, club managers and audiences. For Empress Stah, revivalist burlesque is just 'doing what has been done before, you know and it was, initially exciting because it was a revival and now it's just torturous'. For Empress Stah, it was important to use a term that fitted her performance style which would enable her to market herself as something quite different from mainstream burlesque. One difference is that she pushes boundaries, and this can be seen both in the combination of styles she appropriates *and* within the provocative content that narratively structures her shows.

Empress Stah outlined that using a sideways approach to communities and cultures has allowed her to establish herself in her own terms, without being neatly aligned to one specific social group. This in-between area – the sideways approach – implies there are a variety of contributing factors that contextualize identity. For example, gender is only one aspect of who we are; yet, wider social norms frame gender as all-encompassing (see Ms T on gender being only a small aspect of our identity). Describing how this approach appears in her work, Empress Stah explained that it is about someone not completely identifying with or fitting into socially ascribed boxes. This is particularly important for Empress Stah in terms of her marketability and the uniqueness that has built her career. On being interviewed about her burlesque for a magazine, she said:

> **Empress Stah:** I've never fitted in to any box. Live art people weren't really interested, the fetish scene ... like TG now it's a bit different but go back say ten years, and it was still very much body art and black. And there I was, like I know you have seen it all but have you seen it in pink done to ABBA. It's taking like a sidewards approach which is the uniqueness that's built my career ... I did some thinking about what I wanted to say about myself; this is like nearly two years ago now that that was made, and this is where burlesque was becoming really mainstream. I was trying to explain what I did and yeah, the circus world I don't get many circus gigs they think I'm aaaaaah [gestures] too scary, the fetish scene, outside of TG perceive it to be too colourful ... the live art scene too entertaining.

What the reactions show is that within any social group individuals need to convey a specific approach to gender and sexuality that is commonly accepted and recognized as normal. However, being different to any standard within any group gives a certain visibility to Empress Stah, making her identity and performances non-conformist and individuated. Here there is a commercial likability because she does stand out. Nevertheless, it is vital to examine how Empress Stah approaches femininity and self-identity in her performances, particularly *The Queen of the Night*. *The Queen of the Night* is a significant piece in showing the tensions inherent in gender normativity and sexual expression. This striptease uses humour and

a story like other burlesque I observed, but orifices are seen and the
show is sexually explicit.

Empress Stah actively demonstrates a way to approach gender
and sexuality differently, whilst still retaining a femininity which
she does not compromise, specifically as she does not judge, make
strange or Other women. The importance of this piece is reiterated by
Empress Stah through her battle to perform the show at the *Feminist
Neo-Burlesque Symposium* in 2007 at the Central School of Speech
and Drama in London. In the ethnographic discussion Empress Stah
maintained that there were discussions as to whether include *The
Queen of the Night*. This was due to content and how long it took
to perform. As the conceptualization of the show is built through
personal experiences and her self-identity, censorship takes away
agency and rights. On censorship, Empress Stah stated that the show
they wanted was *Glamour Pussy*.

> **Empress Stah:** At first, I was like yeah whatever and my friend
> Ryan Styles said no way, you can't do that, that's not what you do …
> you need to do The Queen of the Night! She was like, it's too long
> in the programme and I'm like, it's only an extra seven minutes. She
> [said], oh but there's all these feminists and a lot of them haven't
> seen burlesque and what are they going to think. I'm like, well this
> is burlesque, what are you talking about! This is a seminal piece!
> [pokes the table and laughs]

What this exchange demonstrates is that what people value depends on
the degree of solidarity between what is visible and what is acceptable
to perform in specific social contexts. *The Queen of the Night* is an
example of neo-burlesque and instead of revivalist burlesque Empress
Stah's shows do not repeat the femininities present in burlesque parody.
Instead, she parodies wider cultural norms regarding gender, identity
and sexuality. The content and themes of shows do confront negative
perceptions, specifically in regards to associations or practices that

are seen to devalue dirty female sexuality. Being naked and sexual have not always been seen to be scandalous, but also offence and acceptance always depend on context, history, the social standing of the person and taste. Empress Stah highlights this by saying that:

> **Empress Stah:** back in the day to be naked behind some feather fans or show some ankle or to hint at sexuality was scandalous, completely scandalous and now it's beautiful. The way Dita Von Teese does [burlesque] is beautiful and it's been a real pleasure to watch. But it's exactly that, it's a renaissance ... it's just revivalist so it's really important to have this element of work in the discussion of burlesque.

What Empress Stah does is develop burlesque rather than repeating an idealized standard of femininity which is already established and parodied. This highlights that there are other approaches which offer a variety of ways of doing gender (see Butler, 1990a, 1990b, 1993), but instead of just showing the artificiality of gender (i.e. through drag), *The Queen of the Night* also demonstrates that self-identity and self-expression are comprised of multiple aspects of who we are. We are not irreducible to one set reading or box. The sensual and the experiential are means to new embodied knowledge, and the inclusion of modern primitivism and experimentation enables queer journeys. These journeys position self-identity as an evolving thing, rather than a person arriving at a set destination that essentializes their experience. For example, you learn and respond to the situations you find yourself in and you can grow and transform (i.e. the body is a site for transformation, as we explored in Chapter 1 in regards to body modification). Identity is not fixed: it is an ongoing process. Burlesque and other forms of performance art are vehicles to communicate biography and embodied knowledge. Biography and embodied knowledge can upend binary discourse and elevate dirtiness to providing space for possibilities to be felt, realized and embodied.

Styling gender, sexual expression and bad femininity

Challenging stigma was a central theme observed in Empress Stah's performances. Framed through humour and the absurd, Empress Stah places herself in a space where cultural norms surrounding identities, gender and sexualities that are perceived to be bad and dirty are challenged. As we will see in the following sections, situating herself in the role of the jester, the fool and the alien enables Empress Stah to confront and expose the artificiality of sexual and gendered norms. This opens space for possibilities, where Bad Women can occupy space on their own terms *as they are*, without having to compromise.

The Queen of the Night

The Queen of the Night was highlighted by Empress Stah as an important piece for her and one of her favourite acts to perform. The act is significant due to the use of neo-burlesque, but also how femininity and non-heterosexual desire are articulated. *The Queen of the Night* was situated within the twisted cabaret (now cabaret performer) section of Empress Stah's website. The description on the website (below) gives a detailed overview of themes. This description is atmospheric and sets down her vision:

> I put a spell on you … because you're mine!! The Queen of the Night summons to her underworld an innocent sailor so she can unleash more sadistic desires. She is soooo evil she has razor sharp horns, eats fire and ejaculates champagne. Her sense of humour is exquisite …. but is the Queen really a She? Skills and props include a male blow-up doll, body piercing, fire eating, flogging, dildoes, sodomy and penetrative sex. Music includes snippets from songs including I want to be evil – Eartha Kitt, I put a spell on you, The Queen of the Night – Mozart, Peaches and Peggy Lee's Is that all there is? (www.empressstah.com, 2007–10)

The Queen of the Night was initially produced for TG with links to her experiences which have built the concept of the show. Empress Stah explained: 'David TG [said] you should do a more fetish show, something that would translate to European touring and fetish clubs. I decided to do a fetish show, so it's got whips in it, it's got enemas, it's got stuff in it that's a bit fetishy.' The show is comedic, horny and pornographic, with references to masturbation, non-normative sexual expression, bisexuality and modern primitivism (i.e. such as the insertion of temporary piercings/needles in her forehead). The way in which the show is styled combines high art references, such as ballet and the aria in Wolfgang Amadeus Mozart's *The Magic Flute* (1791) which is used before a full striptease to horny electro-beats. The combination of fetish and BDSM with references to high art destabilizes normative representations of authority and intelligence. This highlights agency even within identities that are seen to lack this, such as bisexuality (Harris, 1997; du Plessis, 1996; Weeks, 1991, 1995) and being a sexual woman. However, the combination also reflects Empress Stah's biography and also being inspired by the aria. Empress Stah further explained how the show was made, referencing real-life experiences and how she uses these to encourage performance development.

> **Empress Stah:** The Queen of the Night itself: I was involved in a production of Mozart's The Magic Flute at the Royal Opera House in London which I did three times through three runs. In that opera is the Queen of the Night and that music, the aria is the Queen of the Night's aria. During that performance in the opera house, I would come on veiled with this dagger and at this point I'd had to hand her [the queen] the dagger and she'd take it and she'd be off [gestures] doing this amazing thing and I'd used to just trip out every time and be like wow, you know looking at the audience at the Royal Opera House and this woman singing one of most complicated songs for the human voice to do. I used to imagine my

power. She would take this thing from my hand and [gestures and mimics] to the sky and I'd be like: are you listening mission control [amused] you know put it out there, you know very sense ... [of] self. So I always wanted to use that piece of music in the show as well and The Queen of the Night, she was really evil and she was trying to get one up on the son god Sarastros so the eating of fire [in] that part of the show [her show] is a reference literally to that.

The Queen of the Night uses humour and a story like other burlesque I observed during field research, but orifices, explicitness and taboo were woven into the narrative. The second time I saw this performance was at The Brickhouse in 2008, with only the facial piercings omitted. The facial piercings are usually included in an uncensored show. The props used included a dildo in a harness, one male blow-up doll dressed as a sailor (PVC white shorts with an anchor on, and a sailor's hat), a glass bowl containing a lighter and other fire-eating equipment, a silver crystal ball, a black velvet drape, a small syringe with liquid (not the same as the comedic floppy syringe in Chapter 5), a condom and a whip.

Empress Stah entered the stage cackling like a witch. Dressed in an all-black ruff, long black coat/cloak and heels to match, and silver glitter adoring her head, she picked up the crystal ball and danced with it. Whilst casting a spell as she looked into the crystal ball, a clap of thunder echoed over the speakers. As she cackled, a male blow-up doll was thrown onto the stage. Picking up the blow-up doll, this revealed its outfit: a black S&M harness strapped around its chest and white PVC shorts adorned with a single anchor. Comedically – provoking laughter from the audience – Empress Stah placed a sailor's hat on the doll and sat him down by the back wall. The striptease began. The music changed to 'I want to be Evil' by Eartha Kitt (1953) and her body became animated. She stomped her feet and mimed the words like a drag queen, mirroring the camp style of make-up around her eyes. As the lyrics expressed 'I want to go to the devil, I want to be evil', she dramatically lifted her hands to her head and flipped horns. She started to take her opera gloves off, and as the gloves were removed she pulled the front of the jacket apart, transforming the outfit into a cloak. The chorography linked with traditional forms of striptease, but the first 'reveal' was not cute tassels; instead, she revealed a strip of material that covered her breasts and a black strap-on dildo in a harness. Vampiric connotations emerged through holding up two halves of the cloak like bat wings.

The Queen of the Night's Aria by Mozart (1791) engulfed the stage and the rituals begin. These rituals resembled foreplay, highlighting desire and intimacy, but these are queered through the juxtaposition of Empress Stah and the sex doll. As the music played, Empress Stah started to take off her outer clothing and all what was left was the ruff, the strap-on in a harness and the material covering her chest. Connecting to themes in the re-emergence of burlesque, Empress Stah began to perform fire-eating, tipping her head back and putting the fire out. She is the vampire, the devil, the Bad Woman from the underworld. The effect of the ruff made it seem that her head had disappeared as she ate the fire. Bringing her head back to face the audience, they clapped. 'Low' carnivalesque is meshed with 'high culture' with the selection of music, blurring rigid distinctions. Picking up a flogger, Empress Stah snapped it between her hands and paraded with it up to the blow-up doll. With a smile on her face she picked up the doll, held it to the audience and in time with the music, she flogged him. Taking off his hat she licked her lips and she dragged him to the foot of the stage by his ludicrously pink penis. Turning the doll upside down, she bit into the penis with a snort, and roughly took off his pants whist looking directly at the audience. The type of tease and narrative is different from what is presented by burlesque in popular culture, but also the commercialization of burlesque in subcultural spaces too (see Chapter 5). The Queen's approach is fun, and her attitude towards sex, the body, desire and intimacy is not serious. Femininity and self-expression do not need to be aligned to heterosexual narratives, linear stories or heterosexual vanilla sex. A theme which connects Empress Stah with Ms T (indeed all case studies of Bad Girls in this book) is that of not Othering any women who may identify (or not identify) with the themes expressed in performances (i.e. themes of deviancy and the Bad Woman).

Picking up the syringe, she pushed the contents into the doll's anus, giving the anus a clean and lubeing it up ready for penetration. She placed the doll on the seat, took off her ruff and the music changed to the highly orgasmic electro-pop song *I U She* by Peaches (2003). She started to thrust the strap-on towards the audience, whilst she lip-synced the words extravagantly and licked her lips. Confronting the audience, she pointed at people as the lyrics turned to: 'I, you she together, come on come on baby let's go' and 'you me he together come on come on baby let's go'. Significantly unlike any mainstream burlesque narratives seen, Empress Stah references, embodies and explores bisexuality, taboo practices and a wider scope of gender play. She directly involved the audience by breaking the fourth wall in such a way that heteronormative expectations are upended. The campness, comedy, ludicrousness and the exaggeration in performance trouble discourses surrounding bisexual stereotypes, kinkyness and the Bad Woman (see Weeks, 1991, 1995). Satire thus ridicules normative power. The terminology of bisexual aesthetics and performativity used in *I U She* is easily understood by audience cultural understandings and associations with bisexual stereotypes. Although the lyrics state 'I don't need to have the choice I like girls and I like boys, come on come on baby let's go', the tongue-in-cheek humour applied by Empress Stah and the use of the blow-up doll revel that perceptions about bisexuality are exaggerated and ludicrous.

Appropriating the extreme through the lens of comedy makes bisexuality, taboo sexual acts and kink seem fun and dirtily daring. The choreography cleverly and creatively links BDSM with bisexuality (as we saw with Weeks (1991, 1995) in chapter one), which is further represented in the lyrics: 'whips crops, chains whatever, come on baby let's go; I, you, she whatever come on baby let's go'. Sexual excitation, horniness and confidence flow from this performance. The uniqueness and branding of the performance individuate Empress Stah. The inclusion of comedy and tongue-in-cheek humour questions assumptions and reveals a space where binaries are shaken making them unstable. This is seen through Empress Stah over-exaggerating facial expressions when she roughly sodomizes the blow-up doll during the performance. The issue of a woman sodomizing a *male* sexual object and using a dildo to do this does not correspond to the femininities present in mainstream burlesque, nor does this correspond to vanilla sex. The scope of femininity is opened rather than reduced, and the 'lack' associated with femininity, sex and having a vagina (de Beauvoir, 1949; Brownmiller, 1975; Dworkin, 1994; Millett, 1977) is troubled. There is no 'Othering' of women in the performance, as the Queen just 'is'. The Queen is of her own design and she does not devalue or make abject any other women. The Queen presents the 'both/and' rather than 'either/or' (as we also saw with Ms T).

As the performance continued, Empress Stah placed the doll down and picked up a condom. Whilst licking her lips she placed the condom on the penis of the doll, symbolizing safe sex and sexual intent. She then straddled the doll and ironically made a lasso motion, making the act not a serious erotic representation of sex, but something silly. After de-straddling the doll, Empress Stah walked to the opposite end of the stage and sat down on a chair as the song *Is that all there is?* (1969) by Peggy Lee came over the speakers. What is demonstrated here is that these acts are not as outlandish as wider social assumptions and attitudes might project. This links to what was discussed in the interview, where Empress Stah commented on how wider cultural assumptions and attitudes about people who identify with BDSM are usually out of context and only based on exaggerated behaviours that are seen to be somehow at odds with the norm. The finale of the performance was the money shot, symbolized through her shaking a bottle of champagne and releasing the cork as the bottle was placed between her thighs. On the other hand, the lack of masculine presence and associations with objectification contradicts the cultural assumption that bodies are always destined 'for another' (de Beauvoir, 1949:345) and that women are only objects of male desire. Although the ejaculation was orchestrated through an external object, the inclusion of 'is that all there is' and the tongue-in-cheek exaggerated comedy demonstrates pride in sexual expression. This pride may be narrated through the Queen of the Night not being satisfied. 'Is that all there is' highlights that non-vanilla sex is not actually frightening, dangerous or dirty. What is implied is that sexual expression is fun, there is nothing bad about it and there is nothing wrong in exploring self-identity through a variety of activities. As the performance drew to a close, she drank some of the alcohol, wiped her mouth with the back of her hand, dropped her hands to the side of her body, smiled and nodded. The music stopped, she took a bow and exited the stage to applause and cheers from the crowd.

The questioning of gender and of femininity through the Queen does not fall neatly into presupposed ideological readings of Bad Girls lacking agency. Instead, the careful use of comedy and the blatant showcase of sensual and sexual scope allow agency which does not compromise her femininity or self-expression. Although the themes and issues within Empress Stah's performance can be seen in threatening ways, replicating the status of bisexuality as critiqued by Weeks (1995), vitally she does not distance herself or parody women, which the majority of mainstream burlesque narratives do (see Chapter 5). Therefore, sexuality and marginalized sexual tastes do not always have to be seen in threatening ways (i.e. they are nothing to be scared of). As Empress Stah does acknowledge cultural assumptions regarding specific sexualities like bisexuality and kink, and the behaviours attached, it is essential to explore if the need for readability compromises new ways of destabilizing norms.

Disengagement and readability

Discussing *The Queen of the Night* and why she used the material, Empress Stah explained that the social role she plays corresponds historically to clowns and the freak show (see Lee, 1995; Mannix, 1999). One of the key tools Empress Stah uses is shining a light onto inconsistences. Through comedy, crudeness and camp Empress Stah addresses problems with the world, especially attitudes towards certain bodies, behaviours and femininities. Empress Stah identifies dominant morality as the main contributor which tells people what they should do with their own body.

> **Empress Stah:** It's like the clown, the fool, the court jester. Take the court jester from medieval times. They had a way of, in jest, could point or poke a finger at anything, and highlight anything that was amiss. Only [they] could criticise the king by making a joke out of something and shining a magnifying glass on it until it was so like blatantly obvious what the flaws were, that it exploded and was able to be addressed. That is how I feel. I feel through comedy and in the ancient role of the fool magnifying these idiosyncrasies, these kinks, perversions, desires and just going, what the fuck? Why? What's the big deal? What's the problem? Why've we got all this moral bullshit surrounding human sexuality on what you should and shouldn't do to your own body?

The contexts of performances and the way in which sexuality is presented demonstrate self-ownership of the body, specifically through the conscious approach Empress Stah takes to sexuality. Empress Stah maintained that using the position of the jester allows her independence because she is coming from a space which allows more scope to question heterosexuality as the only means to express femininity and sexual purity. In the ethnography, she specifically highlights religion and heterosexuality imposing social attitudes that demonize bodies and sexualities that exist outside of the norm. In being the alien, she states:

> **Empress Stah:** I have observed your planet and you've got this belief that there is only one God, you've got a belief that homosexuality is a crime against nature, that recreational drug use is bad and reducing carbon emissions is gunna save you from extinction … all these different things and to go: [mimes] hmm … curious. That might make people go: oh, yeah you're right actually … yeah to make some profound stuff but in a very comic way again.
>
> **GC:** Again, with the whole lighting up what's kinda wrong with the world and amplifying it?
>
> **Empress Stah:** Yeah, amplify it and going: ha ha! Aren't you all stupid! Look at what you think, look at what you believe: it's ridiculous! You know … we just really need to turn the page. Live in the moment, look around you. Look at what is real, look at size, look at evolution, look at concepts, look at everything that's happening in the modern world; the reality of the modern world, not what God said two thousand years ago.
>
> **GC:** You define yourself, you know: fluid.
>
> **Empress Stah:** Yeah, just fluid. Let … humanity … be more fluid

This exchange correlates to repeating themes present in fieldwork (see Rebecca Drury in Chapter 1) concerning the editing of femininity through institutions such as the church, the workhouse and home (see Chapter 1). Amplification makes assumptions and stereotypes appear ridiculous. This exposes what is constituted in language as socially and culturally constructed. Failing to abide by cultural definitions and 'norms' is actually important, as these acts give assurances that there are multiple ways in which women can challenge stigma. The non-uniform attributes presented by Empress Stah's femininity and self-identity highlight that gender transformation can be found within inconsistencies. This relates to Butler (1990a:141) on the possibilities of gender transformation that are found 'in the arbitrary relation between such acts, in the possibility of a failure to repeat, a deformity, or a parodic repetition that exposes the phantasmatic effect of abiding identity as a politically tenuous construction'. What Empress Stah seeks to demonstrate – through her position as someone who can magnify – is that social and cultural constructions of gender can be undermined.

The weaknesses of heteronormative binaries are not necessarily always demonstrated through people doing things differently; rather, it is the grey areas and tensions which expose the fragility of binaries and the inadequateness of stereotypical perceptions (i.e. failures). Although inconsistencies are highlighted and presented through performances on stage, the permanency of Empress Stah's identity in her everyday life and within the themes repeated in performance demonstrates that gender has scope, providing more ways to sexually express. Also highlighted in the dialogue are the problems faced by individuals who do not identify with binary gender positions and individuals who do not conform to heterosexual normalcy. Empress Stah is, however, still in a privileged position but she does recognize this. She identified in the interview that women should realize the privileges they have, regarding access to their own bodies and using their sexuality to make money and to express themselves. There are women in the Western world who do have the opportunity and contexts available to re-address femininity and how they can express sexuality. This happens even in the confines of commercialization and objectification.

> **Empress Stah:** It's like Dita [von Teese] and people who are like 'I want to be objectified', 'I want to be like a sex symbol' and 'I wanna exploit that for money'. A lot of women these days are really in control of that as well … lot of people aren't, it's granted, and

there are hideous things like the sex trade and that's a completely different kettle of fish. The war hasn't obviously been won you know, female circumcision in Third World countries, but again it's a different thing to what we are talking about [in the interview], what we experience in our First World.

Through magnifying issues concerning perceptions of the female body and sex, and by showing that women's experience cannot be reduced to one overreaching presumption (i.e. lack, empowered, etc.), what Empress Stah is calling for is recognizing context. What is seen on stage is not a repetition of normative femininity; rather, what constitutes 'femininity' depends on context, life experience and the individual's embodied knowledge. Context can undermine presumptions that categorize women as either good or bad, rather than just recognizing grey areas where women challenge and exist outside of language (i.e. the both/and frame can be recognized here). The use of magnification in *The Queen of the Night* and themes within other performances is significant because Empress Stah draws out the socio-cultural factors that shape gender in ludicrous ways. In Empress Stah combining intelligible aspects of identity (i.e. the bisexual, the witch, the deviant, the queer, etc.) but with a 'sidewards approach', she is able to question normative social attitudes as limiting, ineffective and things to laugh at. This is presented by Empress Stah through the themes of the jester and humour, and through re-presenting sexual desire in context, demonstrating the presence of inconsistencies which question normative social attitudes informed by labelling (Becker, 1963).

The impact of the unknown

In the interview Empress Stah explained that her shows were transitioning as she was developing more shows for a wider audience. In the interview, the theme of the unknown arose as a central concept to her self-expression and how she situated her identity. The concept of the unknown is more prominent in her transition to new shows under the banner of 'Stah-Lite' in late 2009 in her new performances titled *Zero G*, comprising trapeze, comedy and tease set in outer space on a space station in the future. Shows under the category of *Stah-Lite* are less sexually explicit than other performances to suit a wider audience. Empress Stah still maintained that she would not restrict her self-expression because if she wanted to pull something out of her vagina, she would. Consistency is present, with the unknown still prominent throughout her work in the form of the jester and 'magnification'. Empress Stah explained that one of her focuses now was to get sponsorship to be the first person to trapeze in space because outer space was something she identified with. This is consistent with her identity and performances in the 1980s and 1990s. 'Alien' and outer space were recurring themes throughout the ethnography, including how she felt when listening to the queen's aria in the production of Mozart's *The Magic Flute*. In response to alien, she said that it is not something to do with alienation, but something which is from the unknown. This character was also inspired by the *1970s My Favourite Martian* who she said was a 'really silly comic character'.

> **Empress Stah:** Empress Stah way back in the eighties and nineties was like alien; like Empress Stah Power Girl and then I matured out of it … and now it's come back the full circle. I'm going to be this alien character, the character in Zero G floating around the stars, is from space or from another planet or another dimension. I haven't worked it out yet exactly, or is coming down or maybe is just a hologram selling space tourism.

Contextual themes in *Stah-Lite* focus on the future, which is actually consistent with her approach to neo-burlesque and sexuality (i.e. forward thinking and an open attitude to gender, sexuality and sexual self-expression, etc.). This sideways approach is now incorporated in the figure of the 'alien' in her new shows (i.e. this can be linked back to her use of the jester/clown). She argued that the alien is not something that is based on the image of a 'savage', rather a person who is advanced, has wisdom and is liberated. Describing the alien, she expressed:

> **Empress Stah:** That which is unknown, so I could come from anywhere; from the afterlife, from outta space, from another planet because we don't know. So, it gives me complete freedom to make up what I want but it also means that I come back, comment socially from a perspective of someone that has no agenda, no interest, has never [seen] it before.

Although Empress Stah's interpretation of 'alien' is freeing for her to perform and allows her to comment without a heterosexual perspective compromising self-identity, this space is still constructed. The freedom expressed in this space (out of space and metaphorical space) is constructed by her own conditions which do not necessarily translate or have the ability to transfer to other women's lives. This space is a grey area, where she has the ability to continually queer and undermine social scripts. As the shows connect to her self-identity and experiences, this is an example of embodied knowledge from an individual perceptive. To ensure that audiences 'get' shows and are entertained, Empress Stah's shows include wider social contexts that are intelligible for audiences. This is combined with a sideways approach and the application of the unknown. The combination of intelligibility and magnifying inconsistencies gives her access to style the space in which her stories are expressed and told. Her notoriety as an extreme performer also gives her an advantage to present her self-identity in non-conformist ways, so she actively *creates* space (much like Ms T). The proposition is that this space is created in order to sustain her identity and performance style, which correlates to her inclusion of relatable identities, such as the jester, allowing her to perform in particular ways.

We can, therefore, interpret Empress Stah's position on gender and sexuality through the style and types of performances she does. Not only can this demonstrate her having a sense of control over her body, she also recognizes that if you have the opportunity to carve out your own space to occupy then this is achievable (i.e. but only if you have the networks, cultural capital, funding, recognition, etc.). The queering of space opens possibilities and undermines heteronormative 'certainties' through the body and self-identity being an ongoing project. Although a sense of control over gender and sexuality is a common theme expressed in revivalist burlesque, Empress Stah does not gain this through demonizing women or distancing herself from Bad/Dirty women. The approach of her performances is conditioned through Empress Stah's openness to sexuality and a vital *awareness* of her privilege as a Western white woman. This specifically concerns choice, but is also about taking advantage of that privilege and using it as a platform to expand scope and the possibilities that are there for women's self-expression. The space Empress Stah creates is inclusive of identities that are devalued, seen as dirty or made strange by dominant social discourses that continue to stick to certain types of women.

From the ethnography, Empress Stah's 'unknown' does not draw upon usual body politics and discourses which shame or other women, even if the unknown is conditioned by her own distinctions and privilege. What the unknown does show is the impact and influence heterosexuality has on women's struggle to gain self-respect, even from the gender they are part of. The control Empress Stah takes from constructing the contexts of her performances is a form of defence and defiance. What this can highlight is the problem that women can face, namely having to *justify* their actions and their self-identity to men *and* women. Attwood and Holland (2009:173–4) articulate this through one of their participants, a professional pole dancer, who was worried about people getting to know about her career. This specifically concerned the negative portrayal of pole dancing, which her friends differentiated her from (i.e. for instance pole fitness can be sometimes viewed as more valid than pole dancing). Therefore, the mainstreaming of a particular image of pole dancing as sanctioned, fun and respectable builds pressure on women to disguise their careers or desires. This is an issue because context is abandoned and not recognized. Context is lost when agency is questioned making the 'status' of women (who perform for money) remain 'precarious' (Attwood and Holland, 2009:1740). The queering of space and opening up possibilities enable Empress Stah to comment on social construction, because in outer space there are no such restrictions. Part of this space and vision is conditioned by how Empress Stah sees the world and the self-confidence she possesses. Empress Stah maintains that she has the confidence to be open about her gender and sexuality in public and *not* just behind closed doors. She stated:

> **Empress Stah:** People that are ashamed of what they might do behind closed doors are people who are going to criticise and point fingers and be like [mimicking] oh that's disgusting, you mustn't do that. Seeing you be so open, free and happy and joyous about doing whatever the fuck you like really pisses them off. So, in order for them to feel better about themselves about it, they want to stop you from doing it as well because they haven't got the guts to do it themselves or be open about it.

Empress Stah does not see a problem with doing what she does on stage but maintains that people's issues with sexuality are centred on specifics found within religion and in society.

> **Empress Stah:** It's about just letting people be … be whatever you want to be, harm no one else, do what you want … who says I can't be naked on stage, who says I can't fuck a blow-up doll, who says I

can't pull something out my arse or [put] something up my pussy, [or] stick something through my body. It's mine! It's my body! I don't believe in religion and God and morality in that sort of a sense. I have a very good moral code that I live by, but if I want to get my clothes off, be naked in front of thousands of people and stick something up my arse, that's completely up to me. It's funny … do what you want to do, live your life.

The above statement is a personal manifesto, and as a public figure and entertainer she has significant power and authority to undermine and disturb gendered and sexual boundaries. Although this happens within a particular context and site, thus limited and restricted, the performances do go beyond the micro as she is a global artist famed for her ability not to be categorized in one specific box. This maps neatly to her statements in the popular press on not fitting in completely with the arts scene, the fetish scene and the burlesque revival. Although the unknown opens scope and space for Empress Stah to express herself, the problem is that this space needs to be created in the first place, showing a tension between her manifesto and the global appeal of her work. What the unknown also demonstrates is the weakness of heterosexuality as an approach that people should continue to abide by. Nevertheless, Empress Stah's performance and position still do not totally overcome these problems as they are still inherent in the way people communicate, something which is externally binding. However, she constantly disrupts and queers heterosexual predispositions and narratives. What her performances engage with is the need to constantly challenge norms in all areas of society, and to keep audiences entertained. We can expand this idea to identity and the body as an ongoing project, where the journey of self-identity is embodied, changeable and open to possibilities. Identity never sits still, even though external hierarches and social systems try and repeat ways of seeing the world and performing self-identity in a world that tries to reduce people to generic universal categories.

What Empress Stah highlights is the vital importance of including *context* which allows women to approach gender and sexuality in ways that should not need justification. In consequence, how Empress Stah articulates femininity and sexual expression demonstrates that if women have the chance to be sexual and to use their gender, then they should be able to choose this without justification, albeit this position being a privileged one.

In conclusion, through an ethnographic study of Empress Stah and her performances, it has been established that gender conformity does not always correspond to established heterosexual social identities. What Empress Stah demonstrates is that women who are sexual and do not follow the main characteristics of ideal femininity are not strange or lack agency. The extent to which Empress Stah's approach is translatable and transferable is questionable as this depends on case to case, people's life experiences and the opportunities they have had access to, but it is significant nonetheless. It has been vital for the book to include Empress Stah's performances and experiences as they demonstrate that heterosexual normalcy is weak and that this weakness need not be highlighted through Othering or poking fun at women as the majority of revivalist/mainstream burlesque does in its narratives and stylistic approach. The scope of femininity, which Empress Stah demonstrates in *The Queen of the Night* through a non-heterosexual approach to sex, gender and social reality, shows the inherent weakness of heterosexual legitimacy. This weakness is shown through the visibility of inconsistencies in how femininity in styled, lived and identified as. Heterosexual legitimacy therefore becomes something that is only real through the articulation of it and by its application in modes of communication, social interaction in physical spaces and within expression. In critiquing how Empress Stah does this through the jester, magnification, the alien and the unknown, it was found that the space she had created to do this in could justify her identity and how this identity exists outside of language. This does provide scope but this scope is carved out by Empress Stah herself and the opportunities afforded to her. Not all women have this opportunity to perform for a living, but also it is important to remember we cannot carbon-copy women's experiences. Instead, we should celebrate women like Empress Stah and the ways in which she uses the stage to narrate important stories about gender, sexuality, attitudes and belief systems.

Empress Stah addressed herself as a neo-burlesque artist to pitch and describe herself to clients as her shows are not revivalist and who she is on stage is not a parody of anyone. Consequently, Empress Stah contradicts the revivals focus on preserving respectability, through expanding agency via penetrating, accessing and controlling her *own* body by the use of sex toys, piercings and overt sexual display. Being one of the 'futures' of burlesque allows Empress Stah to direct herself through her own experiences, rather than relying on the formulas presented in revivalist burlesque. Through *The Queen of the Night*, gender articulation is blurred allowing the presence of femininity in its own terms, rather than always relying on purity, masculinity or misogyny to explain what is expressed. Therefore, the themes projected from Empress Stah's performances do not compromise her femininity or self-expression. Through the ethnography it was established that if a woman has the chance and opportunity to use her body, talent and sexuality in a way she identifies with or wants to express by, she should be able to do this without having to continually justify these choices.

RubberDoll: Success and the significance of sexual otherness

RubberDoll is a world-renowned hard-core latex and fetish model, performance artist and full-time kinkster. Through exploring RubberDoll (her performance repertoire, self-management and her sexual self-identity), the chapter will argue that Bad/Dirty (i.e. 'Other') women should be valued as socially and politically significant because women like RubberDoll are actively producing alternative routes to success. This idea of success connects to employment, creativity and the carving out of space for her femininity and sexual identity to exist on her own terms. The chapter draws upon aspects of *The Queer Art of Failure* (Halberstam, 2011) and entrepreneurship literature (e.g. Grandy and Mavin, 2011; Berg, 2016; Pajnik, 2015 and others), but primarily what can be learnt from RubberDoll's own words, her entrepreneurial empire and performance art, some of which utilize aspects of burlesque. What will be addressed is: how do women like RubberDoll actively produce alternative pathways to support desires and creative careers often sneered at or seen as a commodity for heterosexual men?

The central theme in this chapter is how RubberDoll's entrepreneurial skills and self-management of her own kinky-latex empire are important factors to consider when re-examining the gendered and political significance of Bad/Dirty (i.e. Othered) women. Here, entrepreneurship is not just a positive and creative means to support alternative pathways to employment, but a tool to continually carve out space for her self-identity to exist by her own direction/terms.

We will see how heterosexual normalcy is challenged by RubberDoll's presentation of femininity and sexual identity. The significance of kinky Bad Women will be explored through the ways in which RubberDoll queers burlesque narratives and intersects the personal, the biographical and the sensual. Here, it is important to highlight that the main themes in her performances include latex, domination, striptease, medical scenarios, military outfits, the use of orifices, fetish, angle-grinding and sensual use of the skin. Themes of Dirt, pornography, perverse expressions of femininity and breaking the limits of orifices are included through performances viewed on *YouTube* and onstage at Erotica in London in 2009.

Expertise, career and craft

Based in Florida, RubberDoll is a touring model who headlines large-scale fetish events (e.g. Fetish Factory, Erotica UK, Montreal Fetish Weekend, etc.), nightclubs, music venues and adult lifestyle shows. Sometimes she performs with other models (girl on girl), but she is well known for her solo stage shows.

> In addition to modelling, RubberDoll has established a reputation as one of the most explosive and sought after live performers on the fetish and adult club circuit. She has performed all across the globe, with appearances at all the top fetish events and gentleman's clubs in the US, Europe and beyond ... RubberDoll's one-of-a-kind shows are erotically charged and filled with sexy surprises that include extreme fetish outfits, magic tricks, humour, and outrageous visual effects. (RubberDoll.net, Biography)

On her website (https://www.rubberdoll.net), she is described as having a high-end latex style with a 'raw sexuality' which has enabled her to become a 'fixture on the worldwide fetish scene' (RubberDoll. net). Her career spans several decades with the RubberDoll brand starting in the late 1990s with her modelling rubber clothing in a range of photography sets built and designed by herself. Originally, RubberDoll started off modelling for gothic-styled photoshoots but her growing love for latex meant that shoots became more fetish-orientated. Named as a prominent fetish figure in Access All Areas, RubberDoll started as a screen name on AOL due to her strong interest in latex clothing. Through an emerging online fan base, she was continuously being asked to perform and be a guest at fetish clubs on the merit of her images. In her own words, RubberDoll wanted to take this online fantasy 'that existed in the Internet and make her real' (https://www.browardpalmbeach.com/news/rubber-doll-6311792). Much like Empress Stah, this is a full-time career for RubberDoll and she has developed an extensive portfolio of work, including owning and managing ShinySluts.com. RubberDoll is well respected and there is a high demand for appearances, with some clubs fitting the date and schedule of their event around her diary. RubberDoll has a range of social media accounts, which she manages to mainly promote events she will be appearing at, merchandize, and images of her getting ready to go to shows/events. This allows fans to have an intimate insight into her career and everyday life.

Her fan base is diverse, which reflects the ways in which she uses certain websites and platforms to distribute her material. For example, fans can pay per month for private membership to her website. She has also been a member of NITEFLIRT since 2002, where clients can pay to call her for a 1-2-1 session (i.e. she lists her services and expertise) or offer her tributes from $5 to $500. The links on all her social media accounts and NITEFLIRT all direct visitors to RubberDoll.net. For example, there is a link on NITEFLIRT for merchandize, which means if you had a session you may want to continue your fantasy or fan support through purchasing a DVD, such as *Rubberised*. She makes and sells her own videos, with her website being one of the ways in which she distributes her content.

RubberDoll.net is extensive, even without private membership access, and is the central hub of her empire. This empire also includes the model call and casting page for ShinySluts, which is an offshoot company that she manages. Being a creative director for shoots and sometimes appearing alongside other models in both pictures and films means that RubberDoll is a producer, director and artist (i.e. she has a foot in front of the camera and also behind it too). This showcases her as an industry expert, a success story and someone who applies a variety of skills and knowledge to her business empire. In an article on RubberDoll in *Night Magazine* she is described as a successful entrepreneur, a canny businesswoman and an authentic fetishist (i.e. fetish is personal and not just about the clothes). But who is RubberDoll and what can we see when we peek into her latex-encased lifestyle in the kinky corners of the web and beyond? The personal is important to explore as it enables us to situate femininity and self-identity in context.

Journeys and life history

In interviews RubberDoll explains that she sees her career as a personal journey shaped by her own evolving desires, kinks and tastes. From an early age RubberDoll identified as a goth and was active on the goth scene. Much like Ms T, RubberDoll started going to fetish clubs and liked the diversity of people there. She realized she had a preference for rubber clothing. It is important to note that RubberDoll does not identify as a rubber sex doll, nor does she transform into a rubber sex doll, unlike some performers like Steffy the Rubber Doll. The naming of RubberDoll is about her looking sexy in latex. RubberDoll explained in an interview for Access All Areas that she could not transform into a rubber sex doll because she is more dominant than submissive, which is evident in her stage shows, photosets and DVDs.

RubberDoll: For me, calling myself RubberDoll is more about just looking very sexy in latex, and not transforming into an actual rubber sex doll. In the first place, I tend to be much more dominant than submissive, so the concept of being a doll that is controlled by someone else is not really a natural fit for me. I also tend not to go for the 'completely encased in latex' look, and I typically don't wear hoods since I like to be creative with hair and make-up.

RubberDoll describes latex as a flexible subject, where she can embrace classy and elegant couture, whilst also allowing herself to explore 'pervy heavy rubber' and kinky toys for a specific session. RubberDoll identifies as bisexual and mainly performs alongside other women who are submissive to her. Her style is flexible and she embraces different ends of the rubber-kink spectrum. For RubberDoll it is important for her to be inspired by a prop or item of clothing she wants to wear as she builds up a concept for the stage design and her stage performances. To support this, RubberDoll expressed in Access All Areas:

RubberDoll: I do try to constantly keep the moods and feelings of the scenes changing as much as possible. I do this not only to keep the venues interested, but also to keep up with my own changing tastes and ideas.

This sex-positive and experiential attitude resonates further when RubberDoll was asked in an interview for *Night Magazine*, what she would say to vanillas interested in exploring the scene. She expressed:

RubberDoll: Don't be intimidated by the Unknown. Explore and be surprised by how much you enjoy it.

Positive attributes RubberDoll gives to the potential feelings of intimidation towards the Unknown may firstly appear to be transgressive, because the allure of sexual transgression (Halberstam, 2011) has become normatively sexy, naughty and profitable in consumer culture. As Halberstam (2011:150) states 'that which seems off-limits becomes sexy, and in indulging our interest in the taboo we feel naughty', and one could argue that the allure of commodified transgressive sexual behaviour allows a temporary disruption of heterosexual scripts. This suspension, however, has negative attributes, much like attitudes towards bisexuality (particularly in relation to women). Something temporary can suggest instability or a temporary position from where you will – at some point – return back to a linear stable state of identity (i.e. heterosexuality and monogamy). There is, however, potential in being Dirty and Bad because RubberDoll can continually be playful with her self-expression in a range of communities she is part of, but also continue to earn a living. This is done in a playful and creative way through hybridized forms of technologies and leisure-time environments, which sustains RubberDoll as a brand through her presence online, on stage, via social media and her merchandize. Playfulness also connects hand to hand with entrepreneurial skills, which will be explored later in this chapter in relation to her wanting to continually capture her adventures and adapt her empire. Playfulness and fun with transgression are a lifelong commitment for RubberDoll, so the idea of her identity being temporary before she 'settles down' is short-sighted. Temporality takes on a different meaning in the context of RubberDoll because her desires and tastes now are not endpoints. Connecting to Halberstam's critique of the unpredictability, RubberDoll's journey and success manipulate and destabilize heteronormative discourses. RubberDoll enables us to see opportunities and alternatives to hegemonic norms/systems (see Halberstam (2011) on queer studies).

RubberDoll identifies that the fetish and BDSM scenes she is involved in (both personally and professionally) will never be fully mainstream for a variety of reasons, but she feels that it should be a celebrated identity and a celebrated space, because it offers an important way to express yourself. These modes of expression connect with Halberstam's (2011:147) discussions about the social worlds we inhabit, which are never inevitable and where the production of one type of reality means that 'many other realities, fields of knowledge, and ways of being have been discarded and, to use Foucault's (2003) term, "disqualified"'. In the contexts of RubberDoll and the scenes she is involved with, the social spaces allow more possibilities for people to explore not only self-identity, but also desires which have yet to be experienced (even if certain desires have been internally recognized as something a person identifies with).

Experience and mixing with a range of diverse identities are an enabling factor when connecting to and developing new fields of knowledge. For one reality to be disqualified, there needs to be space for other forms to develop, even if these realities are formed as counter to mainstream practices and beliefs. To open one's eyes to diverse and different forms of sexualities, it is important to have a space that allows this mix and for a person to interact with a range of sexual realities, something which was central for Ms T. The continual playfulness of RubberDoll's desires and self-expression has been facilitated through her journey into fetish clubs, the development of RubberDoll.net, her rise to popularity and the continuation of her performance portfolio. RubberDoll argues that in fetish clubs, she felt the encounters she had with other people enabled her to develop her creativity, but also was an enabling factor in becoming part of the community:

> **RubberDoll:** I started to meet a lot of new people and my eyes were opened to many different forms of sexuality. I experienced everything from gender-bending cross-dressers to strict dommes to submissive sissies to bisexual swingers. I loved every new experience and embraced each unique encounter as another step into my journey into the fetish world. (RubberDoll.net)

What is evident is RubberDoll's passion and creative drive for what she does for a living. Her flexible attitude to sexuality and sensorial experiences resonates with queer potentiality. This is an area where we will now explore the themes in her performance art and how her performances showcase the importance of Bad Girl visibility and embodied knowledge.

Live shows

RubberDoll has an extensive performance portfolio and some of her burlesque-styled stage shows can be viewed through YouTube. The mix of latex, lights in costumes, magic, pop songs and horny beats and metal music creates an exciting space where expectations are upturned and Bad/Dirty (i.e. Other) women are celebrated. In general, RubberDoll's performances on stage combine striptease, comedy and magic, with a fetish, S&M and sex toy twist. Most of the kinky burlesque performances have a focus on the vagina, with objects such as umbrellas, cum confetti and beads being pulled out of orifices, but also a metal dildo in a harness which she angle-grinds, throwing sparks over the stage or over another (female) performer. The performances are entertaining, horny, and they reflect RubberDoll's own personal desires and tastes, such as hot women, domination and sexual dissidence. Her website clarifies her success as a stage performer, listing awards and other accolades. These reinforce her expertise and craft, as well as her popularity on the fetish and porn scene.

> RubberDoll's live shows have earned accolades and awards including 2016 FetishCon Awards Live Performer of the Year, Nightmoves Magazine 2012 Feature Entertainer of the Year, 2016 Exotic Dancer Invitational East Champion, and 2012 & 2016 Exotic Dancer Magazine Feature Entertainer of the Year Nominee. (RubberDoll.net, Biography)

The art of illusion

One tease-styled performance titled *'Birdcage'* sees RubberDoll – in a skimpy latex outfit – sit back on a chair, open her legs wide and pull two metallic birdcages from her vagina (or maybe like a magician, out of a carefully concealed pocket in her outfit). RubberDoll's genitals are covered by latex (i.e. imagine the strip of material covering the genitalia on a swimming costume) but the focus on the genital area showcases RubberDoll's confidence in her own body, agency and sexual self-identity. Like a magician, the art of illusion through smoke, sparks and tricks enables RubberDoll to craft routines that comment on the power of the vagina, female sexuality and women's creativity.

The art of illusion resonates well with queering because RubberDoll uses the unconventional in her performance art, articulates a fearless love of sex and embraces Bad Girl identity as agentic and individuating. Masturbation is recurring theme in RubberDoll's performances, and combining this with tease and magic destabilizes heteronormative assumptions around lack, pornography, linear romance and desire as reducible to binaries. The focus on the vagina, with objects such as umbrellas, cum confetti and beads being pulled out, is not necessarily for titillation or produced to satisfy men. Instead, the replacement of bodily fluids with objects out of context turns focus back to RubberDoll and her self-expression. Towards the latter end of *Birdcage*, sexual appetite is also communicated via the music chosen for the performance and in this case, *Freak* by Klass (2011), extenuates sexual fun and directly addresses sexual excitation from a woman's point of view, with the lyrics stating:

> Give me a freaky boy/I'll make him sit & beg/I'll put a chain around him / Wrap him between my legs/I like it bouncy bouncy, so Throw me up and down/Just keep on moving through me and turn my world around.

Her performances, the networks of adoring fans and co-performers, and her online presence, offer a distinct and continual disruption to these assumptions as her self-identity is visible, she is in control and present no matter if she is celebrated or dismissed. RubberDoll is RubberDoll, irrespective of external heteronormative discourses which may interpret her as failing femininity because of her still being part of an industry that some consider as morally corrosive and dangerous. RubberDoll is still part of the adult entertainment business but it is important to note that she has privilege and status that allow her to be visible and open about who she is. Other performers may not have this luxury, and if they want to get a job outside the industry, they might face discrimination or harassment because of their previous careers (see Jizz Lee 2015). Although from a privileged position, what is interesting about RubberDoll is her openness to sexual expression, with commentary on this present in online interviews, performances, her engagement with a range of kink and fetish scenes, and on her website. The multiple ways in which RubberDoll communicates her sexual self-identity are counter-hegemonic and a practice that undermines heteronormative common sense about female sexual passivity, intimacy and self-pleasure.

Most of the themes in performances see RubberDoll self-pleasure with her hands, but also this self-pleasure goes beyond the vagina to other erotogenic zones such as the breasts and nipples. Pleasure and sexual expression are also displayed throughout her performances with other female performers, where she dominates them, humiliates them and uses her large strap-on to simulate masturbation. Much like burlesque humour there is a tongue-in-cheek playfulness with body parts, with her angle-grinding her strap-on, confetti fired out of a phallic-styled tube and sparkler bazooka breasts akin to Madonna in the 1980s. The layering of humour, the horny and her notoriety queers straightforward reading of the meaning behind her performances and indeed her sexual identity. Although gender may be seen to be fixed through the use of attributes commonly associated with women (breasts) and men (penis), the inclusion of both within the use of RubberDoll's body causes a tension. The tension is also regarding latex love versus blatant orifice use as a right for men, situating agency directly back to RubberDoll. RubberDoll continues to destabilize the legitimacy of heterosexuality and normative gender relations as the only eligible way to perceive, feel and express. There is no special place held for a man or vanilla sex. In RubberDoll's performances there is a heavy emphasis on the senses and the importance of sensuous experiences. This conceptualizes femininity as having the ability to be refined on a case-by-case basis. These experiences are personal, demonstrating the diversity of gender and sexuality through re-presenting agency in articulating individualism via a femininity which holds no shame and does not Other.

Erotica stage performance

Watching the stage show produced by TG at Erotica 2009, the burlesque performances rolled into one another, creating no difference, and as ballet was included, this made the shows appear high cultured and decadent. Not knowing who was coming onto the stage next, as my brochure was tucked into my bag, RubberDoll was announced. The show being analysed is the second performance RubberDoll did at Erotica, after the first performance seeing her encased within and coming out of an inflatable white latex balloon, simulating the birth of something 'naturally' perverse. During the second performance RubberDoll came on in a red and black latex outfit to the foot of the stage to *Smack My Bitch Up* by The Prodigy (1997). This song is used frequently in RubberDoll's performances when she is on stage with another woman who she is humiliating, dominating or carrying out fantasies with. After she teased the audience, by constantly revealing her breasts under her jacket, she removed the jacket and walked to the middle of the stage, approaching a chair. RubberDoll sat on the seat and then slouched, bent back slightly and did the splits. This image was unapologetic and highly stylized. The position she was in seemed uncomfortable and not a position for sex, rather the position magnified her individuality through disrupting the use and meaning of the vagina. RubberDoll exuded power, presence and control as she started to slap and rub her vagina through the latex barrier. This barrier is clean, expensive and safe as nothing can penetrate through it. Latex can be viewed as clinical, sensual and erotic. Without having anything penetrating her, she produced a string of large balls from between her legs, symbolizing individual pleasure and the power and flexibility of the vagina. This offers a challenge to and destabilizes the devaluation of the 'leaky' vagina presented by menstruation (de Beauvoir, 1949). The encasement of these items within her vagina and genital stimulation demonstrates an active sexual intent and a woman who was directing the sexual content of her performance. Embodied knowledge shapes self-identity and how this is communicated. Self-pleasure also derived from the presence of this sex toy, making sexual context directed by her desire. Desire, excitement, pleasure and entertainment are open to be shared mutually between the audience and performer, mirroring Ms T and Empress Stah.

As RubberDoll flung the string of balls around her head, she stopped and started to deep-throat each ball. As she sucked and then licked the balls animatedly from side to side, her assistant came on stage dressed in heavy-duty latex with inflatable breasts and a wig. Although the inflatable breasts and playing with orifices highlight parts which women are 'reduced to', these normative assertions do not acknowledge the contexts where rubberists and latex lovers place significant value on wearing outfits like this and the sensuous experiences they get from wearing rubber.

Context needs to be applied and reflected upon here because viewing this performance cannot adequately allow re-presentation to happen in the context of those wearing the outfits, specifically as experiences in rubber are personal. What this mirrors is the difficulty for women to demonstrate and justify their own sexual arousal, so mediums have to be used to convey agency and the personal. At the foot of the stage RubberDoll placed goggles around her eyes and strapped a metal phallus to her body. She started to simulate masturbation with this hard and large black penis. She picked up an angle grinder and walked to the chair again. The 'woman' encased in heavy latex, the inflatable breasts and wig, placed herself on the floor a few feet away from RubberDoll and bent back. RubberDoll touched the angle grinder on the sides of the metal phallus producing sparks which were aimed at the woman before her feet.

The sparks symbolized RubberDoll 'cumming', in time with the beat, over the woman who writhed on the stage floor. These sparks do not burn and are not unsafe unless they go into the eyes so danger is only implied, not actually real. The difficulty of getting this across can spoil the illusion created by the show. This also comments on the inability of showing how it feels wearing rubber and the embodied knowledge produced through the experience of encasement and having a second skin. Like the latex outfits, the sparks were ejected in the contexts of safety. The phallus was not inserted and the 'cum' was not directed by a man which queers leaky bodies, infection and women's performance of sexual expression.

RubberDoll continues to destabilize the legitimacy of heterosexual normalcy and meaning as the only eligible way to perceive, feel and express. This is specifically due to her personal latex fetish which emphasizes sensuous experiences as a means to experience and gain knowledge about the body. Rather, in RubberDoll's performances there is a heavy emphasis on the senses which build upon the themes present in Mouse's performance regarding the body and to emphasize the importance of sensuous experiences. These experiences are personal, demonstrating the diversity of gender and sexuality through re-presenting agency in articulating individualism through a femininity which holds no shame and does not demean other women (e.g. not seeing any woman as lacking something).

Bad/Dirty women hold possibilities, and the queering of Dirt enables more ways to present femininity. The absence of penetrative heterosexual sex, even with the presence of two women and one strap on, symbolized that what was presented was neither straight nor lesbian. Rather what was seen was something embodied, sexual and something which questions binaries. The ease with which patriarchy and misogyny can be applied is also questioned through re-presenting the value of context, which can often be difficult to articulate when contexts are taken away (supported by Attwood (2005, 2007a, 2011b) and Budgeon (1998, 2011)). Highlighted here is another theme found through research, and this is the inability of social definitions to re-present individual's lives in their various contexts. Central to this book and evidenced through the case studies is the importance of lived experience and what this means is that there is space to include possibilities for *all* women. A key aspect of creating, taking up and challenging *all* space is ensuring that no one is dismissed and for women to give themselves permission to do what they want. This is reflected in RubberDoll's performance themes. She does not dismiss any woman as the performance was centred on herself, which is also present on her website, her biography and the repetition of themes throughout her performance repertoire.

What RubberDoll presents is an approach to sex and desire which cannot be reduced to boxes defining what sex is for, namely procreation and heterosexuality, as the performances are centred on herself and her kink. Although her male fans and some of the Erotic events she goes to may complicate her agency, alongside who we might assume her kink videos and performances are designed for, the context of her kink and fetish *still* provides more scope for femininity. This is specifically the case as RubberDoll has become a brand as she manages and directs her work. What RubberDoll presents is an approach which allows the re-articulation of femininity through individualism and casting off the need for heterosexuality, as it is not needed nor life fulfilling for all women. RubberDoll is actively producing alternative routes to success, albeit for some women only (i.e. with money, a large fan base and other forms of privilege). Although this site of privilege might still illuminate aspects of her identity that enable her to do this for a living and reap the success of her business, her presence gives hope and highlights possibilities and futures.

The idea of success connects to employment, creativity and the carving out of space for her femininity and sexual identity to exist in her own terms. We have explored this through what RubberDoll identifies as a life journey, where contact with a range of identities in fetish and kinky spaces – both online and in the physical world – has enabled her to be creative and flexible with her personal and professional desires relating to her career aspirations and self. Enabling factors are not limited to these spaces, but what she does in and to these spaces. So, self-motivation and her business skills are central to her success, and this needs to be recognized as such. Entrepreneurship is also key here and not just as a positive and creative means to support alternative pathways to employment, but as tool to continually carve out space for self-identity.

Rubberised entrepreneurship and alternative income streams

To put the above into context, we need to explore wider discussions that focus on technology as an enabling tool for Bad/Dirty women to navigate alternative income streams. Through RubberDoll, we will see how technology and brand management open up opportunities for success, creativity and self-identity. There are some discussions of alternative income streams and the gig economy in the adult entertainment industry, such as pornography and sex work. Reflections on other forms of entrepreneurship are present in some academic disciplines, with debates focusing on alternative income streams, porn's gig economy (i.e. income from satellite industries, marketing strategies, etc.) and porn entrepreneurs (see Grandy and Mavin, 2011; Berg, 2016; Pajnik, 2015). Fredrik Lane (2001:111) states that sexual entrepreneurship is not your usual part-time job and that 'for sexual entrepreneurs, the primary consequence of the pornography industry's increasing prominence and economic success was to create a wider range of business opportunities'.

Motivation for new forms of self-employment is also a product of changes to socio-economic landscapes of large post-industrial cities that have seen the emergence of leisure and consumption as key sites of the new economy. Portfolio careers also shape employment landscapes and possibilities, with flexibility, valuable skills and informal knowledges identified as key components of enterprising femininity (Grey, 2003). Networked agency and community support enable individuals who work in the sex industry, space to navigate alternative income streams via social media and promotional websites. New opportunities and increased demand have meant individuals can produce, create and distribute their own materials (Lane, 2001). In this climate, we must also note sex-positive and feminist retailers creating new cultural spaces for sexual conscious-raising and social change, which Lynn Comella (2017) explores in a US context (Good Vibrations, Eve's Garden and Babeland) and frames feminist sex-toy stores as counter-publics (i.e. sex-positive entrepreneurship, retail activism and products/information as a route to transformative sexual politics), thus redefining the sexual marketplace.

For Berg (2016:171) marginalized workers in the sex business are more likely to produce their own content, allowing greater amount of autonomy, despite the real possibility of employment discrimination if changing career outside of the sex industry (see Coming Out Like a Porn Star 2015, Jizz Lee). Although some adult performers rely on the gig industry and other alternative income streams, RubberDoll's business is less precarious as she is effectively the CEO of her brand, which is made buoyant by her celebrity and various business ventures. Having control of production and distribution, coupled with knowledge of the industry and the fame her celebrity has brought, means that RubberDoll exists in a privileged position of power. This means that she can take risks and experiment, resulting in her continually creating fresh, exciting and kinky performances.

Diversity and a solid brand connect to discussions in popular culture around the importance of developing an entrepreneurial mindset which also means exhibiting entrepreneurial traits, abilities and behaviours, which, Jones (2014) argues, only happens after entrepreneurial activities have taken place. RubberDoll's career trajectory and online success also sit within the development of the ordinary celebrity, girl power and the emergence of social media stars. Social media has enabled women's success to emerge out of alternative career routes which reflects the presence of *women* being recognized as entrepreneurs in popular culture with terms like 'mum-preneur, etsy-preneur … blog-preneur' (Duffy and Hund, 2015: 1), the social media entrepreneur (Duffy and Hund, 2015:5) and the culturpreneur (Loaker, 2013:130) being widely used. An important element to consider in this context is how RubberDoll's business empire has survived the multiple barriers against female entrepreneurs. Bruni (2005:19) identifies these barriers as the socio-cultural status of women, lack of access to networks that have information and assistance, and access to funding. Bruni (2005:19) argues that these barriers add to gendered subtexts in society that see women as lacking a range of qualities and traits, such as 'status, networks and credibility'. RubberDoll is a survivor of presumptions, particularly as Bruni (2005:19) highlights that assumptions about someone's failure are based on personal characteristics, such as nonconformity.

RubberDoll can also add another dimension to discussions on female entrepreneurs, without seeing the motivations of women entrepreneurs as only being driven by necessity, choice or lack of opportunities. These motivations flatten women's existence and presume that there are no real alternatives, when queering the system is an everyday activity for women like RubberDoll. In online interviews, RubberDoll did not disclose anything about barriers; instead, she discussed how the initial launch of RubberDoll.net was initiated through watching a TV programme about how the internet is a good route to forming a business, which you could start yourself. RubberDoll continues to use the internet to sustain and generate social networks, which enables her to be self-sufficient, in control and in employment. This also allows her to be part of a community, not just for financial reasons but – as we will see – for personal growth. Alternative routes to success for women like RubberDoll are not just based on the freedom to do what they love, it's actually a radical undermining of normative gendered scripts that see any characteristic of 'lack' in a woman to be a negative or bad thing.

Despite RubberDoll's empire reaping the benefits of being in a capitalist system, what she produces does not collude with capitalist ideological moorings to heteronormalizing people, particularly women. Although RubberDoll is privileged in many ways, her performance art, entrepreneurial skills and self-management offer a significant framework that does not marginalize sexual expression, nor does it allow 'lack' to appear as the first trait of non-normative Bad/Dirty femininity. In her performance art, RubberDoll is fierce and she is fun. She demonstrates that her self-identity cannot be evaporated, nor can her femininity and sexual expression be seen as one-dimensional. RubberDoll is hugely successful, enabling us to see a concrete challenge to heteronormativity and to witness the queer potential of women who fall between the binary. RubberDoll continues to want to do what she loves, but also to explore new areas that interest her. This has massive significance for the study of sexuality, desire and intimacy particularly in relation to how these are externalized and communicated via sexy, subversive and political performance art.

5

Commodification of cult and 'alternative' femininities

In this chapter, we will explore how certain revivalist burlesque scripts (i.e. good girls) are replicated in such a fashion that they comment on sexual, bodily and gendered politics in very specific and clean ways. The body as a site for change, progression and commentary is a key component to focus on, especially when the alternative is marketed to such a degree that possibilities are sanctioned, packaged and cleaned. But what happens when you fall into that grey in-between area we discussed in the previous chapters? What if your sexual politics seemingly contravene the 'alternative' because they 'sully' the politics of a creative movement that frames itself as progressive and a site of empowered 'Bad Girl' femininity (i.e. revivalist burlesque)? Before we explore the contexts behind the rise, demise and revival of burlesque, we need to initially explore how revivalist burlesque is contradictory and an example of performing an alternatively safe good girl femininity. We will explore these themes through critically unpacking the mediated femininities found in ethnographic fieldwork to see the ways in which standardization makes 'alternatives to' fall back into heteronormative tropes.

The revival's context has been conditioned through a focus on the glitz, glamour and comedy of retro-burlesque, which distances the revival from elements associated with the 'demise' in the late 1950s and from 'Other' women who contravene 'empowerment'. In performances seen in ethnographic research, the main characteristics associated with burlesque 'femininity' mirror femininities and stories defined by established culturally understood norms. Stories and femininities use cultural assumptions of particular stereotypes (e.g. ditzy blonde, bad goth girl, secret agent, subverting fairy tales and glamour puss), and although performing stereotypical glamorous femininity or the 'good girl gone bad' may highlight gender as a construction, there is no real radical revision or questioning of binaries. No 'new' is articulated. Femininity presented in the revival is refined, styled and shaped by cultural ideals from both within subculture and wider culture too as both are inseparable (i.e. entertainment and consumer culture have blurred these lines).

Cleanliness and purity

Through observations, the central themes/focuses of contemporary burlesque were cleanliness and an agreeable articulation of heteronormative gender and sexuality ideals. From the ethnography, safe and clean performances also included the integration of circus, freak show, magic and illusion, high art and dance, making the burlesque scene incorporate other talents demonstrating the skill and art involved. This raises the value of the performers' tease away from other styles of stripping, through variety and skill. The combination of classic tease alongside other skills includes Red Sarah's drag striptease and twirling tassels that are on fire (i.e. a wonderfully playful and daring adaption of fire-play), and Dani California pulling out ribbons from items of clothing that she is taking off (i.e. classic ribbon dancing in an alternative context).

Although production value may be low for those on the local circuit, burlesque is carefully thought out and stories are constructed, such as the twisted fairy tales of Angel LaVey where Goldilocks turns into a sassy woman after handing out biscuits to the audience.

Opulence can also feature in burlesque, such as Roxy Velvet's tease in a large birdcage and Veronika Valentine teasing out of a costume with large butterfly wings that resulted in a beautiful butterfly dance. Stepping away from negative sexualization can also be seen in the ways in which performers construct their story narrative, such as Sophia Landi's fire poi dance following a tease out of a 'gangster' style suit, and the femme fatale image used by Miss Ruby Fortune, producing a male severed head after her tease. Clean forms of tease were also demonstrated by the tongue-in-cheek slapstick humour of Emerald Ace, playing a strong woman in one performance. In her burlesque, she initially lifted up cartoon-style weights and then – after teasing down to '1 Ton tassels' ('1 ton' was written on each tassel adoring her breasts) – she lifted each breast with her hands whilst flexing her muscles, which resulted in a chorus of laughter from the audience.

Consequently, the skill, humour and burlesque in the examples above reinforce certain stylistic and performative norms around revivalist burlesque. Repeating safe forms of femininity moves revivalist commercial burlesque away from compromising femininity (i.e. not dirtying it) or explicitness (i.e. disempowerment). Most of the burlesque seen in the context of fieldwork did not go beyond the cheesecake, *Carry On*, slapstick or glamorous style, indicating that skills were essential (even if amateurish) and that there was a limit to how much smuttiness was allowed. The performance style and aesthetics of femininity adorning the faces and bodies of performers did not offer an opportunity to contaminate their self-identity. The articulation of empowerment, resistance and celebration is safely narrated, styled and performed.

The repetition of cleanliness and pure femininity were themes which were structurally dependent on careful and informed negotiations of gender *and* the cultural contexts adorning heteronormativity, specifically regarding sustaining forms of feminine value and worth. These cultural contexts are informed by wider social understandings of gender and place, specifically regarding binary oppositions and reference points to heterosexual normalcy. The revival is conditioned through distancing away from associations that are attributed to burlesque's demise and the rise of sexual cultures that revivalist burlesque dismisses. From the ethnography, it was observed that there were visual, stylistic and communicative tools (i.e. style and performance routine) used that distanced burlesquers from Other women who are socially seen as dirty and lacking agency. This is articulated through the presence of culturally understood knowledge embedded in shows and also narratives communicating the effort put in by the performer in the construction of routines, symbolizing that shows have been 'thought-out.'

The inclusion of stereotypes such as the femme fatale and the ditzy blonde, alongside juggling skills, dancing, story-style shows and twisting the outcomes of well-known fairy tales, all add to the entertainment value of burlesque. This value is upheld by burlesque being viewed as an art form and a safe space showcasing multi-talented women who happen to be teasing. The central characteristics allowed convey a specific sexy, sassy, uncompromised and powerful femininity. The absence of sexual intent or explicitness means that any sullying and tarnishing of credible femininities bypass the 'art' of tasteful burlesque. Therefore, what is repeated on stage restricts agency to a certain standard and this standard is fully conscious of the types of femininity needing to distance oneself from (the bad, the pervy, the unclean, the stripper, the whore, the sex worker and so on). What is performed on stage combines readable feminine characteristics substantiated by visible femininities within the burlesque community, the contexts of its revival and the way femininity is seen in wider society. The following performances seen in the field substantiate these claims specifically in relation to femininity and distancing from elements which are seen to compromise agency.

Birmingham Bizarre Bazaar

Several performers who were usually seen on the burlesque circuit were involved in a burlesque demonstration at the Birmingham Bizarre Bazaar (BBB), a day-time fetish fashion market held in Birmingham every third Sunday of every month. The BBB was held in Nightingales, a gay club in the centre of Birmingham's gay village. The first two levels of the club space were used for clothing, BDSM equipment, book and accessory stalls rented by a variety of independent businesses. The third floor was always spare for demonstrations, such as whipping or rope play, but on this particular Sunday the demonstration focused on burlesque. The demonstration included several shows performed by three individual performers and interactive parts where the audience could try teasing with gloves and other props associated with burlesque. The individuals from the audience who chose to physically participate in the demonstration were enthusiastic, and the rest of the audience watching were supportive through clapping and whooping. The normal house lights were on, rather than the usual lighting arrangements seen at club nights when performers appear on stage. The space felt quite clinical rather than sultry or intimate. The audience was smiling and the hubbub of murmuring voices, including my own with participants, demonstrated that this was a social space.

Delilah DeFoe came on stage in NHS scrubs and after a short time started to drink a bottle labelled 'Bad Medicine', linking to the rock and roll song playing. As she stripped away the NHS scrubs she drank more of the 'Bad Medicine', finally revealing a red PVC nurse's dress underneath, which looked like something from Anne Summers rather than something perversely kinky or expensive from such fashion houses as Skin Two, Pretty Pervy or House of Harlot. The costume was socially clean and something which could be worn on a hen night, a distance from the glass dildos being sold downstairs. The kink involved with this performance and the links to excess (i.e. drinking and drugs) were temporary due to the application of slapstick comedy. Although the outfit was easily read as a reference to 'kink', there was a line drawn (i.e. the pseudo-latex, through the stylistics of burlesque and the limitations imposed by parody) between high street kink and more 'authentic' forms. This line was also communicated through the use of a rather large comedy syringe, complete with a floppy needle.

The prop was tongue-in-cheek and as she bent over she placed the floppy end near her bottom. There was no reference to inserting it into any orifice or to pierce herself directly, which we saw with Empress Stah challenging revivalist burlesque by mixing porn, sexual explicitness and irony in her neo-burlesque performances. The large underwear the performer wore covered up any orifice in which the syringe could be inserted. This barrier took away the possibility of her accidently inserting the syringe into herself, even in a tongue-in-cheek manner. Purposely inserting this object, or changing the object into something which could be inserted (like a dildo or sex toy), would take away the tongue-in-cheek attitude and the stylistics of 'mainstream' burlesque into something perverse, 'unsafe' and deviant, thus not feminine. The addition of pants and the humour made her clean, and the messages projected from her body were safe. What the inclusion of Delilah DeFoe demonstrates is how burlesque, in the main, does not compromise the ideals of its re-emergence and its definition through distinguishing clean bodies from dirty ones. Consequently, her body and identity were not compromised either making her performance a reflection of normalcy through applying a specific structure of conforming (burlesque) femininity. This reduces the possibility of being seen as Bad/Dirty (i.e. Other).

As a result, the structure of femininity reduces bodies being compromised and thus sets a definitive gap between clean and Dirty Bodies. Nothing penetrates or damages the body. Instead, items are taken off; they are never inserted or taken out of the body by the performer or another person onstage (e.g. Empress Stah and

RubberDoll). Subsequently there is distancing in the very fabric of performances, away from bodies that can compromise the context of tease, but specifically the performer herself and her femininity. As burlesque is seen to be liberating for many performers, anything which compromises this actually compromises personal agency, purity and respectability (the latter two are definitive characteristics of heterosexual femininity and womanhood). In the context of the floppy needle, this highlights that the skin is never broken and no 'sexual' orifice or intimate part of the flesh – such as the nipples – is shown to the audience in the main body of revivalist burlesque. After the performance ended at the BBB, the burlesquer received applause and cheers from the audience who seemed suitably entertained. The positive reception from the audience and how audience laughed at the right bits signifies that the femininity on display is translatable and draws upon wider cultural readings/knowledge. This shows that what was expressed is mainstreamed and understood, thus is socially invested, and this can easily be accessed and consumed because there is already a place for it.

Although the audience in the BDSM fetish events responded positively to what they saw at the BBB, the male host who had announced the performers commented on how one of the performers did not have huge 'tits'. This comment was announced to the entire room. The contexts of revivalist burlesque may be something unfamiliar to this person but the political contexts of the revival are disavowed because what mattered for this person was the way in which women are considered desirable. Burlesquers cannot escape this despite there being an array of bodily types on the scene, as the ideal image of a woman is still substantiated by busty and skinny burlesquers adorning mainstream and subcultural press/media. The presence of an idealized type of burlesque performer through a specific articulation of femininity is not foolproof specifically as some audience members are not the intended audience. This was also observed at Silk Stockings (Birmingham), where a group of men started to shout inappropriate innuendos towards one performer (e.g. 'I'll give you sugar' in reaction to the performers' sugar cube pasties). Burlesque cannot fully shake free or distance itself from other forms of sexual consumption, nor can readings be controlled in the spaces where burlesque is supposed to be celebrated in particular ways.

London Burlesque Festival: Angela Ryan

Walters (2010) highlights issues for performers through themes of pornography, prostitution and lap dancing, all of which are thought to compromise and complicate the notion of burlesque's 'empowered' image (i.e. misogynist attitudes). However, she does not look at the ways in which some women can execute power through using misogyny as presented within themes in the next performance (although the performance has limitations which need consideration too).

At the London Burlesque Festival, I observed Angela Ryan perform a tease dressed as a man in a suit and hat. She walked across the stage, and at the foot of the stage she grabbed her crotch, ran her hands sexily all over her body and got out a copy of *Playboy*. Intermittently she looked at the audience and the pictures in the magazine. She demonstrated pleasure by insinuating she was turned on by pretending to masturbate, whilst having her back to the audience, placing the magazine on a chair under her body and putting one foot on the seat. She seemed to be masturbating over the women in the magazine but did so in the context of being 'male'. However, the tease revealed her femininity through taking off her masculine clothes, revealing a sexy, delicate and non-threatening woman underneath. Thus, same-sex desire is averted as something non-existent (i.e. temporary or fleeting). Symbolic masturbation is justified through binary gender characteristics sanctioned by the presence of male attire and the magazine, rather than providing visibility for a woman who is turned on by another woman on display. As her jacket and trousers were teasingly peeled off, she sat down, only wearing a white shirt, red tie, hat, red stockings and black heels. She looked incredibly sexy with her top half connoting male authority and bottom half typifying feminine sexiness. These were binary symbols, making gender differences look 'natural' but also the presence of masculine aesthetics sanctions the narrative and leaves little room for other routes or sexual desires.

As she sat back on the chair with her back facing the audience, she undid her hair, let it fall and removed her hat. She removed her white shirt but the cuffs, collar and tie still remained, with a small skirt and black pants covering her genitals and red heart-shaped sparkly tassels covering her nipples. There was a fine line between strip-o-gram and burlesquer. With her tie slightly ajar she looked at the magazine again, and I wondered what she was thinking about when she looked at the women in the magazine and what she thought about us watching her. She seemed to mirror the types of women in the magazine through what she was wearing and potentially hinting at 'dabbling' in same-sex desire. As the performance neared its finale, she took her tie off and put it between her legs. The woman next to me, who I had made friends with at the beginning of the evening, commented that it was like a phallic symbol and that she had executed this choreography well, which I agreed. The red tie between the legs could be interpreted as demonstrating differences between men and women regarding lack through the menstrual cycle (de Beauvoir, 1949) and lacking a penis to visually demonstrate power and sexual excitation. The tie could also mask and cut off access to her vagina.

Through Angela Ryan creating and presenting this show, this can highlight that women can use objectification for their own means and that ownership over their bodies can come through performing sexualized femininity. Therefore, what compromises her body are social attitudes rather than the practices she does. Conversely, there is still a tension regarding how she presents this, specifically as sexual and gendered submissiveness were demonstrated in the finale as she used the tie to bind her hands together and lifted her bound hands above her head. Although this was incredibly sexy and showed a command of desirability, the subtle references to sexual foreplay/ BDSM (but never going further than what is conventional) and the insertion of the aesthetics of masculinity in her performance negate 'alternatives' to heteronormativity. Desire and femininity, here, are negotiated/mediated through binaries. Femininity and female sexual desire are not articulated on their own, but always in reference to and through binary/hegemonic masculinity.

Burlesque in Birmingham: Ditzy Diamond

Heterosexual normalcy was repeated in another performance seen at a burlesque night called Silk Stockings in Birmingham. Ditzy Diamond entered the stage dressed as a young, innocent girl with a basket and book in hand. She spied a bottle of bourbon at the foot of the stage, dropped what she had in her hands, picked up the bottle and took a gulp. After this gulp, the music shifted to some rock and roll and she pulled off her wig exposing a sexy sassy woman. Alcohol and experimentation have connections to excess and temporary youth rebellion within the contexts of rock and roll, even if sex and drugs were not overtly referenced. The reading of this performance correlates to some approaches within subcultural theory linking delinquency to criminal behaviour and pathology, or making subculture appear to be a temporary style of 'subversive' activity (see Aggleton, 1987; Becker, 1963; Carins, 1994; Matza, 1964; Rock, 1973; Schur, 1984). The temporality of the performance and the inherent heterosexuality invested in revivalist burlesques scripts of femininity automatically relocate the performer back to cleanliness as the definitive point of reference. Although genitals were never shown, these can be referenced in a safe way. For example, in another revivalist style burlesque performance by Ditzy Diamond, she used a circus-style sign stating her name and her 'performing pussy'. This is significant as the word 'cat' was absent in the performance, thus initially rendering her 'performing pussy' as something suggestive with naughty undertones, rather than compromising her agency through showing her genitals.

However, in the performance the 'cat' was something she was trying to search for and the cat was only revealed at the end of the story when she turned her back to the audience. She had sat on the cat, symbolized by a squashed 'pussy' sewn onto her pants, provoking laughter and cheers from the audience. In contrast to the more explicit performances seen (i.e. Mouse, Doris La Trine, Ms T, Empress Stah, RubberDoll), Ditzy Diamond did not pull anything out of her vagina or show anything which could be explicit because heteronormative linear scripts demand cleanliness. Clean and safe performances adhering to heteronormative scripts do not reduce the performer to her genital use, allowing her to have agency which does not comprise the performers' self-identity nor does it compromise heterosexual purity. What this assumes (on an ideological level) is that women have to constantly negotiate and distance themselves from genital use, pleasure and Bad/Dirty (i.e. 'Other') women to assert agency via revivalist/mainstream burlesque's connection to clean femininities and heteronormative social scripts.

Although misogyny can affect all women, the way in which clean femininity is used in these examples allows agency, and although performances seen were entertaining, burlesque cannot claim to be radical or inclusive when some women are left out, despite using similar themes, re-styling tease and commenting on bodily politics. Legitimate characteristics connoting femininity mean that revivalist burlesque does not compromise the morality or social standing of the performer; thus, alternative constructions of femininity rely on conforming to norms to protect the legitimacy of revivalist burlesque (i.e. as an art or a tool for empowerment) and to protect performers from compromising their self-identity (both in the scene and beyond, as taint can follow you and is not restricted to one sphere or space only).

Uncompromising clean femininity?

Up to this point, the chapter has established that the language and discourse of popular/mainstream burlesque valorize heterosexuality and clean femininity, just like hegemonic gendered scripts and heteronormative linear narratives. We will now explore the issues that emanate from commodification of cult. The implication this has on women who fall in-between or outside the norms is something we have continually engaged with in this book. Norms are always established by any dominant group, whether in 'subculture' or within the 'mainstream' and this has ramifications on possibilities. Standardization, commercial appeal and sanitized performances do not challenge bodily, sexual and gendered norms even when 'alternative' clean/safe femininity is presented (i.e. style, performance routines, bodies that matter). The 'alternatives to' are still measurable to the norms of the dominant group, even within subcultural spaces (i.e. needs to be intelligible, especially in relation to consumer culture/ economic capitalism). Binaries enforce a sanitized version of lived experience. Subvert and queer at your own peril.

Heterosexual legitimacy and the Good Girl

Through the case studies (Mouse, Doris La Trine, Ms T, Empress Stah, RubberDoll), we have seen that the stigmatization of women who do burlesque/femininity differently mirrors the social sanitization that has been historically applied when policing women's bodies, sexual identities and lived experience. The standardization of burlesque is not just about commercial money making; it is actually a mechanism of prevailing discourse that elevates 'clean' femininity as valuable and agentic. The structure of performances and community/audience expectations restricts anything which may compromise the revival through associations with its demise. What this mainly concerns is 'Dirty' Bodies which are seen to be attached to pornography, misogyny and lack of agency. Dirty Bodies are structured to be contagious, abhorrent and socially unacceptable (see Mort, 2000; Cohen, 2005) but the definition and value of what they stand for and what they demonstrate need visibility beyond assumptions.

The interpretation of femininity within the majority of (revivalist) burlesque performances seen reflected uncompromising, clean and safe ways for contemporary women to be sexually assertive. Part of this is to reclaim space back from misogyny. Although this is something which is positive and demonstrates ways in which women can take control of their bodies and femininity (e.g. supported by Attwood and Holland (2009), Baldwin (2004), Ferreday (2008) and Von Teese (2006)), femininity is sanctioned mediated and safe (i.e. not really reconceiving or opening out femininity). The commodified 'good/Bad' Girl can articulate an 'alternative' to, but there is no space to radically queer norms. The main interpretation of burlesque available in clubs, in consumer culture, in the media and in wider social thought connotes an idealized version of alternative femininity. The revival does not speak for the women who interpret burlesque through other mediums they identify with such as BDSM, pornography and same-sex desire.

Although burlesque does not have to speak for all women, the value it has for women who perform does not transpose onto other femininities, specifically women who are seen to have connections with sex work and Bad femininity. These 'types' and 'sites' of femininity are continually acknowledged as either being victims of misogyny or have little agency. Sex workers and sexual performers do not have the positive visibility burlesque has, nor do they have a history which connotes power, strength and assertiveness. The articulation of femininity within the main body of burlesque is conditioned by the revival's focus on distancing from Bad/Dirty (i.e. Othered) bodies, which we have also explored in Chapter 1 (i.e. themes of lack, dirt and stigma). However, the mediated forms of alternative femininity do not provide sustained ways in which women can contradict, undermine, question and address social attitudes that restrict the ways in which women can express.

Consequently, the vocabulary of performances, in the main, is directed by a certain standard which is culturally understood, actively used and automatically applied to valorize a specific type of femininity. This is bound by heterosexual normalcy and commodification, even if burlesque appears to be liberating for the women who do it and who feel they take control of their body by its application. Burlesque does not have to be political, nor does it have to be an expression of that particular woman's sense of identity and modes of expressing this. However, (revivalist) burlesque does not challenge heteronormativity, even if the 'performance' of gender 'reveals' heterosexual constructions. The absence of taboo and sex in the mainstream and subcultural uses of burlesque (i.e. this includes the references to marginalized groups in some performances seen) does not liberate or open out definitions of femininity and sexual self-expression beyond what is clean. In fact, it confirms this expression through a rigid approach to sex, ignoring any value in BDSM, kink, non-apologetic (i.e. same sex, kinky, bi, etc.) sexual desire and the exploration of the senses seen in the spaces burlesque was performed at. This demonstrates that only parts of subversiveness are used to gain credibility. This comes directly back to how femininity is performed and the visibility of this in performance narratives/scripts. Normative traits seen in wider social contexts and interactions are present in burlesque. Although these have allowed women to express with a variety of identities, these identities are limiting. Therefore, the approach to sex, desire and perversion is continually reliant on universal norms around intimacy/desire/femininity, etc. These are then defined and read through particular social and historical understandings of women and place.

The use of burlesque as a medium to understand femininity cannot adequately destabilize norms or upend clean femininity. Rather this shows the incorporation of normative signs of heterosexual legitimacy that are inherent in the ways in which burlesque is styled. This is through the meanings disposed/circulated by its history and, more importantly, how the revival has been shaped (i.e. linear narratives and the climate of post 90s femininity). As established, the burlesque observed demonstrates how heterosexual values inform femininity and how the revival of burlesque asserts this femininity within structures that do not compromise agency (albeit negative reactions from audience members can question this). Although narratives of burlesque valorize and visualize heterosexuality, there is a limitation to which burlesquers can challenge, give visibility to or offer another approach that celebrates femininity. The structure of performances and popular culture's expectations restrict anything which may compromise the climate of the revival and, indeed, 'empowered' femininity. This is not to say revivalist burlesque is not significant or important, because burlesque is meaningful for the women who consume and perform it. However, narrative and stylistic distancing from associations with burlesque's demise still demonize Bad/Dirty (i.e. Other women). What this mainly concerns is continually attaching 'Dirty' Bodies to negative perceptions around pornography and sexual women (i.e. those who supposedly lack agency). As we have explored in previous chapters, the discourses that frame and structure Dirty Bodies make them out to be contagious, abhorrent and socially unacceptable (Mort, 2000; Cohen, 2005). It is dangerous to continue these assumptions because the Bad and the Dirty have more significance than they are given credit for.

Through the examples above, burlesque is still defined within the social scope of heterosexuality through the dismissal of Bad/Dirty (i.e. Other) women. These women do not demonstrate restraint, thus potentially compromise the elevated status of clean heteronormative femininity (even in subcultural spaces). Consequently, when looking at the rise and popularity of mainstream burlesque, there is no alternative offered to wider cultural descriptions of ideologically clean femininity. This is specifically due to the meaning structures used, which are actually extensions of the heteronormative in the guise of difference. Even if women do feel empowered by using burlesque as a medium to build self-confidence, in the very acquisition of the performance repertoires and the expectations of audiences and clubs alike, femininities are bound to social standards. The struggle for agency and integrity by women, who choose to do burlesque in order to secure both, is a huge problem for all women. This has been produced not only through the sexualization of mainstream culture or the presence of heterosexual normalcy in gender relations, but through an active dismissal of women by women who use the very structures that devalue anything other than heterosexuality (as explored in previous chapters). To dismiss women like Mouse, Doris La Trine, Ms T, Empress Stah and RubberDoll is damaging.

Recognizing contexts as a means to alleviate the pressure on women in having to justify their identity is important, particularly as alternative constructions of femininity are always in constant battle with heterosexual ideals even within subcultural contexts. The consequence of this dismisses the potentiality and scope these identities have, specifically as they can challenge how femininity is perceived and how women should feel about who they are. Although the more extreme performers can be read through the lines of misogyny, they should not be continually reduced to this typical analysis. The value of Bad/Dirty (i.e. Other) women is something that we will always need to explore in more detail and in context to demonstrate permanent agency and scope of non-normative female sexuality and biography.

Resurrection of the 'alternative to'?

In recent years, the resurrection of burlesque in non-mainstream spaces (fetish BDSM clubs and magazines, burlesque events and club nights, etc.) has provided women – within these contexts – another avenue to express identity and a means to showcase positive body politics. Sex positivity and 'empowerment' are key words often associated with the rise and popularity of burlesque even within the mainstream, where burlesque style and 'politics' are trendy and widely understood as a valid means for women to feel good about themselves, their bodies and looks. Although there are criticisms of 'mainstreaming' something from subculture (i.e. becoming inauthentic, politics being removed – see Klein (1999) – and style becoming standardized and losing appeal); it is interesting to explore the rise and proliferation of burlesque in popular culture and its relation to non-mainstream spaces, lifestyles and alternative women (see Attwood, 2011b; Baldwin, 2004; Drury, 2007; Glasscock, 2003; Liepe-Levinson, 2002; Walters, 2010; Wilson, 2008; Von Teese, 2006).

For this chapter, the vehicle into debates and contradictions around the good/Bad, Dirty/clean and possibilities is burlesque. By exploring the rise, demise and revival of burlesque, and also the commodification of other 'alternatives', we are able to examine the kinds of standards and norms that emerge. What happens when women fail expectations and socially approved alternative identities to convey agency, 'feminism', sexual self-confidence and ownership? How and why do some women become complicit in the subjugation of other women (i.e. Bad/Dirty girls, sluts, performers who are seen to be too extreme)? If some women are using socially approved alternative identities to convey agency, sexual self-confidence and ownership, then what does this say about conformity and 'real' alternatives to heteronormativity and good girl privilege? How this plays out in the commodification of alternatives in popular culture is interesting, not specifically in relation to debates on authenticity (be careful of those binaries) and new embodied knowledge, but what commercialization and standardisatizn tell us about clean safe femininities within the 'alternative'.

Although the development of consumer culture and leisure time has opened different avenues for femininity to be expressed in more ways other than the traditional, if these 'new' modes of expression are highly structured, sanctioned and clean, they are still arguably contained within what is socially plausible and intelligible. What happens if you contravene these standards, both in popular culture and 'other' spaces? We will now explore the commercial success of burlesque, the issues stemming from the branding of women's bodies for entertainment, and the gendered implications of the commodification of alternative constructions to the 'norm'.

Clean versus Dirty burlesque

To set the scene, it is important to acknowledge the origins of burlesque, the commercial popularity of this form of tease and its demise in the late 1950s, and early 1960s. The reasons surrounding its demise will help us understand why the contemporary revival of burlesque promotes a safer 'alternative' femininity with standardized looks, despite being hailed as inclusive and open for all bodies to perform (i.e. all sizes, BAME, queer, etc.). Examining burlesque also means examining the socio-cultural history and gendered politics of the cultures that surround this practice (i.e. cleanliness, industrial capitalism, night-time economies, burlesque as empowerment). Although the revival displays a range of styles and interpretations, we will see how these have been commodified and articulated in ways that continue to dismiss Bad/Dirty (i.e. Other) women who are seen as bad, pollutants and 'not burlesque' (see Empress Stah, Ms T, Doris La Trine, RubberDoll, Mouse, etc.). How the revival and mainstreaming of burlesque correspond to heterosexual normalcy through a clean/ good girl aesthetic will be explored through its distance from other types of femininity associated with sex work, porn, bisexuality and same-sex desire (as explored further in Chapter 1 and the case study chapters).

Popular entertainment and controversy

The origins of burlesque emerged through the vaudeville, bawdy working-class humour, cabaret, mime and the theatre in the UK. In the mid-nineteenth century, Lydia Thompson and her troupe, The British Blondes, travelled from the UK to America, where they achieved acclaim and success (see Baldin (2004) and Nally (2009) for a comprehensive history and examination of burlesque). The success of burlesque increased momentum during the 1920s and 1930s, where artists performed in packed-out venues. Burlesque was a hugely popular form of risqué and controversial entertainment in the 1920s and then in the 1930s, where it 'threatened to engulf all of the legitimate theatres on Broadway' (Liepe-Levinson, 2002:2).

We cannot see burlesque and its popularity as stand alone or isolated from the development of the entertainment industry in the post-war period, where youth cultures emerged and disposable incomes enabled entertainment industries to thrive and develop. The popularity of burlesque was never without controversy and despite Clinton-Baddeley (1973) highlighting that performers managed themselves, Michelle Baldwin (2004) maintains that stage names would still be given to the performer by men. The popularity of burlesque and the development of different types of venues for entertainment meant that audience tastes and demands also started to adapt (i.e. audiences are being recognized as diverse and not homogeneous). This adaption is also dependent on individual pleasures and what audience members actively want to seek out, with venues catering for, responding to and – in turn – constructing needs and expectations.

Controversy was never found far away from these developments, with moral crusades against indecency and immoral behaviour in America in the 1930s, 1940s and so on. Anti-sex trade campaigns and the Society for the Suppression of Vice are two examples of the backlash against burlesque and other controversial forms of entertainment that were seen to be immoral and unhealthy. Despite this focus, the 1950s was seen as burlesque's heyday with artists such as Bettie Page hailed as pin-up queens. What is interesting about Bettie Page is not how she is revered as a burlesque superstar and BDSM fetish model (both in the 1950s and now), but how her diverse career highlights a shift in popular culture. This shift correlates to themes in popular culture relating to women's bodies, profit, sexualization, pornography and BDSM/fetish. Bettie Page not only posed in beach wear, she also graced Playboy and underground fetish BDSM magazines. Whilst the latter might be read negatively by moralists as demeaning and not empowering, Bettie Page's style of tease and irony in bondage photos presents her as knowingly playing into and owning sexiness.

Jackie Wilson (2008:148) argues that the way in which Bettie Page performs in her photographs 'marks both collusion and resistance', thus upends and challenges assumptions that women are unknowingly objectified or objectified against their will. Annie Sprinkle's *Anatomy of a Pin-Up* is a really relevant example to intersect here within this discussion, because she blends the image of the pin-up with connotations of subversive potential. This includes the subversive potential in being 'bad' and taking claim over sexual subjectivity.

Anatomy of a Pin-Up Photo deconstructs an image of Annie Sprinkle in thigh-high boots, suspenders, a tight-laced under-bust and a bra. Arrows point to each aspect of her body, including an account of her make-up, and a description of what she is wearing, and how uncomfortable and constructed it is. At the bottom of the photo, to the right and in brackets it states that 'in spite of it all, I'm sexually excited and feeling great!' (Biszek, 2006:312), highlighting that even if the picture and her femininity are constructed and sexualized, she likes it, it is part of her sexual/self-identity, and it is her choice. Sexiness is a construction. Normative perceptions (although not fixed, we are post-structuralist here) are also socially and culturally constructed and frame alternative forms of femininity (i.e. the Bad, the Dirty, the sexual) as subject positions to be saved, to be cleaned and to be policed. This is obviously ideological and contradictory too, as sexiness and the sex appeal of the pin-up (indeed an allegory of the sexually expressive Bad Girl) both invite moral subjugation and commercial interest (i.e. clean alternatives circulate well in popular culture).

Still, the *Anatomy of a Pin-Up Photo* marks potential possibilities for women and how femininity is embodied, conceived and performed. Although Williams (1993:189) maintains that she does not claim that the 'resisting, subversive potential of Annie Sprinkle's strategies' goes beyond the contexts and 'realm' of the sexual, Maria Elena Buszek (2006:311) argues that through the context of Annie Sprinkle's *Anatomy of a Pin-Up Photo*, sexual self-expression *is* a 'progressive issue'. This is important to consider when we are recognizing sexual self-expression as a useful tool to shift negative perceptions around sexual women and that women performing tease are not without agency: instead, what they are doing can be considered sex positive and activism. This has longevity and is not something that can be disconnected from embodiment and self-identity. For Biszek (2006:313), *Anatomy of a Pin-Up* 'suggests that when women are given the opportunity to take control of their sexual representation, they may ultimately expose the very mythology with which women's sexuality and beauty are associated – indeed, to such feminist thinkers, others' judgements of and desire to eradicate them is itself oppressive'.

The knowing wink and spank from Bettie Page in some of her photographs (i.e. burlesque pin-up and BDSM model), for instance, can be viewed as a sex-positive praxis as it exposes how lived experiences of sexual subjectivity are not necessarily aligned to wider bodily politics that assume sexual women are redundant, in need of help or rescue, and not the beneficiaries of the photographs they are part of (i.e. they are paid, they agree for the picture to be taken, the image adds to the management of their public persona, etc.). Nudity and burlesque have shared massive commercial success especially with the development of gentleman's clubs and other leisure venues geared towards men and their wallets, as we will see in the next section.

During the 1950s women took off more clothes than ever (Dita Von Teese, 2006), which really goes hand-in-hand with the expanse of sexual economies, adult entertainment and the strip show in cities (Liepe-Levinson, 2002). Arguably, this was the start of the decline in popularity of burlesque in its traditional form; however, the development of the entertainment business and gentlemen's clubs and top-shelf publications meant that different forms of striptease and nudity were becoming more widespread and accessible. Burlesque may have become an outdated form of entertainment, but the growing commentary from the 1960s onwards around bodily/identity/sexual politics within popular culture renders strippers, pin-ups and women in certain areas of sexual economies as sites of contestation, fragility and failure. This is in stark contrast from the knowing wink and sex-positive activism and praxis seen through the examples of Bettie Page and *The Anatomy of a Pin-Up*.

Sexual economies and body politics

Although Ariel Levy could argue that Bettie Page was knowingly complicit in the objectification of women's sexiness and rendering women as sexual objects (i.e. see Ariel Levy on Female Chauvinist Pigs, 2005), the wink, sexual confidence, breaking the fourth wall and irony arguably offer a challenge to the idea that women are passive objects that cannot choose to take ownership and enjoy their own sexiness (i.e. this includes acknowledging other people's enjoyment of your sexiness being celebrated). We have seen that only certain forms of tease are seen to enable these challenges to happen, when in fact the case studies offer a means to reconceive femininity and sexual subjectivity. The case studies' presentation of Bad Girl femininity, sex and desire is confrontational, dirty and a challenge to palatable 'good' alternatives. The points of contestation in many ways can be viewed as a commentary on and reflection of entertainment culture, divergent feminist politics, women as sexual consumers rather than sexual commodities and the narrow line between socially sanctioned agency and the pollutant.

The inclusion of BDSM imagery and taboo female sexual self-expression merging with burlesque through Bettie Page as an icon adds a layer of contradiction and controversy to the 'Bad Girl' being a site of transformation/consumption. Playfully engaging with taboo brings the binaries of good/Bad and Madonna/whore into view. It also splits burlesque away from its traditions and connects imagery, performance and femininity with new sexual economies that take these aspects and place them elsewhere for different forms of entertainment and consumption: entertainment which the framing of neo-burlesque distances itself from (i.e. pornography, go-go dancing, lap dancing, etc.). However, it is important to note that Bettie Page's notoriety is one part of this history, as Jessica Glasscock (2003:6) outlines that in the 1950s women who did striptease were American idols (i.e. clean girls) and that the ideal burlesquer 'is pink, well fed, and smiling, with tassel-tipped breasts that sparkle like the chrome detailing on a classic car'. The popularity of burlesque in the 1950s was arguably partly due to its risqué imagery, with this then becoming associated with mainstream and underground pornography (i.e. back to the Betty Page BDSM stills again).

For burlesquer Blaze Starr (Glasscock, 2003:160) pornography killed stripping as the 'star quality' was removed from performers due to more clothes being removed, more women in the industry and body parts revealed explicitly in 'problematic' venue spaces (i.e. gentleman's clubs, etc.). In a commercial context, original style burlesque is not actually 'dirty' enough when compared to porn and full stripping. During this period new themes of perversity, sex and women's sexual self-expression were interwoven into wider negative perceptions and attitudes towards burlesque and other striptease imagery. Although negative attitudes were down to wider culture connecting any form of explicitness with the growth of pornography and erotic businesses, the policing of pornography and the interventions made by the US government heightened the sexiness and appeal of this industry. For Dita Von Teese (2006:109) the 1950s was a flagrantly sexy decade and this was largely due to the Society for the Suppression of Vice bringing controversies into the public forum 'with 'sneaking a peek' of a woman 'unawares' developing as one of the burlesque's new themes'.

Interventions by the American government and the Society for the Suppression of Vice into striptease and other 'lewd' acts made more people aware of body politics (Von Teese, 2006), but arguably further entrenched the politics of what is 'dirty', Other and Bad in relation to women's bodies, behaviour and place within new areas of entertainment and economy. The appeal of the erotic therefore intensified around women's bodies in the public forum, especially within marketing and entertainment (both of which have received an abundance of feminist criticism). Yet, certain forms of 'Bad Women' and sexual expression were shunned and made dirty by women (i.e. women Othering other women). The continuation of heteronormativity and the policing of women's bodies can be seen here, with burlesque and other forms of tease framed as taboo, unhealthy and negative (i.e. here there is falling back into discourses that historically bind women as 'lacking' something, etc.). Although Glasscock (2003) maintains that the lack of popularity in the 1960s signalled the demise of burlesque, the integration of pornography into mainstream culture and the intense commercial focus on women's bodies already signal a shift away from one form of taboo to another (i.e. losing appeal to new forms of entertainment, etc.). Go-Go dancing (Glasscock, 2003) and other forms of striptease – notably Playboy style strip clubs – provided the final nail in the coffin for burlesque. Burlesque is seen to be pushed aside due to the popularity of stripping (Baldwin, 2004). Although moral crusades against vice have added to controversies around types of sexual entertainment, the main reason for the demise of burlesque is really the new popular sites of consumerism and entertainment. The stickiness of sleaze, sex-negative attitudes and ideological dismissals still resonate with women who choose to contravene social standards. We have seen how these play out within subcultural contexts, where the policing of women's bodies by other women and the narratives of mainstream revivalist burlesque actually exposes the importance of the embodied knowledge of women who fall between the good/ bad binary. Those who fall in-between do not fit into either category because they redefine their identity on their own terms (i.e. Bad Girls happen to things, Ms T).

Revivalist burlesque: Cleanliness and the commodification of alternatives

The revival of burlesque emerged from alternative spaces and clubs in the 1990s, but also from the sexual revolutions and freedoms contemporary women are accustomed to. These shape the way in which the revival had been framed. We must not forget that sex-positive third wave feminism has also contributed to the revival. Commodification and cleanliness cannot be seen in isolation, nor can the rise of neo-burlesque. Since the 1990s women have been afforded more opportunities to explore their self-identity, and this is recognized through visibility of the sexually empowered woman in popular culture (e.g. single ladies doing it for themselves, pole exercise, sex toys aimed at women, and porn by and for women) and the accessibility of lifestyles and experiences through commodity culture (e.g. affordable sex toys, fast fashion, streaming media services, club cultures and mainstreaming sex). There are many possibilities for women to articulate femininity, which includes alternative forms of femininity that appear to be 'different' from the mainstream such as those found in burlesque. Burlesque femininities are seen to offer an approach to alternative constructions of femininity which are buoyant in contemporary culture. The extent to which these alternatives undermine heteronormative assumptions about the place of femininity within gendered scripts is debatable and something which the book has examined.

Having a visible range of different types of femininities in popular culture is positive in many ways, such as giving young women opportunity to identify with more identities and, perhaps, feel a sense of belonging and legitimacy in how they identify and self-express. The assimilation of aspects of subcultures (e.g. such as style, attitude, political expression) into the mainstream gives somewhat legitimacy to 'alternative femininities' (i.e. tattooed, sex-positive, pin-up style, non-vanilla, etc.). This legitimacy does not sit in isolation from the rest of culture, including developments in gender and sexual politics (i.e. third wave feminism, fourth wave feminism and digital/social media, girl power, women being addressed as sexual consumers, gay rights, same-sex marriage, civil partnership, etc.) and indeed capitalism and consumer culture (i.e. mainstreaming of sex shops, safe shopping spaces for women to buy sex toys in the high-street, suburban sexscapes, etc.). If we take a step back from this celebration, it is evident that positive circumstances are not afforded to all, and this includes women who are berated for expressing their femininity, sexuality and politics beyond what is approved by a dominant social group, even within subcultures.

For Debra Ferreday (2008:49), the defining characteristics of the new burlesque are 'nostalgia for original burlesque performances, as well as a reclaiming of historical burlesque performers as proto-feminists'. This situates the revival (and the past) as powerful, with burlesque being equated to skill, informed body politics, craft and having a history connoting agency and authenticity. The rise and popularity of burlesque in this period signal, to some extent, a backlash against sexualization with women taking back control of sexual self-expression and their bodies. This includes confronting sexist attitudes and creating space that both challenge male gratification (i.e. gentlemen's clubs, etc.) and celebrate femininity in various forms (i.e. diversity in terms of body shape, sexuality, etc.). The framing of revivalist burlesque as empowering, feminist and reclaiming something from negative connotations gives rise to value systems. Contemporary performers such as Immodesty Blaize speak highly of original burlesquers, with performing burlesque seen 'in terms of honouring past performers, [and] as performance of femininity that has survived as a symbol of earlier expressions of independence and freedom' (Ferreday, 2008:50).

Even though the growth of consumer culture and leisure time have given individuals more choice and access to identities and lifestyles beyond traditional femininity, in general, the value some burlesque communities place on past 'proto-feminists' actually acts as a tool of separation. This frames any other form of stripping as disempowering, not feminist and designed for misogynist consumption. Binaries are applied, even if this application is not intentional. However, the reclaiming of space back from gentlemen's clubs is important on the one hand, but on the other it assumes women doing the bump 'n' grind in these contexts are forced to do it, are lacking agency and are doing it for other people (i.e. men) rather than for themselves. To devalue any woman who chooses to strip or lap-dance actually undermines the subversive nature of tease, which we have seen with Bettie Page and the *Anatomy of the Pin-Up*.

We need to note that some moves in lap dancing are also shared with burlesque (see Drury, 2006a, 2006b, 2007) as there is no shame in stripping. Burlesque and the meanings behind tease in the revival have – to some degree – become established as exclusive, politically one dimensional and the only 'rationally' conscious way for women to counter-attack negative sexualization and misogyny. Although it is important for women to reposition femininity and 'women' as central figures in the debates that surround their bodies and choices; if some choices made by women do not fit this political standard, then this means that palatable forms of 'resistance' are actually maintaining heteronormativity and reinforcing binaries. Having a binary assumes there is only one form of femininity to change, resist and collude against. The binary between the good stripper versus the bad stripper does not help when we try to explore new embodied knowledge, especially if we want to be open and listen to women who are articulating their femininity and self-identity in ways that fall between or outside the binary.

Style, confidence and cleanliness

In the 1990s the revival came back full circle to the UK (see Baldwin, 2004; Von Teese, 2006), with popularity and support within BDSM, fetish and other subcultural clubbing spaces. The revival happened in a climate of sex-positivity, girl power and new forms of femininity in conflict with traditional modes of femininity. For Shelley Budgeon (1998:123) femininity in the late 1990s 'could not be considered simple or straightforward', and if we open this wider to consumer culture and the MTV generation we can see a socio-political environment where there were more opportunities 'to do' femininity away from the domestic sphere, men and sexualization. What these opportunities have also opened up, specifically within the revival, is a resistance against femininities and sexual self-expression designed by and for men. The re-emergence of burlesque in popular culture is through striptease becoming mainstream (see Walters, 2010).

Natasha Walter argues that licensing laws in the UK during 2003 helped turn around sleaze associated with lap-dancing venues popularized during the mid-1990s. This allowed striptease venues to be classified as restaurants or bars, rather than sharing the same classification as sex shops. Different forms of tease became normal entertainment avenues for hen-parties, stag-dos and after-work drinks (Walters, 2010). What burlesque means for the individual performer can vary and there are numerous interpretations of burlesque. Interpretations depend on the styles the performer adopts but generally burlesque is a comic or glamorous striptease with an emphasis on *tease*. There are some stylistic and performative differences between burlesque and lap dancing and striptease at gentleman's clubs although moves and tease are arguably similar (see Drury, 2006a, 2006b, 2007). The burlesquer performs at a distance and this performance is situated inside a narrative story constructed through the use of music, props and cultural contexts.

In general, burlesque is not lewd, it does not simulate sex and it is playful rather than exposing skin to intentionally turn people on. This begs the question: if a female audience member is turned on by a female burlesquer, is this 'bad' and objectifying? The lack of recognition of same-sex possibilities disqualifies any other interpretation, rendering celebration platonic. What is seen on stage is quite cheeky, teasingly humorous or glamorous. Burlesque is not dangerous, which distances these performances from other artists performing a striptease with needles, dildos and the extraction of blood, which we explored through Empress Stah and RubberDoll. Performances are not overtly sexual with teasing, winking, comedy and glamour disarming 'negative sexualisation' and this is usually met with laughter and applause from women in the audience, as experienced in field research. Even with the same moves as pole or lap dancing, such as the shimmy and the bump 'n' grind (see Drury, 2006a, 2006b, 2007), the way the burlesquers style their body and the contexts in which they shape their performances are different (i.e. like a sub-genre of 'striptease'). The styles appropriated and seen in field research were mainly 'clean' repeating the permanency of definitive stereotypes and negating any firm links to 'dangerous' cultures present in burlesque history, through the late 1950s and 1960s (i.e. pornography, Go-Go dancing, gentlemen's clubs, other sexual cultures, etc.).

The array of performances seen in field research all included elements of comedy, mime, dance, singing and parodies of stereotypical identities or known figures. The popularity of fakir, the freak show and circus within the subcultures burlesque touches is also included in artist repertoire such as fire eating (see Red Sarah, Lucifire, Miss Behave, etc.). The modern revival brings together an array of tease artists including cheesecake, showgirl style and slapstick, tongue-in-cheek comedy. Tease does not always mean the burlesquer undresses on stage, but in the main fan dances, the slow-seductive removal of gloves and the use of other props, such as umbrellas to convey a tease story, are used to cheekily suggest sexual naughtiness in a coquettishly assertive manner. Performance themes may centre on the bored housewife driven to naughtiness through the very products she is cleaning the stage with, twisted fairy tales, magic tricks, the good girl gone bad through rock and roll music, and the beautiful glamour of showgirls and pin-ups. Recurring themes seen in field research showed that performances and femininities were safe and clean.

The differentiation between stripping and burlesque has someway built the context and value of burlesque in its revival, where women can enjoy watching and feel empowered by performing burlesque without feeling shame or misogyny. The form burlesque expression takes is not closely associated with shame or misogyny, as both of these have no place in performances, club space or mantra of burlesque. Walters's (2010:43) interviews with burlesque performers revealed that these women interpreted burlesque as art and that undressing reflected 'empowerment' and a 'creative way for women to take their clothes off'. This was reiterated by the attitudes of burlesquers in field research, the styles of performances observed and through conversations seen on social networking websites. For Rebecca Drury, tease offers bodily confidence off stage and in the bedroom (Drury, 2007). In the ethnography Rebecca Drury maintained that after teaching burlesque and pole dancing to women (with a focus on posture), she expressed that they hold themselves up high.

> **Rebecca Drury:** I get people to stand in the mirror and to stand normally ... then just push their shoulders back, lift themselves up from the waist and put their head slightly back. They look six inches taller and I [say] that is the difference between girlfriend, girl-next-door and goddess.

Confidence from being sexy and doing sexy is empowering. Rebecca Drury also includes pole dancing and lap dancing as elements which build self-confidence, going against the trend of revivalist/ mainstream burlesque in terms of what it differentiates itself from. This was reiterated in her club night Sirens in Brighton, where burlesque was seamlessly combined with pole dancing. Pink dollars were brought by patrons to give to performers as gifts of adoration and celebration. Pink dollars were also collected at the end of the night and shared equally among performers. Pole dancing and the exchange of money from audience member to performer are not seen on the burlesque circuit, as the only exchange between performer and audience member is the celebration of femininity and normative routes to 'empowerment'. Therefore, the revival's context is situated within an agency and integrity that is only attainable through the expression of safe sexy femininity in 'creative', political, empowered and non-explicit striptease (i.e. due to no money or sexual desire being exchanged).

Burlesque appearing again as a popular means to perform (Glasscock, 2003) and a 'new' style of alternative femininity tries to evade the femininities presented in the 1960s connecting to objectification and 'issues' some argue are prevalent in pornography, lap dance and pole dancing. Nonetheless, a wider scope of acceptability is sanctioned for burlesque and this can be seen through applying the sexualization of mainstream culture, highlighted by Attwood (2006), which includes the acceptability and visibility of tease as powerfully sexy, and being a socially permissible way for young women to dress to connote power and self-representation.

The femininities in mainstream burlesque are not overtly sexual, and performances are generally not explicit: sex acts and genitals/ nipples are never revealed. The 'reveal' at the end of the tease is often tassels that are twirled in an energetic and celebratory manner. The resolution at the end of the performance is euphoric, entertaining and 'nice'. There are no lingering cliff-hangers and the audience is not threatened to think further about the implications of what they have witnessed (which we saw with Doris La Trine): it's pure entertainment. No intimate body parts are revealed and the style of covering these does not always eroticize those parts commonly associated with the 'male gaze', thus the definitive attributes of femininity. Most of the audience in burlesque venues are women, but this assumes women in these venues and indeed the performers are straight. If the audience are straight women, then what are they getting from the performance? In the context of the revival, despite women seeing role models and inspirational women, this celebration is arguably a shared expression of female (hetero)sexuality. Although this enables women to express in safe space, what this does not automatically allow is sexual desire between women. Surely some performers like to strip for women because they are attracted to women (e.g. see Ms T), and in turn some women prefer seeing women doing striptease because they may desire or fancy them. Desirability and accessibility are important, especially for queer, bi, lesbian women, but this is sanitized in the business of revivalist burlesque observed in the research.

Two central themes in modern burlesque include tease and comedy. In the context of the UK, some of the burlesque seen on the scene reflects slapstick humour associated with Britishness, naughty postcards from working-class seaside gift shops and the *Carry On* films, even if some imagery used by the performer might be dark, freak show and slightly macabre. Naughtiness is performed in a choreographed and sophisticated way, with the use of 1940s film star and 1950s pin-up styles, and feminine props such as fans, corsets and opera gloves. The revival is important for many women in the scene, as well as women who use aspects of tease to feel good or to comment politically on self-expression and femininity.

The aesthetics of contemporary performers are based mainly on the fusion of 1940s and 1950s (and 1960s Americana) pin-up style mixed with modern takes on corsetry, tattooing and including elements of goth, rockabilly and punk stylistics and customization (Baldwin, 2004). Hair is normally one block colour namely black, red or blonde which reflects 'natural' looks and basic categories such as the goth girl with black hair and the ditzy blonde. Block colours also look aesthetically better on stage depending on the lighting which is used to emphasize their style (Von Teese, 2006). This stylistic preference is capitalized by Dita Von Teese (2006) in her book on burlesque, which is more of a how to guide. Nearly all the performers seen in field research wore minimal flawless and feminine make-up including red lipstick, black eye liner, flawless 'white' skin and rouged cheeks to various degrees. The repetition of body stylistics seen on stage and within the body styles seen in club cultures, flyers and subcultural magazines, even in mainstream publications, implies that a specific femininity is continually presupposed and desirable (i.e. for profit, commercial appeal and signalling expertise and authenticity).

The visibility of burlesque as trendy within popular and consumer culture sees sexuality, bodily confidence and self-empowerment as something which any woman can obtain on the stage and at home (Baldwin, 2004; Drury, 2007; Von Teese, 2006). The visibility of mainstream burlesque as edgy, sexy, 'dangerous' and naughty has proliferated every aspect of mainstream (consumer) culture (i.e. TV, film, music videos, social media platforms such as Instagram, fan pages on social media and fashion); thus, this sanctioned form of 'alternative' femininity is easily accessible and consumed. Powerful femininity, sexual assertiveness, agency and sexual independence are highlighted by Attwood and Holland (2009:167) through celebrities and 'feisty strippers' strengthening 'a view of body display and erotic performance as a sign of power'. Celebrity endorsement and the proliferation of edgy femininity allow women access to a mediated version of striptease and sexual embodiment which is safe and clean to use. The appeal of this does not take away the agency of the woman choosing it; however, we need to ask: what happens when norms within a community are not challenged? There will always be standards and hierarchies in any (sub)culture, which is why we need to delve deeper into the ethnography to examine how alternative femininity is articulated, lived and expressed. The implication of this – on the valid type(s) and site(s) of alternative constructions of femininity – is profound and exclusionary, especially if certain cultural practices are promoted as inclusive and progressive.

Burlesque striptease, however, is a medium which brings performers/women self-confidence, power and a real sense of sexiness that they can control and style by themselves (Attwood, 2011b; Baldwin, 2004; Glasscock, 2003; Von Teese, 2006; Walters, 2010; Wilson, 2008). This was reiterated by research participants who participated in burlesque striptease on stage or ran burlesque club nights and lessons, and by well-known burlesque artists such as Dita Von Teese (2006), Immodesty Blaize in her documentary film *Burlesque Undressed* (2010) and through the words of Vivienne VaVoom and others in Natasha Walters's (2010) book. Although Walters highlights problems of burlesque associations with what she calls 'dangerous' cultures, like pornography and patriarchy, there is still little said regarding the privileges of more prominent artists, like Dita Von Teese, who tease for a living and are economically funded by product endorsements such as underwear, books and alcohol. Dita Von Teese does not do this for a hobby and is able to utilize her success to employ and manage herself.

The conditions which produce, mould and repeat the themes, types and femininities visible in burlesque present more complex issues which are superficially covered over by the commercial value of burlesque. The revival has been conditioned by a focus on the glitz, glamour and comedy of retro-burlesque, rather than addressing or reframing the issues that subsequently added to its 'demise'. This focus centres on an active distancing from compromising femininities bound in misogyny and lack of agency seen in the refusal of value in pole dancing or overtly sexual aesthetics. The presentation of burlesque femininity in popular culture is accessible for the majority of women to buy into and consume. There is a common aesthetic which emits readings of confidence and sex appeal, without falling 'victim' to misogyny, even if it still confirms boundaries for women and what they can/cannot perform. This can restrict the re-presentation of self-identity on stage and forbid context, the personal biography and sexual self-identity of the performer to be revealed on stage.

6

The shadows of safe femininity

Up to this point, we have explored the significance of the Bad Girl and her Dirty Body. We have also unpicked double standards, the policing of sexual norms, the commodification of 'alternative' constructions of femininity and how revivalist burlesque narratives subjugate women who 'fail' the normative standard. The meaning systems which are used to circulate discourse are pervasive and they try to quash embodied knowledge of those who do not comply. Although Bad Girls happen to things, create their own space and offer ways to challenge heteronormativity (in any social group), they still have a shadow that haunts them. What I mean by this is that 'safe/clean' femininity is still casting judgement on different ways of being a woman. This includes wider social norms and attitudes, but also how femininity is understood and written about in academic discourse. What types of shadows, then, do safe femininities cast?

Safe femininity and the domination of heterosexuality

Although feminist discourses (i.e. the 'waves') have engaged with 'women's realities', the second wave universalization of women's lived experience is problematic for Bad Women. Radical feminists in the 1970s acknowledged that women do not have equal status, privilege or choice in how they express their self-identity (see Brownmiller, 1975; Dworkin, 1994, 2000; Jeffreys, 2005; Millett, 1977). The trend in their critique of femininity is the interrogation of binary terms between the subordination of women and unequal power relations between the sexes. Self-identity is seen (in their view) as being bound, and always in relation to 'lacks' concerning the female body and how it is used and appropriated in culture. The preoccupation with hegemonic patriarchy is problematic as it bypasses femininity as something complex, varied and agentic, especially for women who are labelled Bad/Dirty. What they do, however, highlight the issues inherent in heterosexual domination and how this manifests through patriarchal control over the reality we, apparently, live in.

In wider terms, whatever or whoever contravenes what is normal is seen as having an identity to be suspicious of (i.e. or someone who is not safe, good or stable). These discussions, as we have seen, have implications in the ways in which women's actions, bodies and self-representation are seen, interpreted and engaged with (i.e. in both popular culture, within subculture and how identities are studied and researched, etc.). What the identifying terms (good, Bad/Dirty) do is enable a continuous moral commentary on women's value, how they should behave in everyday spaces (i.e. usually women are expected to take up as little space as possible) and what their 'choices' say about their self-identity. This can even be present in how femininity is critiqued by the various approaches that feminism takes, which we will explore in this chapter in relation to lacks and the conditions that enable safe, clean and agentic femininity to emerge.

Femininity (normative and the conforming) is a historical and socio-cultural construct. How 'femininity' is lived, rejected and 'performed' differs dependent on context and the individual. The everyday level of experience can and does enable women to reconfigure what femininity means to them, but in the broader context there is a stickiness that comes with femininity and this stickiness never seems to go away. This stickiness is affectively felt and flows in, through and on the body of the individual. The stickiness connects to the past and this past is very much present in the wider definitions of femininity and what it is to be a woman. This is even apparent in the tensions between, and the stickiness of, the gender binary. When we begin to look at women's experiences, we can see that feminist commentary on and assessment of femininity is centred on women's struggle to gain access to communicating agency and overt control over their bodies. To be more specific, this is about control over the access women have to their own bodies, sense of self and identity.

This struggle is highlighted by Judith Butler (1990a, 1990b, 1993) in relation to how heterosexuality has been integrated into language and modes of communication, especially through the articulation of heteronormativity in gendered relations. Two 'discrete' and binary genders (i.e. male/female, always cis) continually reproduce heterosexuality as something which is normalized (i.e. internalized as seen as 'natural'), pre-given and an unquestionable facet of the 'human condition'. How this is established and maintained is through social recognition (i.e. this enables other people to understand who you are and what you stand for) and the repetition of certain norms that have become so ingrained that they become sacred. What social recognition highlights is that the characteristics of gender types (in this instance, binary) are pre-given; therefore, gender distinctions are presupposed and socially defined/given. Gender differences between men and women (if we see them as 'discrete' binary categories) are culturally defined through the body being 'sexed' via cultural practices and the compulsion towards needing to embody readable characteristics to enable you to fit in. How gender is conveyed and understood, in general terms, is through social categories supported by cultural, historical and familial contexts. What this means is that heterosexuality, or heteronormativity to be precise, presupposes what women and femininity mean, making both something that all 'females' should 'become'.

However, Butler highlights that even if gender reality appears to be the only reality in which gender can exist, there are many ways to do gender and to challenge it (see also Storey, 2001:140). The notion of drag in Butler's work illuminates the artificiality of gender as performance and enables a space where 'gender' can be questioned. There are, therefore, many ways of doing (and not doing) gender, even if this 'doing' is difficult due to the weight of heterosexual dominance, with rejection from loved ones and society being a real possibility. Butler maintains that gender reality is only real to the extent that it is performed; thus, it is only the repetition of heteronormativity that facilitates the idea that only two genders exist. Coupled with social constructivism, there are certain norms we have to abide by for the 'social good'. The social good is basically what we are told in regards to what constitutes being a good citizen/person, which has been produced by industrial capitalism, institutions – such as the family and heteronormativity – and the rewards gained with positive social recognition. Consequently, what constitutes the social good shapes how society perceives and understands truth, allowing the production of certain accepted identities that are sustained through cultural intelligibility, compulsory heterosexuality and the 'regulation of sexuality within the reproductive domain' (Butler, 1990a:135). The wider historical contexts concerning the domination of heterosexuality, as the pivot in which human relations are measured and measurable by, have a lot to do with this (see Chapter 1 and Jeffrey Weeks on the significance of the nineteenth century, where gender differences and sexual behaviour became fixed). The domination of heterosexuality is something we have continued to revisit in this book, because the history behind heterosexuality and the regulation of sexuality within the reproductive domain are socially produced to elevate certain norms as a means to suppress the transformative power of alternatives (i.e. Bad/Dirty women).

On compulsory heterosexuality and the 'true' woman

On compulsory heterosexuality, Butler (1990b:275) states: 'My point is simply that one way in which this system of compulsory heterosexuality is reproduced and concealed is through the cultivation of bodies into discrete sexes with "natural" appearances and "natural" heterosexual dispositions.' This statement is significant because heterosexuality has become *the* component that is incorporated into definitions that are easily used to convey (and maintain) 'natural' and normative behaviours, genders and lifestyles. This is despite popular culture (i.e. this includes the development of digital culture, the youth economy and gender equality) giving space and visibility to various different ways of doing gender. Although new embodied knowledge and personal accounts offer ways to include more femininities as valid, the shadows of safe/clean femininity are still there, ordering the world. It is a constant battle to take up and make space. Women who reject heterosexual normativity are subject to devaluation which reinforces the view that their self-identity and choices lack credibility. The case studies have revealed the different routes femininity can take to challenge and undermine this view. Undermining heteronormativity is also about challenging women's presumptions about what types of femininity are valid, of value and have transgressive power. It was found in the ethnography that the concealment of the coherence of gender and social performance (repeated as ritual and legitimate; see Butler, 1990a) was used as a way for the more visible femininities and women to gain credibility over other women (see Chapter 5, but also discussions within the case study chapters).

What this indicates is a repetition of ideals that are seamlessly articulated in the production and maintenance of ideals, even within subculture. This highlights that Butler's reflections are not only active in how gender reality is perceived, but how it is *negotiated* and used by women themselves, when trying to gain credibility and visibility. What Butler's critique highlights is the artificiality of gender and sexuality, with Kate Millett (1977:118) asserting that female sexuality is 'subject to social forces'. This is supported by Simone de Beauvoir (1949:428; also see Storey, 2001) on the interpretation of femininity being an 'artificial product that civilisation makes' and that women's instincts 'for coquetry, docility, are indoctrinated as is phallic pride in man' (i.e. good girls). Thus, gender reality is constructed through artificial conditions that all genders are seemingly caught up by. Consequently, the logic of heterosexuality allows intelligibility to comprehend gender differences through cultural standards and stereotypes. However, for de Beauvoir, the characteristics and expectations for women allow greater independence than men, even in a cultural climate which limits their space. She states that 'cooking, washing, managing her house, bringing up children, woman shows more initiative and independence than the man working under orders' (1949:636). This, however, can be complicated by the devaluation of women through sexualization. On the other hand, de Beauvoir still highlights some positivity for the independence and value of women but this does not undermine the logic of heterosexuality because cultural understandings of 'woman' mean that women are required to accept their inferiority and 'Otherness'. Kate Millett (1977) supports this through highlighting the differences between male and female in sexual politics, where female is seen to be passive, ignorant and docile. These 'characteristics' are opposite to male assertiveness and authority. Despite variation and the acknowledgement of contexts (which this book explores), norms still prevail especially in right-wing leaning individuals and groups. Valuing the Bad/Dirty girl through listening to context, voice and embodied knowledge is important as it enables the dismantling of binaries to reveal many ways of being a woman.

An added issue for Bad/Dirty (indeed all) women is the reinforcement of specific attitudes that historically define female sexual desire as lacking, non-existent or produced via male design and needs. For example, Beauvoir's 'true woman' correlates to this issue because a woman is 'required to make herself object, to be the Other' (1949:291). This is actually damaging to the contexts and agency of women who *do* have choices and do recognize their sexual needs and pleasures. Highlighting women's inferiority to men, Millett (1977) critiques femininity under patriarchy and how femininity is a product of male design and needs. These themes can easily (and erroneously) be applied to the history of burlesque striptease and its drift into other forms of sexual cultures from the 1950s onwards, which can be seen as crude, objectifying and sexist. For Millett (1977), social and cultural reality is conditioned by the presupposition of the 'Otherness' (i.e. difference) of women versus male superiority. Millett argues that the construction of femininity, from the needs of men, is actually a product of men fearing the Otherness of women, which in itself presupposes the authority and status of patriarchy (1977:46). This authority is established by men being a referent to the normative, and women subsequently being alien and Other (Millett, 1977:46). What these theories do not highlight or include (although Millett did during the 1970s) is the inferiority projected by women *onto* other women in order to elevate agency and integrity over associations that can compromise both (i.e. the sexual woman, the stripper, the whore).

The presupposition that women have to be seen as always being inferior to men is hugely problematic and far too binary and universalizing. This flattens women's experiences and the intersections of oppression and privilege they experience due to a myriad of factors that build their self-identity (i.e. age, sexuality, gender, race, ethnicity, education/cultural capital and so on). The tensions explored in the above paragraphs were encountered in field research and are present as a key part of the analysis of femininity in this book. The range of femininities and what female sexuality can include is given an increased visibility and can be seen in a positive light through the critiques of gender and sexuality by Attwood (2005, 2007a and b, 2009, 2011a, 2011b), Budgeon (1998, 2011), Harris (1997), Kipnis (2006), du Plessis (1996) and Weeks (1991 and 1995). What these authors demonstrate are wider social, cultural and consumer factors which contribute to the demonization of specific women, but significantly they provide context and variables that situate marginalized women with agency. These ideas have been explored throughout the book, but they need highlighting again as significant in recognizing Bad/Dirty (i.e. Othered) women as having agency and seeing femininity as something complex, varied and not straightforward (i.e. not irreducible).

Invisibilities and exclusions

Several lines of enquiry that emerged as key themes in the ethnographic research included commentaries from performers (and performances) that related to female sexuality (same-sex desire, bisexuality and kink, etc.), sexual agency, pornography and sexual cultures. These themes have already been explored in the previous chapters, through the social contexts and popular/academic discussions around sexuality and sexual self-expression. One area that implicates this are anti-porn sentiments as they continue to depict femininity as always problematic, dirty and lacking. Fieldwork encounters in my own ethnography involved highly sexualized sites and a variety of women (not all) who had affiliations with (by proxy, by association or by choice) or were seen to be part of the sex industry (i.e. due to themes in performances, their gendered and sexual expressions, and viewpoints). Although the sex wars of the 1970s/1980s ended several decades ago, the divide between the anti-porn feminist camp and the sex-positive feminist camp still burns on. The discussions around sexual agency and sexual depiction are still prevalent in the exchanges within and between the sexes, and can be used as a measurement to see which types of women can be valorized (i.e. by popular culture, the mainstreaming of burlesque and 'alternatives' to, between women – as we have seen in previous chapters, and within areas of subcultural resistance), seen as a victim or seen to be a traitor to her sex. In this instance, we will touch upon some of Dworkin's work, as themes in her theoretical approach are invested in taking away agency from women who do have the choice to be sexual, thus ignoring women as having the right to be recognized as having sexual agency.

The problems with oppression and frames of 'lack'

Despite Dworkin's work being influenced by women who have been abused (and this must be recognized too, as this captures some women's experiences), her critique of the sex industry and femininity bypasses a range of women's experiences. Women's experiences are of central importance to this book, so it is important to recognize the issues when experiences are universalized. Sexuality and sexual activity are key concerns, and these concerns have been critiqued by Dworkin to such an extent that they build upon and confirm the rhetoric of what wider socio-historical discourses see as 'dirty' (practices, types of women, types of depictions, etc.). If we explore narratives of dirt, we can see that Dworkin's account of the sex industry and its implications on women's rights to accessing their own bodies and articulating choice narrow the range of femininities to those who ether lack agency (i.e. women *in* the sex industry) and those who are implicated by the existence of pornography (i.e. women and femininity *as* a product *of* pornography). Significantly, Dworkin highlights that all women (i.e. cisgendered) exist in the shadow of pornography because 'whore' and 'cunt' are seen to be definitive of women's reality. She states: 'The definition of women articulated systematically and consistently in pornography is objective and real in that real women exist within and must live with constant reference to the boundaries of this definition' (Dworkin, 1994:201).

Through the above, all women have to struggle to define themselves against heterosexual patriarchy which automatically takes away agency and places them with attributes that they need to constantly negotiate.

This constant reference to pornography and women lacking agency was found in field research and the negotiations some participants made in defining their status and identity, through distancing themselves from other bodies or practices that were socially seen to take away agency (see Chapter 5). This distancing includes how language is used and the preference for certain gendered scripts (e.g. see Chapter 5 and the repetition of revivalist burlesque narratives as reinforcing heteronormativity and the value of the mediated/ commodified 'Bad' Girl). This book evidences how individuals, specifically women, within non-mainstream groups, actively use the methods of distancing and the security of heterosexual normalcy, to vilify certain women already devalued in wider society (i.e. in order to maintain credibility and agency concerning their 'choices'). The struggle for agency and to prove oneself as not being dominated by misogyny or the phallus is something we have explored throughout the book within the case studies, but especially in Chapter 5 (i.e. with mainstream burlesque narratives distancing the performer from harmful attachments such as pornography, same-sex desire and the expression of femininity within pole and lap dancing).

Although the discourses associated with second wave feminism might not be as widespread today, due to their displacement by third (and fourth) wave discussions, wider social norms and popular culture are still playing to the binary and the elevation of the good girl. In this sense, the system of oppression created by pornography and hegemonic patriarchy can be seen as inescapable, because, as Dworkin argues, even sexual penetration is constructed as a male right, taking away any form of mutual agreement or enjoyment. Sex is dirty. Sex as male design and pleasure eradicates sexual satisfaction and enjoyment from the view of the woman. Dworkin essentially removes the clitoris from existence. Rape, misogyny and the damaging effects of pornography are continued to be mirrored in anti-porn sentiments (see Diana Russell, 1998; Susan Griffin, 1988; Susan

Brownmiller, 1975). The presupposition that misogyny is in every space is far too an essentialist view, and does not account for counter-discourse, the multitude of realities and resistance in everyday spaces (i.e. even shouting back to street harassers). However, the contexts of anti-porn arguments are already defined, developed and expected within anti-porn paradigms, which result in problematizing women's choices. By this I mean that women have to continually *justify* themselves from these assertions made by women. The system of anti-porn sentiment is just as inescapable as the misogyny they critique. Although Brownmiller (1975), Dworkin (1994, 2000), Jeffreys (2005) and Millett (1977) critique patriarchy rather than conform to it, their preoccupation with hegemonic patriarchy still lacks the contexts needed to shake and challenge presumptions regarding gender (i.e. sexual women and Bad Girls too), how it is 'performed' and how it is critiqued. The contexts which they are working within have a specific history, which are also substantiated in social reforms, in the differentiation between the sexes and the sexualization of the female body for male ownership and use. These contexts bypass the contexts of women's lived experience, as well as how women explore and express their femininity.

Attacks, absences, exclusion

Another area that complicates choice is around the mediation of beauty and issues even confronting the good girl. Sheila Jeffreys (2005) explores the cultural, bodily and representational implications of the industry (i.e. profiting on lacks). She links pornography and other 'harmful' practices (such as make-up and cosmetic surgery) to patriarchy and misogyny. Jeffreys equates beauty practices to illness, trauma, harm and the butchering of the body (i.e. ingesting lipstick as bad for you, heels massacring the feet and cosmetic surgery as self-mutilation). Jeffreys (2005:150) argues that trauma and self-mutilation are part of misogynistic beauty regimens but are also systematic of hetero-centric (cis) and patriarchal gender positions. Simply put, women's sense of femininity and bodily presence are styled for male enjoyment, power and pleasure. What is ignored in her assessment is women's subjective and bodily experiences: where modifications to the body, whether permanent (tattoos, piercings, cosmetic surgery, etc.) or temporary (corsetry, make-up, etc.), have personal value and enable a deeper understanding of the body, self-identity and possibilities (see Chapter 1 and Victoria Pitts (2000, 2003) on body modification and Mistress Nan (2004) on BDSM and fetish).

Despite Jeffreys outlining that beauty standards rearticulate gender oppression and act as a tool to differentiate between the sexes, her assessment offers no counter-cultural interpretation, nor does she enable a critical assessment of intersectional perspectives on oppression, self-representation and pleasure. Assuming all women are bound by misogyny undercuts agency, ignores a range of struggles and renders any articulation of informed choice as nothing more than wishful thinking. In this instance, no matter how much women think they have choice (i.e. implying agency), what they do and how they do this by continues to be connected to associations with lack and powerlessness. But do all women *actually* feel this every day in their lives? Are we assuming 'women' *always* have to start out on the back foot? Thinking this eradicates possibilities, as it ignores how oppression and privilege are complex and intersectional.

We must take note that these assumptions emerge socially and through how certain expressions and depictions are critiqued (i.e. these are not the only presentations or experiences of 'reality'). What reality 'is' depends on how it comes to us and how we see, feel it and read it. In any case, these generic assumptions envelop all aspects of choice in a system of struggle which, to some degree, is made even more present in Jeffreys's critique. This critique confirms patriarchal oppression, rather than offering other approaches or giving examples of a variety of real-life experiences that women encounter. Therefore, scope is not only restricted by the presence of misogyny but in the re-articulation of its 'presence' in more radical feminist thought.

The problem faced by women here is a constant need to justify their choice to other women, which actually diminishes women's agency by devaluing what some women want (i.e. there are different kinds of good/Bad Girls). It is far too simplistic and essentialist to even presume that women cannot actively or positively choose alternatives, because of a totalizing statement around 'Western culture's founding ideals' concerning sexual difference. There is always dialogue and discursive practices: this is how discourse and, indeed, reverse discourse, works.

Brownmiller's (1975) critique of beauty is an example of another attack on choice and ignoring contexts. Her assessment of beauty is around how it commands passivity, enabling patriarchal systems to dominate. Although her critique offers an important unpicking of patriarchy, this has a detrimental impact on views on sex, intimacy and the erotic: as patriarchal control of women's bodies does not allow sexual agency. The will to desire is framed within a phallic shape: a one-size-fits-all discourse that excludes and never recognizes any utterance of rebellion or agency beyond the confines of its walls. What I mean here is that expressing desire and sexual agency as one sided enables a misrepresentation of how people engage with sexual politics (or not) in the everydayness of life. Brownmiller's argument polarizes the sexes in essentialist categories, which includes men being seen as predators that actively desire (as it is part of their 'nature') and predators that abuse and humiliate women. Consequently, Brownmiller's statements implicate women as not having ownership over their body, that women cannot actively enjoy sexual activity and that women cannot reverse the dehumanization of their gender (e.g. via pornography and patriarchal use of the female body). This synthesis is still present in *some* women's realities; however, these approaches can dominate how we should 'think' and critique gendered positions and possibilities. The repetition of heterosexuality, as a definitive term for the 'subjugation of women', will always be present in academic approaches which do not recognize the multiplicity of experiences and how all our lives are different in a multitude of ways (n.b. there is a parallel here with 'political lesbianism' in the 1970/80s). Therefore, it is also the paradigms and traditions by which women are critiqued that also bind and subjugate them as this.

Challenging these oppressive contexts can be difficult, especially when critiquing subjectivity due to the role 'lacks' have in confirming agency of certain subject positions. Having to articulate the value of those in a position of lack is actually a repercussion of heterosexuality becoming part of 'human nature'. When certain values are seen to be an intrinsic component of everyday life (i.e. it is the 'go to' default that helps differentiate between subject positions, etc.), then any resistance is always in dialogue with the default. This 'go to' default is about measurability (even being 'Other' is socially measurable too) and what is intelligible (i.e. them/us, normal/Other and so on). Heterosexuality has become integrated into the very means in which knowledge, privilege and value are circulated and communicated within society. Whilst there have been social and cultural changes allowing other identities and lifestyles to exist, changes to the law do not undo entrenched discourse or prejudice.

We have explored how certain types of women have to navigate their self-identity and existence through a myriad of discussions focusing on 'lacks'. Obviously, we should not think of women as having lacks in the first instance, as this can mean woman are constantly seen in relation to or having to prove themselves different from this assertion. 'Woman' and 'women' are not monolithic categories: gender identity is complex and is felt, defined and interpreted in different ways dependent on personal circumstance and experience, and other intersections such as age, sexuality, cultural identity, race, class and so on. Gender is also a small part of other attributes that build who we 'are', so we should not really see gender as the all-defining and all-encompassing 'thing' about a person's identity and value. How gender is felt and interpreted by the individual is changeable over their life course due to circumstance, opportunity, location (i.e. socially, culturally, geographically, in the workplace, and friendships or other forms of personal relationships), and having the tools (or social, cultural and monetary capital, etc.) to express in ways they want. The thought of having a lack, or being 'disempowered', is not something all women may think about, as it is not something individuals may always encounter or even consider. Women are powerful instigators of change, and we do not have to see our gender as lacking anything despite surrounding culture is seemingly binary and essentialist (see Meg-John Barker's work in *Queer: A Graphic History*, 2016). This book has encountered a range of women who were exploring self-identity in creative ways and focused on themes which are still seen to be taboo, Bad and contravening safe femininity.

Conclusion

This book is first and foremost interested in lived experience. To understand the ways in which lived experience is negotiated by the individual, the book established the importance of navigating language and meaning systems. These systems inform *and* are challenged/negotiated by the examples the book draws from (i.e. popular culture and the ethnography). The case study chapters evidenced that alternative constructions of femininity offer new embodied knowledge and challenge the restrictions placed on women by heteronormative social scripts in popular culture and within subculture too. The themes found in the case study chapters expose theoretical and social presuppositions that undermine the potentiality of non-normative femininity. The behaviours or gendered practices of some Bad and non-normative femininities not only have the power to shake and challenge normativity; they actually open scope in how femininity can be conceived, lived and experienced. This is located directly in micro-contexts, where agency and self-identity manifest, but they also circulate and are accessed through popular culture, entertainment spaces and digital technology. We have seen that space can produce some sticking points when it comes to positive social recognition of women who are still maligned as Dirty, Bad or perverse.

Disrupting space and expectations, alongside showcasing biography, same-sex desire and the ridiculousness of prejudice, enables women who exist in-between the binary to make visible different routes to success and possibilities (e.g. there are variety of debates specifically relating to how and why bodies connect to or become 'invisible' in certain spaces – see Puwar, 2004; Rahder and McLean, 2013; McNay, 2000; Massey, 2005; Keen, 2006; Jin and Whitson, 2014; Bain, Gray and Rodgers, 2012; Anderson, 2009; Zieleniec, 2007; Knopp, 1995; Lefebvre, 1991; Foucault, 1977). Undermining the socially predictable use of orifices, desire and the body holds transformative power, as demonstrated by Mouse and Doris La Trine (Chapter 1), Ms T (Chapter 2), Empress Stah (Chapter 3) and RubberDoll (Chapter 4). Transformative possibilities were expressed through the questioning (and queering) of pathology, dirt and lacking agency. How this was established was through the inclusion of biography to continually contextualize performances to reflect individuality, permanency and scope.

The conclusions outlined in this chapter will establish and show that non-normative femininity (i.e. Bad Women who disrupt popular notions of safe and sanctioned 'alternative' femininity) disrupts heteronormative linearity and challenges the notion that sexual, assertive and 'Bad' Women lack power and agency. With the current climate of right-wing rhetoric concerning women's agency, sexual rights and citizenship, we need sluts, Bad Women and bitches to occupy space and not shut up (see Sollee, 2017). What this book has established through case studies is that 'Bad'/non-normative femininity can shake, challenge and push the scope of femininity and how it can be conceived and embodied. The holistic and ethnographic approach applied is significant as this enables the research outcomes to re-establish, maintain and make permanent participant/case study self-identity through the mediums they identify with and express through. Supporting ethnographic outcomes, Holland's (2004) study of alternative femininities and Hodkinson's (2002) study of the goth subculture both highlight the ways in which subcultural groups, friendships and space provide room for individuals to diversify how they express their gender and sexuality. Although this study evidences similar themes, what is significant about this book is that fieldwork found how subcultural spaces also restrict identities and demarcate acceptable badness from dirty/filthy femininities.

One key thing found in the popular appeal of burlesque is how agency and scope still retained a grasp on conceivability (i.e. language and meaning systems, but also discourse), linked to mainstream culture and good/safe/clean femininity. Maintaining approved alternative femininity within subcultural contexts was generally through women mediating Bad Girl imagery and politics alongside popular culture, liberal attitudes since the 1990s and distancing performative scripts away from lacks (see Chapter 5). Maintaining a stable and unthreatening identity is about self-preservation but can also be a strategy that never risks or compromises the individual's status within a subculture (or subcultural practice). Maintenance of alternative constructions of femininity within the rise and popularity of burlesque (i.e. the replication of style, the standardization of narrative and the parameters of an approved 'alternative' to) means distancing oneself from lacks or harmful cultures (i.e. burlesque as art, not vulgar, porno and not for men).

What was found in the ethnography through observations, stories and interviews is that 'alternative' femininity was made distinct and intelligible based on acceptable ways of expressing self-identity. This was through intelligence and creativity being valuable commodities in burlesque. The value of these facets is conditioned through their linkages to approved and commercialized narratives, demarcating a type of alternative femininity which reflects wider social norms around empowered femininity and the good agentic girl. This is one of the reasons why mainstreamed burlesque narratives and stylistic conventions use objectification in ways that 'take back' space, rather than reducing women to genital use. The problem with this attitude is binary value systems which are presupposed by it, specifically as this approach brings those 'lacks' discussed in Chapters 1, 5 and 6 into existence. Although meaning and discourse are always negotiated, we need to still address the ways in which power and history operate to continually support regulatory institutions that try to diminish the power of Bad Girl femininity. The re-articulation of good/bad binaries and the use of pervasive heteronormative discourse demonstrate the lengths to which non-mainstream spaces are also implicated in propping up approved identities.

Socially approved femininities and mediating the Bad Girl

The book has found that the majority of participants in the spaces studied (see Commane (2012) for reflections on kink and BDSM, as well as ethnography as a method) were situating self-identity and self-value through mainstream concepts that enabled clean alternatives to be conceived and made plausible. Although it is not new to acknowledge that hierarchies and value systems operate in subcultural spaces as they do in popular culture, it is still important to be reminded of this. Tensions between the clean/dirty and the complexities of who is considered insider/outsider preside over hierarchies with subcultures too, as evidenced in the ethnographic and case study chapters (i.e. similar to wider cultural indicators of agreeable or abhorrent self-identity). Through the analysis of revivalist burlesque and its history (see Chapter 5) it was found that the use of burlesque in subcultural space and popular culture (i.e. consumer culture and night-time economies) mainly adhered to socially approved 'alternative' identities to convey agency, sexual self-confidence (i.e. positive/contemporary sexual politics) and distinctness. This mirrors wider cultural constructions of clean/ approved femininity within the boundaries of commodification, contemporary sexual politics and heteronormative linearity. One of the key contributions the book makes is that Bad/marginalized/

Dirty/Othered women have presence, voice and agency. Bad/ marginalized/Dirty/Othered women addressed by the book (e.g. Mouse, Doris La Trine, Ms T, Empress Stah and RubberDoll) are given visibility in positive ways and this has been achieved through approaching the research holistically and applying ethnographic and reflexive tools to draw out key themes led by the data set.

Importantly, biography and contexts are put at the heart of analysis, as these enable the queering and questioning of the heteronormative and the value of the good/Bad binary, as well as giving visibility to in-between and grey areas. Context and biography also disrupt presuppositions and reject one-size-fits-all stereotypes. Contexts therefore set a new challenge to think of new ways to recognize, capture, research, re-present and interpret femininities. As all chapters have demonstrated, contexts are often changeable and do not always follow a set pattern because friendship groups and relationship dynamics can change meaning, value and status of individuals within groups. It is, therefore, always important to acknowledge variables, tensions and value within subcultural practices and their relationship to popular culture (and vice versa). Acknowledgement gives a range of femininities space and visibility (specifically those maligned as too bad or too dirty) and this is despite the main body of revivalist burlesque expressing an agreeable clean alternative femininity reflecting wider cultural values and restrictions. Attitudes which 'condition' gender and the range of possibilities are changeable and dependent on the individuals participants socialized with. Changeability relies on inclusion and how this varies depending on the location where individuals socialize, who they socialize with and the contexts which allowed them scope to express.

The book found that the visibility of individuals and their self-expression were also based on the dynamics of friendships, which meant that range and inclusion depended on what was accepted by those who participants were close to. Although this scope can expand beyond mainstream expectations, there are still issues concerning conceivability and not compromising the status individuals have in the groups they identify with. Choice, solidarity and access, therefore, centre on specific bodies and how they are made visible in ways that are socially approved and understood, even if there are more ways of doing gender. Consequently, the book contributes an approach to subcultural practice which interrogates how the Bad Girl is appropriated, as well as highlighting the need to continue to explore Bad Women (e.g. sexual cultures, marginal entrepreneurship, the Professional Dominatrix framed as an entrepreneur and creative, oral histories, etc.). Certain types of women can be and are marginalized even within marginalized/subcultural groups. This is why studying and reflecting on alternative constructions of femininity are integral as some women still do not have the presence or visibility they deserve. The book continues the visibility of Bad/marginalized/Dirty/Othered women through critique focusing on exchanges within the ethnography, rather than set theories which preside over the articulation of gender/sexuality and subculture/mainstream.

Revivalist burlesque and alternatives to

It was vital for the research to be open in its approach to femininity and to be critically objective towards the different styles of burlesque seen in research. The research focused on the complexities found within burlesque and alternative femininity, as popular forms of self-expression for contemporary women. It was found that the interpretation of burlesque femininity within the majority of performances seen, reflected uncompromising, clean and safe ways for contemporary women to be sexually assertive and to reclaim space back taken by misogyny (see Chapter 5). Although this is something which is positive and demonstrates ways in which women can take control of their bodies and femininity, as supported by Attwood and Holland (2009), Baldwin (2004), Ferreday (2008) and Von Teese (2006), issues concerning sexual presentation in neo-burlesque and performance art are not addressed. This is partly due to the focus of burlesque literature on the articulation of femininity through 'proto-feminist' artists of the 1950s, and also by a narrow view of the 'negative' attributes which contributed to burlesque's 'demise' (see Chapter 5) rather than burlesque's integration within other forms of legitimate leisure from the 1960s onwards. The interpretation of the revival as preserving agency, power and an innocence, has also had a part to play in maintaining the perseverance and strength of mainstream/ clean burlesque femininity.

It is important to state that sexual self-confidence and self-assertiveness are apparent in revivalist burlesque, as this was seen throughout the performances observed in field research, including the solidarity shared, the support given and the positive responses of the audiences to the performers. It was found that the revival of burlesque and the performative styles appropriated by performers positioned meaning and value through a specific sexual and self-expression which connoted a clean and commodified contemporary alternative. This is further validated through assertive and powerful identities available in consumer society. The question that continues to arise is: what kind of women does capitalism prefer? In the context of this book, the empowered woman is valorized within certain contexts, but she is not actually powerful in a broader context. Bad Women are or, in other words, Bad Women open space for all types of femininity to exist in their own terms. Expanding space for possibilities for women is a radical and political act, enabling women to confront and challenge *all* types of spaces (i.e. work environments, socio-cultural hierarchies, the education system, social and entertainment space, etc.).

Consequently, the meaning of the revival and the interpretation of the femininities within are in reference to and always in association with heteronormativity and the boundaries of what is permissibly dirty/bad. The connection the revival has to consumer society should not and does not always have to reduce performers to temporary trends. The book has not devalued the ways in which revivalist burlesquers have chosen to express femininity. However, what the book did find is that the idealized ways in which women could express femininity through the support of 'alternative' practices did not compromise their self-identity nor were these 'deviant' in ways which could connote harm or excess. In fact, the revival does not speak for the women who interpret burlesque through other mediums they identify with such as BDSM, pornography and same-sex desire (see Chapters 1–4).

Although burlesque does not have to speak for all women, the value it has for women who perform does not transpose onto other femininities, specifically as women who are seen to have connections with sex work are continually acknowledged as either being victims of misogyny or having little agency. Sex workers and sexual performers do not have the positive visibility burlesque has, nor do they have a history which connotes power, strength and assertiveness. What this and the book highlights is the concept of 'choice', which is easily recognized within the burlesque paradigm as women not only tease for a local cultural practice, it has a permanent presence in their self-identity regardless if they perform as a career or not. This further stigmatizes Bad/Dirty (i.e. Othered) women and reinforces heteronormativity.

In Chapter 5 it was established that the main interpretation of burlesque available in clubs, in consumer culture, in the media and in social thought connoted an idealized version of alternative femininity. Holland (2004) argues that alternative femininity sees itself not only as feminine but as more assertive and less anxious (Ferreday, 2008:57) than their traditional 'fluffy' counterparts, meaning that the status of femininity, within subcultural setting and through subcultural style, is elevated beyond the normative and yet it does not go beyond conceivability or beyond what is inappropriate. This resonates within Bludgeon's (1998:123) analysis of 'new' femininity and girl power, where both were breaking away from the traditional modes of what it meant to be a woman, specifically as femininity was not seen as straightforward in the 1990s. Complexity was seen throughout the fieldwork process, particularly when negotiating, learning from and writing-up artists whose work was closely aligned with pornography, 'deviancy' and 'compromisation'. However, in the context of traditional revivalist burlesque, the repetition of particular styles, narratives and norms protects certain 'alternative' and commodified femininities. Consequently, this ensures that Dirty/Bad Women (i.e. pornographic or 'extreme' expressions of femininity) are not included in the spaces that revivalist burlesque is expressed.

Consequently, the context of burlesque femininities mirrors wider societal norms, which means that anything that compromises normativity or does not fit expected standards is still read by the same dominant frameworks which limit how femininity and gender are perceived. The book found that this was problematic, as contexts are continually ignored through presuppositions which do not adequately address how individuals are understood and, most importantly, how they are researched. Consequently, the approach of the book has questioned the continuation of presuppositions by retaining the various and changing contexts, values and meanings participants negotiate. This is supported by Attwood (2005), Bremer (2006), Buszek (2006), Ferreday (2008), Frank (2006), Holland (2004) and Williams (1993) through situating alternative women in context and with an agency which is not affected or reduced by normative presuppositions.

The book therefore does not allow Bad/Dirty (i.e. Other) women to be automatically disregarded and left open to presuppositions which continually cast them as outsiders with no value to add to femininity or zero power to challenge normativity. This approach is continually sustained throughout the book by the continued permanency and value of sexualized women within critique, who use parts of tease and sexual self-expression to demonstrate what they experience, feel and understand about their own self-identity. How this has been established throughout the book is through challenging normative views concerning how specific women are approached, critiqued and written about. It is also challenged through the voices of the case studies and by exploring context.

The research found tensions concerning different types of body performances, who these performances were for, and what they said about the women performing. These tensions were the source of focus for Chapter 5, but specifically in the choice of case studies as they articulated femininity in ways which undermined presuppositions about the body and the tensions caused by the opinion of wider society. What RubberDoll, Empress Stah and Ms T all demonstrate that women can have connections with 'negative' sexualization and still show agency and possibilities. This is supported by the critique of Annie Sprinkle (Buszek, 2006; Williams, 1993) through the 'this/ and' approach to possibilities regarding her self-identity, sexuality and femininity. What the 'this/and' approach means, in Annie Sprinkle's context, is that women do not have to be *either* an artist *or* a whore; they can be both. Consequently, this forcibly questions the presuppositions regarding what individuals think about specific women, their history, their value and their future. Thus, women cannot be defined by binaries as many women share, adapt and use aspects in a variety of categories to express self-identity, as the case studies Empress Stah, Ms T and RubberDoll demonstrate.

The book has demonstrated that burlesque does provide women with a sense of power and agency through articulating femininity within clubs, promoting solidarity in such a way that positive self-esteem is experienced as reiterated by participants and theorists alike (Attwood, 2011b; Baldwin, 2004; Drury, 2007; Glasscock, 2003; Liepe-Levinson, 2002; Von Teese, 2006; Walters, 2010; Wilson, 2008). However, fieldwork found that there were tensions still apparent *between* women and that devaluation of Other women's bodies, already demonized by social exclusion, was being actively used to elevate the status of revivalist burlesque as a 'real' alternative to heteronormativity, when in fact it is not. This exclusion and elevation are not done on purpose or consciously by many burlesquers (i.e. not deliberately excluding others, it is more the matter of thinking everyone else is like them. Here there is a parallel with issues of white feminism too). Norms are incorporated within the language, style and articulation of femininity within the tease paradigm.

What was found in the ethnography, regarding the differentiation between women, highlighted that the articulation of femininity within the main body of burlesque is conditioned by the revival's focus on distancing itself from Other bodies. Not only is this distancing based on the 'causes' of burlesque's demise in the late 1950s and 1960s, but also the context of the revival in the 1990s where its meaning has been conditioned by girl power, women being able to be addressed as sexual consumers (Attwood, 2005) and feminine assertiveness through displaying sexual self-identity. However, the mediated forms of alternative femininity do not provide ways in which women can contradict, undermine, question and address social attitudes that restrict the ways in which women can express. The ethnography found that the main body of revivalist burlesque was situated closer to the mainstream, of which performers drew meaning from and remained related to identities that did not compromise, were highly structured and were styled in ways that highlighted the performers' individuality, creativity and agency. On the other hand, the burlesque artists who drew from personal experiences, from pornography, from social fears and from their own desires pushed the burlesque ideal further. This, then, questions the ways in which women are expected to present themselves in society and how they should use their bodies. The case studies offer a challenge to 'safe' transgression, the naughty but nice woman and the binary of good/acceptable rebellion versus bad/unacceptable rebellion.

The value of lived experience and the inclusion of contexts

It is important to acknowledge the significance of using ethnography in the study of gender and sexuality, especially as ethnography opens up meaning through considering a range of contributing factors rather than relying on presuppositions. Critiquing femininity and the expression of female sexuality is a significant point to start at specifically as discussions of gender and sexuality are fraught with contentions which take away agency and solidarity from women who matter when shaking established ways of doing gender. The book does not make Other women strange specifically as it retains their rights and agency in the contexts experienced in the ethnography, rather than falling into the trap of cultural presuppositions about sexual, sexualized and marginalized women. It was found in the ethnography that the women who open scope and queer normativity are marginalized individuals like Empress Stah, Ms T, Doris La Trine, Mouse and RubberDoll.

Lived personal experience is of great significance, especially highlighting the problems with acquired modes of expression. These case studies demonstrate that women do not have to be ashamed of overt sexuality and that there are many ways of doing gender. What they provide is a showcase of women and their individual sexual self-expression and desire, all of which cannot be automatically reduced to interpretations connoting patriarchy, misogyny and lack. This range undermines the preoccupation that some anti-porn feminists have with hegemonic patriarchy, when in fact their interpretations do not answer all the real problems, issues or challenges the women they are writing about are facing (Egan, Frank and Johnson, 2006:xxvi).

What was found in the literature was a specific trend in the critique of femininity, namely within binary terms between the subordination of women and the power distinctions between the sexes. What second wave feminists like Brownmiller (1975), Dworkin (1994, 2000), Jeffreys (2005) and Millett (1977) highlight and acknowledge is that women do not have equal status, privilege and choice in how they express their self-identity. Although second wave feminism was working in very different social and political contexts, reflections on self-identity as being always in relation with 'lacks' (i.e. concerning the female body) have massive implications on agency, as well as how femininity is appropriated in culture. Although Brownmiller (1975), Dworkin (1994, 2000), Jeffreys (2005) and Millett (1969) critique patriarchy rather than conform to it, their preoccupation with hegemonic patriarchy still lacks the contexts needed to shake and challenge presumptions regarding gender and how it is 'performed' and critiqued. The contexts which they are working within have a specific history which is substantiated by social reforms, the social/ cultural obsession with 'differences' between the sexes and how to negotiate lacks.

It is, therefore, essential to re-present inconsistencies and challenges in context, as well as acknowledging their limitations (i.e. even in the case study chapters in regards to privilege and readability) because gender and sexuality are yet to be fully conceptualized in wider critique and social attitude. This is especially so as all chapters highlighted that issues between women had to become more vocal and central to analysis in order to push theory further on Other women, all of which Brownmiller (1975), Dworkin (1994, 2000) and Jeffreys (2005) ignore. This expression of an idealized and powerful self-assured femininity, within mainstream burlesque identity, is not used purposefully to divide women or to devalue sexual choices. However, heteronormative language and meaning systems (i.e. normative discourse) still play a central role in defining how we understand and recognize femininity. Although popular culture seems to embrace the diversity in how women express their sexual self-identity, this is still very much mediated.

It was found that restrictions placed on women (i.e. patriarchal and in binary relation to men) were also placed *by* women through acceptable ways in which their sexuality is presented and conveyed. A self-policing community of women means patriarchal structures evade blame. Self-identity, sexual self-confidence and sexuality are presented through modes of expression which are highly structured, sanctioned and clean. Although this allowed femininity to be expressed in more ways other than traditional, acceptable femininities are still contained within what is socially plausible (i.e. naughty but nice, bad but not too bad, etc.). The range of femininity and what female sexuality can include is given an increased visibility and can be seen in a more positive light through the critiques of gender and sexuality by Attwood (2005, 2007a and b, 2009, 2011a, 2011b), Budgeon (1998, 2011), Harris (1997), Kipnis (2006), du Plessis (1996) and Weeks (1991 and 1995). What these authors demonstrate are wider social, cultural and consumer factors which contribute to the demonisation of specific women, but significantly they provide context and variables that situate marginalized women with agency. These authors have been a source of support for the direction the book and the variables found in the data chapters concerning female sexuality and the articulation of this through mediums which are socially looked down upon or excluded. Supporting the outcomes of the ethnography, the focus on scope subsequently demonstrates that there were more factors that help define individuals' experiences, their sense of self and their gender.

The book has continued this solidarity, agency and the visibility of participants' self-identity which could have only been achieved through the application of ethnography. Therefore, experiences become the forefront of new contributions to knowledge, rather than established theory presiding over how to read and assess femininity (i.e. we always need to question the canon, how knowledge is shaped and whose voices are included/excluded or who is considered an in/outsider). The critique of femininity and female sexual expression within the book has questioned the foundations of how gender and sexuality are valued. Subsequently, the book found that the re-presentation of femininity and female sexual expression needs to continually draw upon and be directed by the ethnography. Femininities therefore need space to breathe, allowing scope and *inclusion* in written accounts (i.e. academic but also wider discussions in popular culture). In simple terms: your experience is not the same as mine, but equally as valid.

Bad Women and the power of the vagina

Chapters 1–4 established (i.e. through Mouse, Doris La Trine, RubberDoll, Empress Stah and Ms T) that the vagina was something which did not reduce women to sexual use. In fact, the vagina was a source of power and had multiple possibilities that did not always have to be sexual or 'functional' (i.e. childbirth, etc.). The existence of the vagina as something that was not shameful, reductive or dirty allows a wider range of possibilities as to how it is used, specifically for fun, expression and desire. Supporting this is the inclusion of the scope of possibilities highlighted by Annie Sprinkle, who demonstrates that there is nothing wrong or shameful in doing what you want with your body, specifically if you have the choice in doing so. The scope and positivity towards sexual expression and the vagina expressed through the performances created by RubberDoll, Mouse, Ms T and Empress Stah shake the presence of the conditions placed on women by social and cultural attitudes.

Drawing from the outcomes in the ethnography on femininity and female sexuality in field research, the case studies demonstrated that there are many other possibilities for women. These possibilities directly involve sexuality, the body and what individuals do with both. How these possibilities occurred was through the positions and life experiences articulated by the case studies in how they addressed their own self-identity and the attitudes of others. The case studies included the global artists Empress Stah and RubberDoll who performed for a living and Ms T a local burlesquer who did burlesque as a local cultural practice. All three performers identified that what they did on stage and who they were off stage were the same thing, highlighting that they are fully self-actualized. Although what was seen on stage was amplified and designed to suit specific audiences and the performance style used, what they wanted to address, what they liked and what they wanted to perform came through what they identified with.

What was different with these case studies was that they questioned and pushed further femininities seen in revivalist burlesque. Empress Stah addressed herself as a neo-burlesque artist to pitch and describe herself to clients as her shows are not revivalist and who she is on stage is not a parody of anyone. Ms T and RubberDoll's inclusion of sex, BDSM and kink also situates them outside of revivalist burlesque as their performances are far more sexually explicit and they address sexual women in a powerful light. What is significant about the three main case studies is that they celebrate women who express their gender and sexuality beyond the binary. Consequently, there are more possibilities than just two distinct genders, meaning that social attitudes and restrictions about gender are not fully acknowledging or giving space to the multitude of ways that women embody femininity.

Through the ethnography and throughout the book, the main theme which has recurred is that women give their own permission to do they want. What Empress Stah, Ms T and RubberDoll have in common is their approach to the body and asserting choice. Access to their own bodies and what they do to them is their choice, and through constructing highly stylized shows, these choices are not forced but highlight individuation. Their shows highlight individuation because of the mix of burlesque tease with desire, non-normativity and a sexual self-identity which is not part of the revivalist tradition or wider cultural stereotypes. This Bad Girl/filthy femininity, although seemingly explicit, does not fully correspond to definitions which devalue, make dirty and problematize women who like to express self-identity through sensual and sexual means. The approach Empress Stah and RubberDoll take to disregard the status of heteronormativity, through the use of the body, enables them to demonstrate that women who do not correspond to idealized femininities are not strange or lacking agency. Recurring throughout the ethnography was the concept of 'possibilities' specifically found within an engagement with BDSM and fetish communities.

Although all three performers interpreted the communities they were from through their own contexts, Ms T, Empress Stah and RubberDoll present sex and sexual expression beyond the clean sexual products society creates (see Attwood, 2005 on the latter aspect). What Ms T, Empress Stah and RubberDoll address is how female sexuality and sexual expression can be fun, through behaviours and styles which are not always socially seen to be clean or feminine. Ms T, Empress Stah and RubberDoll re-present femininities that are informed through the various contexts and spaces they have negotiated self-identity through. These spaces and contexts involve behaviours, identities and sexual tastes which have more room to express without wider social concerns devaluing them as dangerous or tainted. Therefore, the main case studies question explicitness and show that the critique of women through binary presuppositions, 'lack' and dirt is not inclusive of context and that these themes do not adequately re-present the value of Bad Women.

Context is vital and including this helps to deter interpretation from reducing participants or their self-expression to one set meaning. Variables and various desires are allowed to be expressed without restraint or reduction. This is supported by Attwood (2009, 2011b), Bremer (2006), Buszek (2006), Ferreday (2008), Frank (2006) and Holland (2004, 2009) who all give context and range to individuals' sense of femininity, instead of reducing all non-normative expressions of sexuality to pathology, lack and male ownership. Consequently, how femininity is critiqued and who is doing the critique/study affect the ways in which femininity is presented in social thought, which means that visibility is yet to be fully acknowledged, specifically in wider culture where concepts, identities and values are still cleaned, mediated through binaries and policed. Therefore, the use of the case studies within the ethnography and their visibility through context means that the knowledges produced within the book draw from the varieties present in society. What the case studies demonstrate is the permanency of marginalized gendered and sexual identities as ways to undermine and shake normativity. This was seen through directly challenging how femininity is seen, how sexualities are defined as and through demonstrating that women do have access to their bodies even within sexualized sites.

Consequently, Empress Stah contradicts the revivals focus on preserving respectability, through expanding agency through penetrating and accessing her *own* body by the use of sex toys, piercings and overt sexual display. Being one of the 'futures' of burlesque allows Empress Stah to direct herself through her own experiences, rather than relying on the formulas presented in revivalist burlesque, which means that the replication normativity is challenged. Through *The Queen of the Night*, gender articulation is blurred allowing the presence of femininity in its own terms, rather than always relying on purity, masculinity or misogyny to explain what is expressed. Therefore, the themes which penetrate and project from Empress Stah's performances do not compromise her femininity or self-expression. This was due to the meaning of performances being carefully considered by Empress Stah, even though she maintained that she did not theorize them. Through the ethnography it was established that if a woman has the chance and opportunity to use her body, talent and sexuality in a way she identifies with or wants to express by, then she should be able to do this without having to continually justify these choices. This includes same-sex desire, kink and various forms of sex work. Empress Stah rightfully argues that not all women have the opportunity to make choices but, essentially, she acknowledges the scope of choice in sex work which the majority of anti-porn feminists ignore due to their preoccupation with hegemonic patriarchy.

The approach the case studies take to disregard the status of heteronormativity, through the use of the body, enables them to demonstrate that women who do not correspond to idealized femininities are not strange or lacking agency. The implication of the research is that the women who do have the choice to do what they want with their body, gender and sexuality in spaces they identify with or want to perform at, should be able to without justifying their actions. This means that more women can be included in the same space, without any woman feeling that they need to change in order to fit in. However, Ms T, Empress Stah and RubberDoll create their own space in order to try to win ground back from cultural assumptions. In the ethnography, it was found that although shows are conceivable and do link to meanings in wider culture, the case studies still push both further through challenging the approach to gender and sexuality. For example, Empress Stah's achievement of creating her own space means that she can structure her beliefs and approaches in a feasible way, through using historical figures such as the jester and the fool, to allow her to question concepts by using the medium of entertainment. Consequently, questioning is still limited by what the case studies use to condition and convey meaning. However, Chapters 1-4 found that creating this space still gives the case studies room to express in the ways they want and identify with, highlighting the variability of how gender and sexuality can be embodied.

Therefore, the status of their identity is not compromised by their own principles or by elevating themselves above any other women, making the case studies different from the revivalist femininities seen in Chapter 5 and good girls in popular culture. For example, Ms T's approach to her body and to marginalized femininities is about the re-definition and re-articulation of the Bad Girl. This re-articulation by Ms T situated the Bad Girl and overt sexual expression as not something negative, and that if women have the opportunity to express themselves and take advantage of their own bodies, then they should be able to do so. This was established was through Ms T's performances being informed by her negotiations, difficulties and experiences in subcultural spaces, highlighting that what was presented on stage was something personal. Unlike the majority of mainstream burlesque, it was found that Ms T did not parody Other women in such a way that would further ostracize or stigmatize them. Instead, sexual assertiveness, sexual display and sex are given context which allows women to have space to express these without falling into heteronormative, homonormative or mainstream-based ideological presuppositions.

Recurring themes in Ms T, Empress Stah and RubberDoll's work and self-identity were the concept of 'possibilities', specifically found within an engagement with BDSM and fetish communities. By using vintage lingerie, kink, elegant props and dildos but applying them through an alternative approach to their utilization undermines the 'fashionable, safe, aesthetically pleasing and feminine' (Attwood, 2005:2) products which mainstream society delivers to allow women to address themselves as sexual consumers. Yet, the inclusion of an alternative approach to feminine products does not detract from the performers' femininity as expressed by Holland (2004) on alternative femininities. Instead, the case studies re-present a femininity which is informed through the various contexts and spaces they have negotiated their self-identity through. These spaces and contexts involve behaviours, identities and sexual tastes which have more room to express without wider social concerns devaluing them as dangerous or tainting.

What Ms T, Empress Stah and RubberDoll highlight are different routes to express femininity away from the mainstream and mediated alternative, particularly as they did not totally fit into the subcultures they were associated with. This is significant, specifically as the outcomes of research found that the spaces ethnography was conducted in were highly structured, with etiquettes and tensions within groups binding the potentiality of identity to social expectations. Therefore, the visibility and impact these case studies have do not always depend on challenging the mainstream or specific types of critique, but the very social scenes they frequent, perform at and articulate their self-identity within. This affects the ways in which transfiguration can happen within the mainstream and in subculture. All spaces are potentially open to be challenged, and maybe they need to be, regardless of context.

It is always vital to reflect upon the factors that constitute self-identity, specifically wider cultural and social influences that try and restrict how gender and sexuality are researched, felt and conceived. The dynamics of social spaces and how participants negotiated their self-identity within demonstrated that although there were variables, the value of these variables to the community was measured by what was appropriate. What this relies upon is conceivability and solidarity, both of which were substantiated by negotiating social groups, styles and concepts in a way which did not go beyond the dominant mantra of the group. The marginalized women who straddled the social groups studied, such as Mouse, Doris La Trine, RubberDoll, Ms T and Empress Stah, are also caught up in this tension as they have had to create space for themselves and a context which gives them agency. What these performers and the wider scenes they are connected to have in common is the need to preserve and project self-identity which had permanency. As these marginalized performers used objects, themes and concepts which challenged the norms and expectations in both wider society and subculture, it was essential for the ethnography to continue to preserve agency, context and self-identity. This is specifically the case as presuppositions can persist in covering alternative interpretations. Consequently, throughout the negotiations in the field and their re-presentation in written critique, it was essential to allow the visibility of hidden interpretations and for these interpretations to hold their value and context.

It is vital to include individual approaches/contexts when critiquing social spaces and the wider contexts which preside over how individuals negotiate their gender and sexuality. The inclusion of inconsistencies (i.e. the Bad/Dirty case studies) and the values placed on marginal identities (i.e. through personal stories of case studies) demonstrates that Bad Girls can transfigure and challenge gender norms around femininity. Marginalized women, who have the choice to be perverse, sexual and use their bodies in dirty ways, can undermine normativity (despite having to be conceivable) and reject mainstream mediation (i.e. revivalist burlesque) and cleanliness (e.g. the commodification of the Bad Girl aesthetic).

Rethinking bad femininities

Future research needs to be undertaken to assess the potential of new femininities within burlesque, BDSM, fetish and kink to claim space and legitimacy for alternative sexualities and non-standard gender identities. Future research identified in the outcomes of this book, regarding power and agency of women who have the choice, concerns developing how gender and sexuality can be perceived and articulated in ways which expand the use of femininity beyond heteronormative and misogynist paradigms. The value of bisexuality, the vagina and non-normative identity also present a challenge to the automatic removal of their visibility, power and value. Therefore, it is vital for future research to continue the work of the book through maintaining the agency and value of marginalized and excluded identities. This has to continually be re-worked and synthesized through ethnographic research being combined with theoretical positions to promote permanency, agency and the integrity of knowledges found. There is scope for people who are not white (or cis) to explore the meanings in the burlesque scene from their own positionality. Importantly, this contributes something different (i.e. embodied knowledge and power) especially when it comes from those within their own spheres, who are part of the meaning making. This correlates to the nature of ethnography and the method as lived experience. For example, there needs to be more research exploring trans and non-binary performers and BAME burlesquers. I am an ally, but it is not my place to discuss those practices as my positionality (being white, cis, queer, etc.) would interpret meaning in ways that may take voice away. Ownership needs to go to those communities.

What the book identified, through an ethnographic study, highlights visibility and worth in including marginalized identities through the variety of ways in which femininity can be re-presented. As insiders and outsiders depend on location, group allegiance and attitude, then the book opens up more routes for the integration of a variety of embodied knowledges which acknowledge the irreducibility of human experience. Therefore, presuppositions regarding sexualized women need not always be reduced to standardized interpretations connoting tainting a community or lack of choice. Rather, the integration of women who have the choice to be sexual without being reduced to insignificance or demonized demonstrates the need to continually question the purity/dirt paradigm as the definitive point to which all characteristics are set. How women are expected to study and how particular types of women are framed/depicted/researched are important areas to continually address in future research because how both are conceived through theory and attitude affects the ways in which participants can be re-presented. Consequently, this continually needs to be addressed in order to progress knowledge, how we understand various social positions and how particular social positions can shake the limits of gender and sexuality.

One key area of research that I will continue to explore is the Bad Girl, by opening critique into the lived experiences of creatives, entrepreneurs and activists within the sex industry (namely Professional Domination). In addition, future research should seek to challenge how ethical approval is gained for ethnographic research, specifically as ethical committees have a specific quantitative view on what ethics looks like. The future of research depends not only on the continuation of agency and truthfulness within all aspects of the research process, but on ethnographic research into gender and sexuality actually taking place.

Bibliography

Addington, Deborah (2006) *Play Piercing*. California: Greenery Press.

Adrian, Werner (1976) *Freaks: Cinema of the Bizarre*. London: Lorrimer.

Aggleton, Peter (1987) *Deviance*. London: Tavistock Publications.

Ahmed, Sara (2004) *The Cultural Politics of Emotion*. Edinburgh: Edinburgh University Press.

Arnold, Rebecca (2001) *Fashion, Desire and Anxiety*. London: I.B. Tauris.

Anderson, Tammy (2009) *Rave Culture: The Alteration and Decline of a Philadelphia Music Scene*. Philadelphia: Temple University Press.

Assiter, Alison and Avendon, Carol (eds) (1993) *Bad Girls and Dirty Pictures: The Challenge to Reclaim Feminism*. London: Pluto Press.

Attwood, Feona (2005) *'Fashion and Passion: Marketing Sex to Women'*, in *Sexualities*, 8(4), pp. 395–409. Available at: http://feonaattwood. com/feona_attwood_fashion_and_passion_sexualities_submission.pdf (Accessed: January 2011).

Attwood, Feona (2006) *'Sexed Up: Theorizing the Sexualisation of Culture'*, in *Sexualities*, 9(1), pp. 77–94. Available at: http://feonaattwood.com/ feona_attwood_sexeduppaper.pdf (Accessed: January 2011).

Attwood, Feona (2007a) *'Sluts and Riot Grrls: Female Identity and Sexual Agency'*, in *Journal of Gender Studies*, 16(3), pp. 231–45. Available: at http://feonaattwood.com/feona_attwood_slutpaper.pdf (Accessed: January 2011).

Attwood, Feona (2007b) *'Other' or 'One of Us?': The Porn User in Public and Academic Discourse*, in *Particip@nts*, 4(1), May 2007. Available at: http:// www.participations.org/Volume%204/Issue%201/4_01_attwood.htm (Accessed: November 2007).

Attwood, Feona (ed.) (2009) *Mainstreaming Sex: The Sexualization of Western Culture*. London: I.B. Tauris, London.

Attwood, Feona (2011a) *'Sex and the Citizens: Erotic Play and the New Leisure Culture'*, in Peter Bramham and Stephen Wagg (eds) *The New Politics of Leisure and Pleasure*. London: Palgrave Macmillan, pp. 82–96.

Attwood, Feona (2011b) '*Through the Looking Glass? Sexual Agency and Subjectification Online*', in Rosalind Gill and Christina Scharff (eds) *New Femininities. Postfeminism, Neoliberalism and Subjectivity*. London: Palgrave Macmillan, pp. 203–14.

Attwood, Feona and Holland, Samantha (2009) '*Keeping Fit in Six Inch Heels: The Mainstreaming of Pole Dancing*', in Feona Attwood (ed.) *Mainstreaming Sex: The Sexualization of Western Culture*. London: I.B. Tauris, pp. 165–81.

Avedon, Carol and Pollard, Nettie (1993) '*Changing Perceptions in the Feminist Debate*', in Alison Assiter and Carol Avedon (eds) *Bad Girls and Dirty Pictures. The Challenge to Reclaim Feminism*. London: Pluto Press, pp. 45–56.

Baddeley, Victor Clinton (1973) *The Burlesque Tradition in the English Theatre after 1660*. London: Methuen.

Bain, Lesley, Gray, Barbra and Rodgers, Dave (2012) *Living Streets: Strategies for Crafting Public Space*. Hoboken: John Wiley & Sons.

Bakhtin, Mikhail (1984) *Rabelais and His World*. Bloomington: Indiana University Press.

Baldwin, Michelle (2004) *Burlesque and the New Bump-n-Grind*. Denver: Speck Press.

Barker, Meg-John (2016) *Queer: A Graphic History*. London: Icon Books Ltd.

Barthes, Roland (1993) *Mythologies*. London: Vintage.

Barthes, Roland (2006) *The Language of Fashion*. Oxford: Berg.

de Beauvoir, Simone (1949) *The Second Sex*. London: Picador.

Becker, Howard S. (1963) *Outsiders: Studies in the Sociology of Deviance*. New York: The Free Press.

Bell, David (1995) '*Perverse Dynamics, Sexual Citizenship and the Transformation of Intimacy*', in David Bell and Gill Valentine, *Mapping Desire; Geographies of Sexualities*. London: Routledge, pp. 304–17.

Bell, David and Valentine, Gill (1995) *Mapping Desire; Geographies of Sexualities*. London: Routledge.

Bennett, Andy and Kahn-Harris, Keith (eds) (2004) *After Subculture: Critical Studies in Contemporary Youth Culture*. Basingstoke: Palgrave Macmillan.

Benninan, Frances (1991) *The Sex Code: Morals for Moderns*. London: Weidenfeld & Nicolson.

Berg, Heather (2016) '"A Scene Is Just a Marketing Tool": Alternative Income Streams in Porn's Gig Economy', in *Porn Studies*, 3(2), pp. 160–74.

Berger, Maurice, Wallis, Brian and Watson, Simon (eds) (1995) *Constructing Masculinity*. New York: Routledge.

Bhabha, Homi K (1995) '*Are You a Man or a Mouse?*' in Maurice Berger, Brian Wallis and Simon Watson (eds) *Constructing Masculinity*. New York: Routledge, pp. 57–65.

Blackman, Shane (1998) '*The School of 'Proxy Cupid. An Ethnographic and Feminist Account of a Resistant Female Youth Culture: The New Wave Girls'*, in Tracy Skelton (ed.) *Cool Places: Geographies of Youth Cultures*. London: Routledge, pp. 207–28.

Blackman, Shane (2004) *Chilling Out: The Cultural Politics of Substance Consumption, Youth and Drug Policy*. Maidenhead: Open University Press.

Blackman, Shane (2007) '*Hidden Ethnography: Crossing Emotional Boarders in Qualitative Accounts of Young People's Lives'*, in *Sociology*, 41(4), pp. 699–716.

Blackman, Shane (2010) '*Youth Subcultures, Normalisation and Drug Prohibition: The Politics of Contemporary Crisis and Change?*' in *British Politics*. London: Palgrave Macmillan, Vol. 5, No. 3, pp. 337–66.

Blackman, Shane (2011) '*Rituals of Intoxication: Young People, Drugs, Risk and Leisure'*, in Peter Bramham and Stephen Wagg (eds) *The New Politics of Leisure and Pleasure*. London: Palgrave Macmillan, pp. 97–118.

Blackman, Shane J. (2005) *Youth Subcultural Theory: A Critical Engagement with the Concept, Its Origins and Politics, from the Chicago School to Post Modernism*, in *Journal of Youth Studies*, 8(1), pp. 1–21.

Blackman, Shane and Commane, Gemma Ruth (2011) '*Double Reflexivity: The Politics of Friendship, Fieldwork and Representation within Ethnographic Studies of Young People'*, in S. Heath and C. Walker (eds) *Innovations in Youth Research*. London: Palgrave, pp. 229–46.

Blood, Janet and Sinclair, John D. (2004) *Rubber: Fun, Fashion, Fetish*. New York: Thames and Hudson.

Blyth, Maggie (2007) *Young People and 'Risk'*. Bristol: Polity Press.

Bobette (2007) *FleursduMal: 1*. London: Dirty Pictures, Ltd.

Bolton, Ralph (1995) '*Tricks, Friends and Lovers: Erotic Encounters in the Field*', in Don Kulick and Margaret Wilson (eds) *Taboo: Sex, Identity and Erotic Subjectivity in Anthropological Field Work*. London: Routledge, pp. 140–62.

Bourdieu, Pierre (1982) *In Other Words: Essays towards a Reflexive Sociology*. Cambridge: Polity Press.

Bourdieu, Pierre (1991) *Language and Symbolic Power*. Cambridge: Polity Press.

Bourdieu, Pierre (1993) *Sociology in Question*. London: Sage.

Bourdieu, Pierre and Wacquant, J. D. Loic (1992) *An Introduction to Reflexive Sociology*. Cambridge: Polity Press.

Bramham, Peter and Wagg, Stephen (2011) *The New Politics of Leisure and Pleasure*. London: Palgrave Macmillan.

Brand, Clavel (1970) *Fetish: An Account of Unusual Erotic Desires*. London: Senate.

Bremer, Susan (2006) '*The Grind*', in Danielle Egan, Katherine Frank and Merri Lisa Johnson (eds) *Flesh for Fantasy: Producing and Consuming Erotic Dance*. New York: Thunder's Mouth Press, pp. 35–52.

Brod, Harry (1990) '*Pornography and the Alienation of Male Sexuality*', in Jeff Hearn and David Morgan (eds) *Men, Masculinities and Social Theory*. London: Unwin Hyman.

Brownmiller, Susan (1975) *Against Our Will: Men, Women and Rape*. London: Penguin.

Bruni, Attila et al. (2005) *Gender and Entrepreneurship: An Ethnographic Approach*. New York: Routledge.

Budgeon, Shelley (1998) '"*I'll Tell You What I Really, Really Want*": Girl Power and Self-Identity in Britain', in Sherrie A. Inness (ed.) *Millennium Girls. Today's Girls around the World*. Oxford: Rowman & Littlefield Publishers, pp. 115–43.

Budgeon, Shelley (2006) '*Friendships and Formations of Sociality in Late Modernity: The Challenge of "Post Traditional Intimacy"*', in *Sociological Research Online*, 11(3). Available at: http://www.socresonline.org.uk/11/3/budgeon.html (Accessed: January 2011).

Budgeon, Shelley (2011) 'The Contradictions of Successful Femininity: Third Wave Feminism, Postfeminism and "New" Femininities', in Rosalind Gill and Christina Scharff (eds) *New Femininities. Postfeminism, Neoliberalism and Subjectivity*. London: Palgrave Macmillan, pp. 279–92.

Burkitt, Ian (1999) *Bodies of Thought: Embodiment, Identity and Modernity*. London: Sage.

Burr, Vivien (2003) *Social Constructionism*. London: Routledge.

Bussel, Rachel Kramer and Pierce, Christopher (eds) (2006) *Secret Slaves. Eroticist: Stories of Bondage*. New York: Alyson Books.

Buszek, Maria Elena (2006) *Pin-Up Grrrls: Feminism, Sexuality, Popular Culture*. London: Duke University Press.

Butler, Judith (1990a) 'Performative Acts and Gender Construction: An Essay in Phenomenology and Feminist Theory', in Sue-Ellen Case (ed.) *Performing Feminisms: Feminist Critical Theory in Theatre*. London: The Johns Hopkins University Press, pp. 270–82.

Butler, Judith (1990b) *Gender Trouble: Feminism and the Subversion of Identity*. London: Routledge.

Butler, Judith (1993) *Bodies That Matter: On the Discursive Limits of 'Sex'*. London: Routledge.

Calefato, Patrizia (2004) *The Clothed Body*. Oxford: Berg.

Campbell, Anne (1981) *Girl Delinquents*. Oxford: Blackwell.

Carins, Robert (1994) *Lifelines and Risk: Pathways of Youth in Our Time*. London: Harvester Wheatsheaf.

Carter, Angela (2000) 'Polemical Preface: Pornography in the Service of Women', in Drucilla Cornell (ed.) *Feminism and Pornography*. Oxford: Oxford University Press, pp. 527–39.

Cash, Thomas and Pruzinsky, Thomas (eds) (1990) *Body Images: Development, Deviance, and Change*. New York: The Guilford Press.

Coffey, Amanda (1999) *The Ethnographic Self. Fieldwork and the Representation of Identity*. London: Sage.

Cohen, Phil (1972) 'Subcultural Conflict and Working Class Community', in *Working Papers in Cultural Studies*. CCCS, Birmingham: University of Birmingham, pp. 5–51.

Cohen, Stanley (1973) *Folk Devils and Moral Panics.* Oxford: Basil
    Blackwell.

Cohen, William A. and Johnson, Ryan (eds) (2005) *Filth. Dirt, Disgust, and
    Modern Life.* Minneapolis: University of Minnesota Press.

Colosi, Rachel (2010) '*A Return to the Chicago School? From the Subculture
    of Taxi-Dancers to the Contemporary Lap-Dancer*', in *Journal of Youth
    Studies,* 13(1), pp. 1–16.

Comella, Lynn (2017) *Vibrator Nation: How Feminist Sex-Toy Stores
    Changed the Business of Pleasure.* London: Duke University Press.

Commane, Gemma Ruth (2010) '*Bad Girls and Dirty Bodies: Performative
    Histories and Transformative Styles*', in Burkhard Scherer, and Peter Lang
    (eds) *Queering Paradigms,* pp. 49–64.

Commane, Gemma (2011) *The Transfigured Body: Fetish, Fashion and
    Performance.* Canterbury, Uk: University of Kent.

Commane, Gemma (2016) '*Temporary Reflexive Disempowerment: Working
    through Fieldwork Ethnography and its Impact on a Female Researcher*',
    in Shane Blackman and Michelle Kempson (eds) *The Subcultural
    Imagination: Theory, Research and Reflexivity in Youth Cultures.* London:
    Routledge, pp. 108–21.

Cooper, David B. (ed.) (2000) *Alcohol Use.* Abingdon: Radcliffe Medical
    Press Ltd.

Copstick, Kate (2000) *The Illustrated Book of Sapphic Sex.* London: MacHo
    Ltd.

Corbin, Juliet and Strauss, Anselm (1990) *Basics of Qualitative Research:
    Grounded Theory Procedures and Techniques.* London: Sage.

Cornell, Drucilla (2000) '*Pornography's Temptation*', in Drucilla Cornell
    (ed.) *Feminism and Pornography.* Oxford: Oxford University Press,
    pp. 551–66.

Cornell, R. W. (1995) *Masculinities,* 2nd edition. Polity Press.

Cressey, Paul (1932) *Taxi Dance Hall: A Sociological Study in
    Commercialised Recreation and City Life.* Chicago: University of Chicago
    Press.

Deloffre, Claude (ed.) (1998) *Mugler, Thierry: Fashion, Fetish, Fantasy.*
    London: Thames and Hudson, Ltd.

Diamond, Lisa (2008) *Sexual Fluidity: Understanding Women's Love and
    Desire.* London: Harvard University Press.

Dollimore, Jonathon (2001) *Sex, Literature and Censorship*. Cambridge: Polity.

Doty, Alexander (1993) *Making Things Perfectly Queer: Interpreting Mass Culture*. London: University of Minnesota Press.

Douglas, Mary (1966) *Purity and Danger: An Analysis of the Concepts of Pollution and Taboo*. London: Routledge.

Downs, Donald Alexander (1989) *The New Politics of Pornography*. London: The University of Chicago Press.

Drury, Rebecca (2006a) *Lap Dancing: The Naughty Girl's Guide*. London: Connections Book Publishing.

Drury, Rebecca (2006b) *Pole Dancing: The Naughty Girl's Guide*. London: Connections Book Publishing.

Drury, Rebecca (2007) *Strip Tease: The Naughty Girl's Guide*. London: Connections Book Publishing.

Dubisch, Jill (1995) '*Lovers in the Field: Sex, Dominance, and the Female Anthropologists*', in Don Kulick and Margaret Wilson (eds) '*Taboo: Sex, Identity and Erotic Subjectivity in Anthropological Field Work*'. London: Routledge, pp. 29–48.

Duffy, Brooke Erin and Hund, Emily (2015) '"*Having It All" on Social Media: Entrepreneurial Femininity and Self-Branding among Fashion Bloggers*', in *Social Media + Society*, 1(2), pp. 1–11.

DuPret, John and DuPret, Linda (2000) *The Sins of Our Fathers: A Study of Victorian Sexuality*. London: MacHo Ltd.

Durkheim, Emile (1982) *The Rules of Sociological Method and Selected Texts in Sociology and its Method*. London: Macmillan.

Dworkin, Andrea (1994) *Pornography. Men Possessing Women*. London: The Women's Press, Ltd.

Dworkin, Andrea (2000) '*Pornography and Grief*', in Drucilla Cornell (ed.) *Feminism and Pornography*. Oxford: Oxford University Press, pp. 39–44.

Egan, Danielle, Frank, Katherine and Johnson, Merri Lisa (eds) (2006) *Flesh for Fantasy: Producing and Consuming Erotic Dance*. New York: Thunder's Mouth Press.

Ellis, Carolyn (1991a) '*Sociological Introspection and Emotional Experience*', in Norman Denzin (ed.) *Symbolic Interaction*. Greenwich: JAI Press, Vol. 14, Issue 1, pp. 23–50.

Ellis, Carolyn (1991b) *'Emotional Sociology'*, in Norman Denzin (ed.) *Studies in Symbolic Interaction*. Greenwich: JAI Press, Vol. 12, pp. 123–45.

Ellis, Carolyn and Flaherty, Michael G. (eds) (1992) *Investigating Subjectivity. Research on Lived Experience*. California: Sage.

Entwistle, Joanne (2000) *The Fashioned Body. Fashion, Dress and Modern Social Theory*. Cambridge: Polity Press.

Evans, Caroline (2003) *Fashion at the Edge: Spectacle, Modernity and Deathliness*. London: Yale University Press.

Evans, Adrienne and Riley, Sarah (2014) *Technologies of Sexiness: Sex, Identity and Consumer Culture*. Oxford: Oxford University Press.

Ewing, William (1996) *Blumenfeld: A Fetish for Beauty*. London: Thames and Hudson Ltd.

Fausto-Sterling, Anne (2000) *Sexing the Body: Gender Politics and the Construction of Sexuality*. New York: Basic Books.

Ferreday, Debra (2008) '*"Showing the Girl": The New Burlesque'*, in *Feminist Theory*, 9(1), pp. 44–65.

Foucault, Michel (1977) *Discipline and Punish: The Birth of the Prison*. London: Penguin.

Foucault, Michel (1997) *The History of Sexuality: The Care of the Self*. London: Penguin.

Foucault, Michel (1998) *The History of Sexuality: The Will to Knowledge*. London: Penguin.

Foucault, Michel (1998) *The History of Sexuality: The Use of Pleasure*. London: Penguin.

Frank, Catherine (2006) *'Keeping Her Off the Pole? Creating Sexual Value in a Capitalist Society'*, in Danielle Egan, Katherine Frank and Merri Lisa Johnson (eds) *Flesh for Fantasy: Producing and Consuming Erotic Dance*. New York: Thunder's Mouth Press, pp. 203–11.

Freud, Sigmund (1961) *Beyond the Pleasure Principle*. London: Hogarth Press and IPA.

Freud, Sigmund (1973) *The Future of an Illusion*. London: Hogarth Press and IPA.

Freud, Sigmund (1977) *On Sexuality: Three Essays on the Theory of Sexuality and Other Works*. New York: Penguin.

Freud, Sigmund (1991) *1. Introductory Lectures on Psychoanalysis*. London: Penguin.

Freud, Sigmund (1991) *2. New Introductory Lectures on Psychoanalysis*. London: Penguin.

Gamman, Lorraine and Makinen, Merja (1994) *Female Fetishism. A New Look*. New York: Lawrence and Wishart.

Gates, Katharine (2000) *Deviant Desires. Incredibly Strange Sex*. New York: Juno Books.

Geertz, Clifford (1973) *The Interpretation of Cultures*. New York: Basic Books.

Geertz, Clifford (1983) *Local Knowledge*. London: Fontana Press.

Gill, Rosalind and Scharff, Christina (eds) (2011) *New Femininities. Postfeminism, Neoliberalism and Subjectivity*. London: Palgrave Macmillan.

Glaser, Barney G. And Strauss, Anselm L. (1967) *The Discovery of Grounded Theory: Strategies for Qualitative Research*. New York: Aldine De Gruyter.

Glasscock, Jessica (2003) *Striptease: From Gaslight to Spotlight*. New York: Harry N. Abrams.

Grandy, Gina and Mavin, Sharon (2011) '*Occupational Image, Organizational Image and Identity in Dirty Work: Intersections of Organizational Efforts and Media Accounts*', in *Organization*, 19(6), pp. 765–86.

Gray, A. (2003) '*Enterprising Femininity: New Modes of Work and Subjectivity*', in *European Journal of Cultural Studies*, 6(4), pp. 489–506.

Greta, Christina (ed.) (2004) *Paying for It. A Guide by Sex Workers for Their Clients*. Oakland: Greenery Press.

Griffin, Susan (1988) *Pornography and Silence: Culture's Revenge against Nature*. London: The Women's Press.

Halberstam, Jack (2011) *The Queer Art of Failure*. London: Duke University Press.

Hall, Stuart (1997) *Representation: Cultural Representations and Signifying practices*. London: Sage.

Hall, Suzanne (2012) *City, Street and Citizen: The Measure of the Ordinary*. London: Routledge.

Hammersley, Martyn (1992) *What Is Wrong with Ethnography? Methodological Explorations.* London: Routledge.

Hammersley, Martyn and Atkinson, Paul (1995) *Ethnography. Principles in Practice.* London: Routledge.

Harris, Laura and Crocker, Liz (1997) 'Bad Girls: Sex, Class, and Feminist Agency', in Laura Harris and Elizabeth Crocker (eds) *Femme: Feminists, Lesbians and Bad Girls.* London: Routledge.

Hart, Christopher (2001) *The Illustrated Book of Queen Victoria's Secrets.* London: MacHo Ltd.

Heath, Joseph and Potter, Andrew (2006) *The Rebel Sell: How the Counter Culture Became Consumer Culture.* Chichester: Capstone.

Hebdige, Dick (1979) *Subculture: The Meaning of Style.* London: Methuen.

Hillier, Bill and Hanson, Julienne (1984) *The Social Logic of Space.* Cambridge: Cambridge University Press.

Hite, Shere (2006) *The Shere Hite Reader. New and Selected Writings on Sex, Globalisation, and Private Life.* New York: Seven Stories Press.

Hodkinson, Paul (2002) *Goth: Identity, Style and Subculture.* Oxford: Berg.

Hodkinson, Paul (2005) '"Insider Research" in the Study of Youth Cultures', in *Journal of Youth Studies*, 8(2), pp. 131–49.

Hodkinson, Paul (2007) 'Youth Cultures: A Critical Outline of Key Debates', in Paul Hodkinson and Wolfgang Deicke (eds) (2007) *Youth Cultures: Scenes, Subcultures and Tribes.* New York: Routledge, pp. 1–21.

Hollway, Wendy and Jefferson, Tony (2000) *Doing Research Differently. Free Association, Narrative and the Interview Method.* London: Sage.

Holland, Samantha (2004) *Alternative Femininities: Body, Age and Identity.* Oxford: Berg.

Holland, Samantha (2010) *Pole Dancing, Empowerment and Embodiment.* New York: Palgrave Macmillan.

Howard, Parker, Aldridge, Judith and Measham, Fiona (1998) *Illegal Leisure: The Normalization of Adolescent Recreational Drug Use.* London: Routledge.

Howard, Parker, Aldridge, Judith and Measham, Fiona (2001) *Dancing on Drugs: Risk, Health and Hedonism in the British Club Scenes.* London: Free Association Books.

Jackson, Phil (2004) *Inside Clubbing. Sensual Experiments and the Art of Being Human.* Oxford: Berg.

Jackson, S. and Gilbertson, T. (2009) '*Hot Lesbians*': *Young People's Talk About Representations of Lesbianism*', in *Sexualities*, 12(2), pp. 199–224.

Jeffreys, Sheila (2005) *Beauty and Misogyny*. New York: Routledge.

Jin, Xiuming and Whitson, Risa (2014) '*Young Women and Public Leisure Spaces in Contemporary Beijing: Recreating (with) Gender, Tradition, and Place*', in *Social and Cultural Geography*, 15(4), pp. 119–469.

Jones, S. (2014) '*Gendered Discourses of Entrepreneurship in UK Higher Education: The Fictive Entrepreneur and the Fictive Student*', in *International Small Business Journal*, 32(3), pp. 237–58.

Kappeler, Susanne (1986) *The Pornography of Representation*. Cambridge: Polity.

Kaufman, Michael (ed.) (1987) *Beyond Patriarchy: Essays by Men on Pleasure, Power and Change*. Toronto: Oxford University Press.

Keen, Catherine (2006) '*Boundaries of Belonging: Imagining Urban Identity in Medieval Italy*', in Christian Emden, Catherine Keen and David Midgle (eds) *Imagining the City: The Politics of Space Volume 2*. Oxford: Peter Lang, pp. 65–86.

Kidwell, Claudia Bush and Steele, Valerie (eds) (1989) *Men and Women. Dressing the Part*. Washington: Smithsonian Institution Press.

Kipnis, Laura (1999) *Bound and Gagged. Pornography and the Politics of Fantasy in America*. Durham: Duke University Press.

Kipnis, Laura (2006) *The Female Thing. Dirt, Sex, Envy, Vulnerability*. London: Serpents Tail.

Kinsey, Alfred (1948) *Sexual Behaviour in the Human Male*. London: W.B. Saunders.

Kinsey, Alfred (1953) *Sexual Behaviour in the Human Female*. London: W.B. Saunders.

Klein, Malcolm (ed.) (1967) *Juvenile Gangs in Context: Theory, Research and Action*. New Jersey: Prentice-Hall.

Klein, Naomi (1999) *No Logo: No Space, No Choice, No Jobs*. New York: Picador.

Knopp, Lawrence (1995) '*Sexuality and Urban Space: A Framework for Analysis*', in David Bell and Gill Valentine, *Mapping Desire; Geographies of Sexualities*. London: Routledge, pp. 149–61.

Krauss, R. (1999) '*The Destiny of the Informe*', in Y.-A. Bois and R. E. Krauss (eds) *Formless: A User's Guide*. New York: Zone Books, pp. 234–52.

Krieger, Susan (1996) *The Family Silver. Essays on Relationships among Women*. California: University of California Press.

Krips, Henry (1999) *Fetish. An Erotics of Culture*. New York: Cornell University Press.

Kristeva, Julia (1982) *Powers of Horror. An Essay on Abjection*. New York: Columbia University Press.

Kulick, Don (1995) '*The Sexual Life of Anthropologists: Erotic Subjectivity and Ethnographic Work*', in Don Kulick and Margaret Wilson (eds) *Taboo: Sex, Identity and Erotic Subjectivity in Anthropological Field Work*. London: Routledge, pp. 1–24.

Kunzle, David (2004) *Fashion and Fetishism. Corsets, Tight-Lacing and Other Forms of Body-Sculpture*. Stroud: Sutton Publishing.

Lane, Frederick (2001) *Obscene Profits: The Entrepreneurs of Pornography in the Cyber Age*. New York: Routledge.

LaCaritilie, Major (ed.) (2007) *Masterpieces of Victorian Erotica*. New Milford: Magic Carpet Books.

Laws, Richard. D. and O'Donohue, William (eds) (1997) *Sexual Deviance. Theory, Assessment, and Treatment*. New York: Guilford Press, Ltd.

Lee, Joe (1995) *The History of Clowns for Beginners*. New York: Writers and Readers Publishing.

Lee, Jizz (2015) (ed.) *Coming Out Like a Porn Star: Essays on Pornography, Protection, and Privacy*. Berkley: ThreeL Media|Stone Bridge Press.

Lefebvre, Henri (1991) *The Production of Space*. Oxford: Basil Blackwell.

Liepe-Levinson, Katherine (2002) *Strip Show. Performance of Gender and Desire*. London: Routledge.

Lim, J. and Fanghanel, A. (2013) '*Hijabs, hoodies and hotpants': negotiating the "slut" in SlutWalk*', in *Geoforum*, 48, pp. 207–15.

Lindemann, D. (2011) '*BDSM as therapy?*', in *Sexualities*, 14(2), pp. 151–72.

Loach, Loretta (1992) '*Bad Girls: Women Who Use Pornography*', in Lynne Segal and Mary McIntosh (eds) *Sex Exposed: Sexuality and the Pornography Debate*. London: Virago.

Loaker, Bernadette (2013) '*Becoming "Culturpreneur": How the "Neoliberal Regime of Truth" Affects and Redefines Artistic Subject Positions*', in *Culture and Organization* 19(2), pp. 124–45.

Loftus, Brian (1996) '*Biopia: Bisexuality and the Crisis of Visibility in a Queer Symbolic*', in Donald E. Hall and Maria Pramaggiore (eds)

Representing Bisexualities. Subjects and Cultures of Fluid Desire. London: New York University Press, pp. 207–30.

Lorde, Audre (2000) 'Uses of the Erotic', in Drucilla Cornell (ed.) *Feminism and Pornography*. Oxford: Oxford University Press, pp. 569–74.

Lumby, Catherine (1999) *Bad Girls: The Media, Sex and Feminism in the 90s*. St Leonards: Allen and Unwin.

Luther, Jeffrey (2000) *Thrill-Mad Pussycats: High-Voltage Temptresses from the Pulp Classics*. London: Piron Books Limited.

MacRae, Rhoda (2007) '"Insider" and "Outsider" Issues in Youth Research', in Paul Hodkinson and Wolfgang Deicke (eds) (2007) *Youth Cultures: Scenes, Subcultures and Tribes*. New York: Routledge, pp. 51–62.

Mahon, Michael (2002) *Foucault's Nietzschean Genealogy: Truth, Power, and The Subject*. Albay: State University of New York Press.

Mannix, Daniel (1976) *Freaks: We Who Are Not as Others*. Oswego: eNet Press.

Mannix, Daniel P. (1999) *Freaks: We Who Are Not as Others*. New York: Juno.

Marcuse, Tanya (2005) *Undergarments and Armour*. Arizona: Nazraeli Press.

Mason, Michael (1994) *The Making of Victorian Sexuality*. Oxford: Oxford University Press.

Massey, Doreen (2005) *For Space*. London: Sage.

Matza, David (1964) *Delinquency and Drift*. New York: John Wiley and Sons, Ltd.

McKay, George (ed.) (1998) *DiY Culture: Party and Protest in Nineties Britain*. London: Verso.

McNay, Lois (2000) *Gender and Agency: Reconfiguring the Subject in Feminist and Social Theory*. Malden, MA: Polity Press.

McRobbie, Angela (2009) *The Aftermath of Feminism: Gender, Culture and Social Change*. London: Sage.

Merck, Mandy (1993) *Perversions*. London: Virago.

Mercury, Maureen (2000) *Pagan Fleshworks*. Vermont: Park Street Press.

Millett, Kate (1977) *Sexual Politics*. London: Viraco.

Mort, Frank (2000) *Dangerous Sexualities: Medico-Moral Politics in England since 1830*, 2nd edition. London: Routledge.

Muggleton, David (2002) *Inside Subculture. The Postmodern Meaning of Style*. Oxford: Berg.

Munice, John (1999) *Youth and Crime: A Critical Introduction*. London: Sage.

Munro, Surya (2005) *Gender Politics. Citizenship, Activism and Sexual Diversity*. London: Pluto Press.

Nally, Claire (2009) '*Grrrly Hurly Burly: Neo-burlesque and the Performance of Gender*', in *Textual Practice*, 23(4), pp. 621–43.

Nally, C. and Smith, A. (2012) *Naked Exhibitionism: Gendered Performance and Public Exposure*. London: I.B. Tauris.

Nan, Mistress (2004) *My Private Life. Real Experiences of a Dominant Woman*, 2nd edition. Los Angeles: Daedalus Publishing Company.

Nickell, Joe (2005) *Secrets of the Sideshows*. Kentucky: The University Press of Kentucky.

Nietzsche, Fredrik (1994) *On the Genealogy of Morality*. Cambridge: Cambridge University Press.

Nietzsche, Fredrik (2001) *The Gay Science*. Cambridge: Cambridge University Press.

Odzer, Cleo (1997) *Virtual Spaces. Sex and the Cyber Citizen*. New York: Berkley Books.

O'Reilly, Karen (2005) *Ethnographic Methods*. London: Routledge.

Pajnik, Mojca (2015) '*Merchandizing Sex on the Web: Gender Bias in Profiling Actors and Services*', in *Gender, Technology and Development*, 19(2), pp. 181–203.

Park, Robert (1925) *The City: Suggestions for Investigation of Human Behaviour in the Urban Environment*. Chicago: University of Chicago Press.

Picerno, Doralba (2007) *Girls*. London: Pictoropia, Ltd.

Pitts, Victoria (2000) '*Body Modification, Self-Mutilation and Agency in Media Accounts of a Subculture*', in Mike Featherstone (ed.) *Body Modification*. London: Sage, pp. 291–304.

Pitts, Victoria (2003) *In the Flesh. The Cultural Politics of Body Modification*. New York: Palgrave Macmillan.

Du Plessis, Michael (1996) '*Blatantly Bisexual; or, Unthinking Queer Theory*', in Donald E. Hall and Maria Pramaggiore (eds) *Representing Bisexualities. Subjects and Cultures of Fluid Desire*. New York: New York University Press, pp. 19–43.

Polsky, Ned (1967) *Hustlers, Beats and Others*. London: Penguin.

Puwar, Nirmal (2004) *Space Invaders: Race, Gender and Bodies Out of Place*. New York: Berg.

Queen, Carol and Schimel, Lawrence (eds) (1996) *Switch Hitters*. San Francisco: Cleis Press.

Queen, Carol and Schimel, Lawrence (eds) (1997) *Pomosexuals. Challenging Assumptions about Gender and Sexuality*. San Francisco: Cleis Press.

Rahder, Barbara and McLean, Heather (2013) 'Other Ways of Knowing Your Place: Immigrant Women's Experience of Public Space in Toronto', in *Canadian Journal of Urban Research*, 22(1), pp. 145–66.

Redhead, Steve (ed.) (1993) *Rave Off: Politics and Deviance in Contemporary Youth Culture*. Avebury: Ashgate Publishing Limited.

Reger, J. (2015) 'The Story of a Slut Walk: Sexuality, Race, and Generational Divisions in Contemporary Feminist Activism', in *Journal of Contemporary Ethnography*, 44(1), pp. 84–112.

Roberts, Brian (2006) *Micro Social Theory*. London: Palgrave Macmillan.

Roberts-Hughes, Rebecca (ed.) (2007) *True Decadence*. London: Erotic Review Books Ltd.

Rock, Paul (1973) *Deviant Behaviour*. London: Hutchinson University Library.

Russell, Diana E. H. (1998) *Dangerous Relationships: Pornography, Misogyny, and Rape*. California: Sage.

Schacht, Steven (2000) 'Gay Female Impersonators and the Masculine Construction of "Other"', in Peter Nardi (ed.) *Gay Masculinities*. London: Sage, pp. 247–64.

Schneider, Rebecca (1997) *The Explicit Body in Performance*. London: Routledge.

Schur, Edwin M. (1984) *Labelling Women Deviant: Gender, Stigma, and Social Control*. New York: Random House.

Segal, Lynne (1992) 'Sweet Sorrows, Painful Pleasures: Pornography and the Perils of Heterosexual Desire', in Lynne Segal and Mary McIntosh (eds) *Sex Exposed: Sexuality and the Pornography Debate*. London: Virago.

Segal, Lynne (1994) *Straight Sex: The Politics of Pleasure*. London: Virago.

Shlain, Leonard (2004) *Sex, Time, and Power: How Women's Sexuality Shaped Human Evolution*. London: Penguin.

Simmel, Georg (1971) *On Individuality and Social Forms*. Chicago:
University of Chicago Press.

Sinclair, Nicholas (1996) *The Chameleon Body: Photographs of
Contemporary Fetishism*. London: Lund Humphries.

Skelton, Tracy and Valentine, Gill (eds) (1998) *Cool Places: Geographies of
Youth Cultures*. London: Routledge.

Sollee, Kirsten (2017) *Witches, Sluts, Feminists: Conjuring the Sex Positive*.
Berkley: ThreeL Media.

Solomon, Robert (2006) *Love and Sexuality*. Colorado: Madison Books.

Spooner, Catherine (2004) *Fashioning Gothic Bodies*. Manchester:
Manchester University Press.

Spooner, Catherine (2006) *Contemporary Gothic*. London: Reaktion.

Sprinkle, Annie (1998) *Post-Porn Modernist. Annie Sprinkle: My 25 Years as
a Multimedia Whore*. San Francisco: Cleis Press.

Steele, Valerie (1985) *Fashion and Eroticism. Ideas of Feminine Beauty from
the Victorian Era to the Jazz Age*. New York: Oxford University Press.

Steele, Valerie (1996) *Fetish: Fashion, Sex and Power*. New York: Oxford
University Press.

Stein, Arlene (1997) *Sex and Sensibility. Stories of a Lesbian Generation*.
London: University of California Press.

Steintrager, James (1977) *Bentham*. London: Allen and Unwin Ltd.

Storey, John (2001) *Cultural Theory and Popular Culture: An Introduction*.
London: Prentice Hall.

Suleiman, Susan Rebin (1990) *Subversive Intent: Gender, Politics, and the
Avant-Garde*. London: Harvard University Press.

Sullivan, Nikki (2006) *A Critical Introduction to Queer Theory*. Edinburgh:
Edinburgh University Press.

Sumner, Colin (1994) *The Sociology of Deviance: An Obituary*. Buckingham:
Open University Press.

Taylor, Ian, Walton, Paul and Young, Jack (1973) *The New Criminology: For
a Social Theory of Deviance*. London: Routledge.

Thompson, Bill (1994) *Sadomasochism. Painful Perversion or Pleasurable
Play?* London: Cassell.

Thompson, Kenneth (1998) *Moral Panics*. London: Routledge.

Thrift, Nigel (2004) '*Intensities of Feeling: Toward a Spatial Politics of Affect*', in *Geografiska Annaler*, 86, pp. 57–78.

Tyler, I. (2009) '*Against Abjection*', in *Feminist Theory*, 10(1), pp. 77–98.

Vason, Manuel, Watson, Gary and Wilson, Sarah (2001) *Franko B*. London: Black Dog Publishing Ltd.

Visweswaran, Kamala (1994) *Fictions of Feminist Ethnography*. Minneapolis: The University of Minnesota.

Von Teese, Dita (2006) *Burlesque and the Art of the Teese/Fetish and the Art of the Teese*. New York: Regan Books.

Walter, Natasha (1998) *The New Feminism*. London: Little, Brown and Company.

Walter, Natasha (2010) *Living Dolls: The Return of Sexism*. London: Virago.

Warner, Michael (1993) *Fear of a Queer Planet*. Minneapolis: University of Minnesota Press.

Weeks, Jeffrey (1991) *Against Nature. Essays on History, Sexuality and Identity*. London: Rivers Oram Press.

Weeks, Jeffrey (1995) *Invented Moralities. Sexual Values in an Age of Uncertainty*. London: Polity Press.

Weimann, Gabriel (1999) *Communicating Unreality: Modern Media and the Reconstruction of Reality*. London: Sage.

White, Emily (2000) *Fast Girls: Teenage Tribes and the Myth of the Slut*. New York: Berkley Books.

White, Ralph (2007) *BDSM Primer*. Las Vegas: The Nazca Plains Corporation.

Williams, Linda (1989) *Hard Core: Power, Pleasure and the 'Frenzy of the Visible'*. London: University of California Press.

Williams, Linda (1993) '*A Provoking Agent: The Pornography and Performance Art of Annie Sprinkle*', in Pamela Church Gibson and Roma Gibson (eds) *Dirty Looks: Women, Pornography, Power*, pp. 46–61.

Williams, Raymond (1980) *Culture and Materialism*. London: Verso.

Williams, Raymond (1989) *Resources of Hope: Culture, Democracy, Socialism*. London: Verso.

Willson, Jacki (2008) *The Happy Stripper. Pleasures and Politics of the New Burlesque*. London: I.B.Tauris.

Wilson, Elizabeth (1993) *'Is Transgression Transgressive?'* in Joseph Bristow and Angelia R. Wilson (eds) *Activating Theory: Lesbian, Gay, Bisexual Politics*. London: Lawrence and Wishart, pp. 107–17.

Wilson, Margaret (1995) *'Afterward. Perspective and Difference: Sexualization, the Field, and the Ethnographer'*, in Don Kulick and Margaret Wilson (eds) *Taboo: Sex, Identity and Erotic Subjectivity in Anthropological Field Work*. London: Routledge, pp. 251–75.

Wood, David (ed.) (1996) *Torture Garden: From Bodyshocks to Cybersex. A Photographic Archive of the New Flesh*. London: Creation Books.

Wood, David (ed.) (1999) *Body Probe: Mutating Physical Boundaries*. Creation Books.

Znaniecki, Florian (1940) *The Social Role of the Man of Knowledge*. USA: Harper Torch Books.

Zouravliov, Vania and Findley, Marie (2000) *Mediaeval Baebes. Songs of the Flesh*. London: The Erotic Print Society.

Zieleniec, Andrzej (2007) *Space and Social Theory*. Los Angeles: Sage.

Zpira, Lukas (2005) *Onanisme Manu Militari II*. Mexico: Editions Hors.

Index